MULTI-SEASON
SHRUBS AND TREES

D1209310

by the same author

with Thomas Rochford

THE ROCHFORD BOOK OF FLOWERING POT PLANTS
THE ROCHFORD BOOK OF HOUSE PLANTS
ROCHFORD'S HOUSE-PLANTS FOR EVERYONE

MULTI-SEASON
SHRUBS and TREES

RICHARD GORER

Gardeners Book Club
Newton Abbot 1972

perm

Copyright © 1971 Richard Gorer

First published by Faber & Faber Limited

This edition was produced in 1972 for sale to its members
only by the proprietors, Readers Union Limited, PO Box 6
Newton Abbot, Devon, TQ12 2DW. Full details of
membership will gladly be sent on request

Reproduced and printed in Great Britain
by Hollen Street Press Slough Bucks
for Readers Union

❧ Contents

❧ Illustrations

7

All the photographs, except for plate 3, are
reproduced by courtesy of Dennis Woodland;
plate 3 is courtesy of J. E. Downward

🦁 Introduction

It is possibly significant that there is no one word in our language to describe the plants about which I want to write. It is also possible that one can place too much emphasis on language; the fact that the French have no word to correspond to our 'home' does not necessarily mean that they have no home-life. It is, perhaps, slightly odd that a nation of gardeners should lack certain essential terms. If we want to refer to the various hybrids of *Rosa chinensis* that continue to flower throughout the summer, we have to borrow a French word and call them 'remontant'. Repeat-flowering roses sounds grotesque, while perpetual-flowering roses is not only inaccurate, but also is liable to cause confusion with the race known as hybrid perpetuals. Since it is quite easy for me to explain the type of plants about which I intend to write, my main objection to our poverty of language is that it prevents me giving the book an informative title.

What this book is intended to be about is plants that have more than one season in which they are attractive. If you think of a popular plant like lilac, you will appreciate that it looks absolutely stunning for two or three weeks in the year, but is remarkably unexciting for the remaining 49 or 50 weeks. Compare this with *Koelreuteria paniculata*. As its leaves unfurl in the late spring, they are a delightful pinky-bronze in colour; as handsome, in my opinion, as such plants as *Acer pseudoplatanus* 'Brilliantissimum'! As they mature they turn green, but are still attractive with their graceful pinnate form. In late July, if the plant is sufficiently mature, it will bear conspicuous panicles of yellow flowers that are succeeded by the curious bladder-like fruits; then in the late autumn the leaves will turn a fine golden colour before they fall. In fact one may say that the plant is attractive for at least 30 weeks in the year. There are not many plants that have quite such an array of attractions as the koelreuteria, but there are a surprisingly large number that have seasons of interest for longer periods than such favourites as forsythia, lilac or Japanese cherries.

9

One stipulation that I have made in deciding what plants to include and what to exclude is that the seasons of interest must be reasonably widely spaced. A plant such as *Pieris forrestii*, which has the most brilliant scarlet young growth and agreeable white lily-of-the-valley-like flowers, has been refused admission because both phenomena occur more or less simultaneously. In the same way, many of the rhododendrons with attractive young growth have been excluded, if this growth appears as soon as the flowers are over. There is a gap of about two months between the flowers and the young growth of *R. lutescens*, so that can be admitted, but the beautiful silvery leaves of *R. argyrophyllum* appear so soon after the flowers that the whole display might be considered together. However, in this case the foliage display is sufficiently prolonged to give an additional attraction.

Perhaps the most valuable part of this book will consist of observations of the obvious, but neglected. I think the subject was first put into my mind by seeing a tree festooned with glowing rubies. Closer inspection showed that these rubies were, in point of fact, the berries of the wild honeysuckle, *Lonicera periclymenum*. It struck me with some force that no gardening book that I had ever read, had drawn attention to the beauty of honeysuckle berries. It then slowly dawned on me that the honeysuckle was more useful in the garden than, say, a large-flowered clematis. The clematis might be more showy in flower, but once over it had, so to speak, shot its bolt, unlike *Clematis tangutica*, which would cover itself with its smoke-like seed-heads after flowering.

My other glimpse of the obvious concerned flowering cherries. I had in my garden, not only one of the *Prunus serrulata* cultivars, that look, when in flower, as though they had been manufactured in an ice-cream parlour and should be given a name like 'Marshmallow Delight', but also a tree of *Prunus sargentiana*. This covered itself with flowers as exuberantly as the Marshmallow Delight; though the single flowers gave it a grace that the sundae lacked, the sundae gained slightly by the fact that the large sterile flowers hung for rather longer on the tree. However, come the autumn, *P. sargentiana* turned gold and scarlet and looked marvellous, while *P. serrulata* remained as dull as it had been ever since the flowers had dropped. It was obvious that *P. sargentiana* gave better garden value than *P. serrulata*, but I could not recall any book that had stated this self-evident fact.

Apart from their flowers, trees and shrubs can attract through the colour of their bark or of the young wood. They may also have an attractive habit, although this is a somewhat imponderable advantage. They can certainly have very attractive fruits, be they berries or less colourful and succulent seed-cases. They can have the leaves delicately coloured as they emerge in the spring and they can be brilliantly coloured before they fall in the autumn. It is not very probable that all these features will be present on the same plant. *Stewartia sinensis* has attractive flowers, good autumn colour and, once the plant is sufficiently mature, very attractive bark; *Acer palmatum* 'Senkaki' has attractive young foliage, mature foliage and wonderful coral-pink young wood through-out the winter; *Rhododendron thomsonii* has attractive glaucous leaves, attractive flowers and good bark, but the number of plants that can equal these attainments is small and one must usually settle for rather less than is offered by these prize examples.

There is a tendency in writing gardening books to assume that every-thing is going to be perfect and that every plant will behave with text-book exemplariness. Alas, this is far from being the case and I suspect that, with a laudable desire for honesty, I have sometimes emphasized the possible disadvantages that may occur to an extent that might discourage any rather timid person. Let us, for example, consider the question of autumn colour.

Now this appears to be an imponderable, depending on a large number of factors. As a result some plants will colour wonderfully in some years and fail to oblige in others. Again, in some localities plants will colour well, but fail to do any such thing in other situations. The classic example of this is *Cercidiphyllum japonicum*, which will light up the garden in one district, while in another it fails to justify its situation at all. With this particular plant there does not appear to be any very plausible reason for its failure to oblige. Plants in the same vicinity with similar soil in which to grow and the same seasonal weather will behave with this baffling inconsistency. It may be that some clones will colour over here, while others do not—apparently they all colour well in the wild—or it may be a question of some trace element in the soil. I do not know if anyone has ever moved a cercidiphyllum from a garden where it did not colour to one where others did. But an experiment such as this might throw some light on the subject.

There are not many plants which are quite so unreliable as this one, but the occurrence of good autumn colour does appear to be controlled to a large extent by the soil and by the kind of summer that has been experienced. Even so there are uncertainties. In my old garden *Acer palmatum heptalobum* 'Osakazuki', which can usually be relied upon to turn the most brilliant pillar-box red of any tree, never coloured, regard-less of what sort of summer had been experienced, while on the other hand, *Cornus mas*, which is not usually thought of with regard to autumn colour, would turn a brilliant purple.

However this may be, there does appear to be some correlation between a dry summer and good autumn colour. This is probably because a dry summer will cause more rapid maturation of the current year's growth, while during wet seasons the plants will tend to make more growth which may not ripen well. This would account for the fact that the Sugar Maple, *Acer saccharum*, will incarnadine the landscape of New England, with its Continental climate of very cold winters and hot dry summers, while it is usually unsatisfactory in old England, with its insular climate of mild winters and wet summers. In any case, the incidence of autumn colour is very odd. Why are some plants expected to colour well, while others are not? Presumably there is a chemical explanation, but what chemical does *Malus tschonoskii* contain, which other malus species apparently do not? Why do almost all the Japanese sorbus species colour well, while plants from Europe or China rarely do so? Indeed, the provenance of the wild plant will often give some indication as to how reliable the appearance of autumn colour will be.

There are, of course, many exceptions to any generalization, but as a general rule it may be assumed that plants from Japan will generally colour well, while plants from North America tend to be much more dependent on the conditions during the summer. Chinese plants also seem to be more affected by the seasonal conditions than most Japanese plants. European and western Asian plants are usually reliable in all seasons. Sometimes the age of the plant appears to have some effect. *Liquidambar styraciflua* colours much better when the plant is fairly mature. Again, the soil reaction may also have a bearing. In spite of the brilliance of such plants as the wild cherry and the spindle tree on the chalk downs, it is usually on acid soils that the most brilliant displays are seen, and the majority of plants that are grown for their autumn colours are native on acid soils. However, many of these will grow and colour well even if the soil is alkaline, so the distinction is not quite so clear cut as this fact might suggest. There are, of course, plants, notably most of the *Ericaceae*, which will not grow on alkaline soil at all in this country, but many plants which normally grow on acid soil will tolerate some alkalinity, although they may refuse to grow in shallow chalky conditions. It can thus be seen that the presence of autumn colour among the list of attractions is a pleasure that cannot be guaranteed. I think I have tended to over-emphasize this fact, but, as a general rule, it should be pointed out that in most years plants will oblige and, to me at any rate, the very uncertainty gives a certain spice to autumn.

In the same way, the production of ornamental fruits is not always a very long-lived pleasure. In some districts small berries, such as those of various sorbus spp., pyracantha or *Sambucus racemosa*, may be taken by the birds so rapidly that the gardener has no time to enjoy them. There is a ray of hope in the manufacture of bird-repellent sprays, which we may hope will soon be effective. At the moment they are rather liable to be washed off in the first heavy shower and they require a mechanical sprayer for application to large specimens. However, it is only in some parts of the country that the birds are liable to be so voracious. In other parts, in towns and near busy roads, the damage they cause will be insignificant. If you do live in a place that is badly bird-ridden, you can either spray your trees with repellents or decide not to grow berrying plants at all. There are, of course, a few plants, notably *Hippophaë rhamnoides*, that the birds will not touch, but there are not very many of these. Districts that are badly bird-infested are also generally unsuitable for growing most of the prunus species, as the buds are removed in early spring, just as they start to swell. In these circumstances the only really satisfactory thing is to cut your coat according to your cloth and, if you want fruits in the autumn grow a plant like *Rosa moyesii*. The large heps of these and other rose species will not be attacked for a long time. Town gardeners usually do not have these problems and their gardens can be scarlet with cotoneasters in the autumn and these may well hang on right through the winter. If I appear in the following pages to hark rather on the damage that birds can do, it is because I garden in a particularly bad area for these pests.

I have included a number of plants with attractive bark or coloured young wood, even if the plants do not have many other attractions. For example, *Salix alba vitellina* will ornament the garden from November to March, which is far longer than most flowering shrubs do. I have rather tended to think that if a plant is attractive for a period longer than eight weeks, it merits inclusion, and so you will find descriptions of such plants as *Cornus alba* and *C. stolonifera*, as well as many willows, which are not particularly outstanding at other periods, although they are by no means unsightly. Plants with attractive bark such as the various snake-bark maples and *Prunus serrula* have similarly been admitted, although they usually have some further attraction to offer.

Green is also a colour, as Gertrude Jekyll so sapiently observed, and I have included a number of plants with particularly attractive foliage. Many people seem to find enjoyment in leaves which have some colour other than green. My own feeling is that such plants must be used sparingly to make their best impression. The various purple-leaved trees and shrubs in particular are liable to give rather a heavy effect. Plants with variegated leaves have an attraction to many that I personally find myself unable to share. However, I am completely illogical in that I like most grey and glaucous-leaved plants, as well as many that have a golden variegation, while I dislike plants with white variegation or with very dark purple leaves. Since it is obviously imbecile to recommend a plant which colours in the autumn while taking an upstage attitude to plants with coloured leaves in the summer, I have tried not to let my prejudices interfere in my selection of plants to describe. A medieval proverb states that *de gustibus et coloribus non est disputandum*. Like so many proverbs, this is not correct; one can dispute endlessly about tastes and colours, but it is quite true that no disputation will induce anyone to change their opinions on these matters. Why indeed should one wish to? Surely it is one of the main pleasures of gardening that one can grow what one likes, regardless of the approval or disapproval of others. If you would like to parallel the contemporary fashion for indoor Victoriana, by filling your garden with beds of yellow calceolaria and scarlet salvia, with an edging of blue lobelia, by all means do so. We are already seeing a revival of the Victorian fernery, which, as that great gardener Shirley Hibberd observed, 'belongs to the truly rustic, rather than the rural department of gardening', and it is probably only the lack of plentiful, ill-paid labour that will prevent us seeing Carpet Bedding revived. There is room in the country for all kinds of gardening and if your taste lies in a direction that is currently unfashionable, take heart with the reflection that nothing goes out of date so fast as today's fashion.

When walking round a garden one is liable to lose one's way down some attractive by-path that leads nowhere and this appears to have happened to me. Let us return to our muttons. A few shrubs that normally flower in the spring will often have a second flowering in the autumn. This is rarely so extensive a display as the spring one, but gives a pleasant bonus and such plants will be mentioned here. The most reliable would seem to be the rhododendron hybrid known as 'Yellow Hammer'.

It is by no means simple to make a list of plants attractive, or even tolerable reading. It is all too easy for the writer to fall into a quasi-somnambulistic state and reel off botanical jargon that is even more tedious to read than it is to write. However, the alternative may often be worse. Even Farrer, that master of plant description, sometimes lost his balance on the narrow tightrope that separates good descriptive writing from bad beautiful writing, using the word 'beautiful' here in a pejorative sense. There are very few Farrers writing at any time and I am certainly not to be numbered among them. Although there seems to be no good reason why it should not be possible to combine accuracy of description with readability, in practice it turns out to be very difficult. I have attempted to add interest to my descriptions of plants, from time to time, by saying who was responsible for their introduction and giving a little information about these plant hunters. This may make the book seem a little diffuse, but I hope will add to the interest.

To sum up, this book will enumerate and describe trees and shrubs that have attractions additional to their flowers. These may lie in the bark, which may be attractively marked or coloured, or in the young wood which is often brilliant during the winter months. Attraction can also lie in the foliage which may be brilliantly coloured when it is unfurling, unusually attractive when mature or brilliantly coloured in the autumn. Very many plants also have attractive fruits, be they berries, as in a very large number of genera or in other forms of fruit, such as the swollen fruits of *Staphyleaceae* or the samarae of some maples. I do not propose to give cultural details for these plants, but will make some mention of any special soil or climatic requirements they may have. Some of the plants discussed will only be possible in sheltered districts, but there are not very many of these. The genera will be listed in alphabetic order but not necessarily the species. It seems easier to discuss, for example, all the snake-bark maples together, rather than to search through the list of acers in order to find out which species have this attractive bark. Similarly, it is more convenient to list all the Aria section of *Sorbus* distinct from the Aucuparia section.

It is not always easy to discover the rate of growth of all the trees and shrubs, but where I have information I will give it. Many people are sometimes shy of planting trees, because of the long time that will elapse before they are sizeable plants. With a good many trees such fears are unjustified. There are very few that will not look fairly handsome after seven years and after 10 most will be extremely decorative. Moreover, unlike herbaceous plants, they will improve each year and, after the first few years, will demand practically no attention. During the first few years it is necessary to see that they are not smothered by weeds, but once they have grown sufficiently tall, the weeds will do them no harm. They will still look unsightly and have to be controlled, but as the tree or shrub increases in size it will tend to discourage the appearance of annual weeds and you yourself, if you are wise, will have destroyed the perennial weeds before you inserted your plants. There is no such thing as trouble-free gardening, but shrubs and trees will eventually require far less attention than herbaceous plants or such time-consuming plants as hybrid tea roses that require annual pruning and fortnightly spraying.

Within reason, the smaller the plant the more rapidly it will grow away. With some exceptions, most notably rhododendrons, a large specimen of a tree or shrub is very liable to receive a check on being moved and this will certainly reduce growth the first season; sometimes this slowing down of growth will persist for the second season as well.

Small plants that are lifted with all their roots intact should get away immediately and suffer no check at all. Of course, you must take reasonable precautions for the first season with any plant, be it woody or herbaceous. It must not be allowed to dry out before its new roots have penetrated your soil, and it must be so secured that high winds do not dislodge it.

If your soil is very stiff, it is obviously helpful to the new roots if some peat, leafmould or compost is incorporated in the soil that is immediately in contact with the roots of the newly purchased plant, while if the soil is sandy and liable to dry out very rapidly it is again useful to mix in material that will help retain moisture. Well-rotted farmyard manure is the best, if this is obtainable, but if not, leafmould or compost are acceptable substitutes. Once your plant is established and growing away well, you can leave it to its own devices. You can, of course, encourage more rapid growth by manures, whether they be organic or inorganic, but there is always the possibility that you may get leaf and stem growth at the expense of flowers. If your soil is very poor, this is probably an acceptable risk, but with reasonably fertile soils, manuring may delay flowering. This is not necessarily a bad thing and it really depends on your patience. If you are prepared to have a better specimen which may take a couple of years longer to produce flowers than a plant that has not been so lavishly fed, you will almost certainly be better off in the long term. When the well-fed plant does eventually flower it may well make a larger display than the plant that has had no feeding at all.

In theory shrubs and trees should be mulched annually in order to keep the soil around the roots moist and in good heart. This is well worth doing for the first two years, when drought may have fatal results and will, in any case, seriously curtail growth. After that period, it is certainly helpful, but not really essential and most gardeners, who have only limited time, may decide to dispense with it. The type of material you use for mulching will depend on what is available. Grass mowings are liable to bring a lot of weed-seeds in their train, and should not be used if the lawn has recently been treated with any weedkiller; nor should they be applied too thickly, as they generate a certain amount of heat while rotting down. Chopped green bracken is highly recommended and the dried dead stems are also useful. Farmyard manure is naturally to be commended, but is in very short supply and is only practicable for a comparatively small number of gardeners. Peat is always purchasable, but after a prolonged drought it may become so desiccated that it fails to absorb the rain when it does eventually fall. This fault can be obviated by mixing the peat and grass mowings together; this is rather laborious, but is probably the best substitute for farmyard manure. If you store your lawn mowings during the summer, you can mix them with peat during the winter and have a good mixture to put around your shrubs the following year.

Once your plants have got sufficiently large they will deposit their own mulch in the form of fallen leaves. If these are not blown away, many of them will be pulled into the soil by worms during the autumn and winter and will there rot, improving the soil both chemically and texturally. If they are blown on to paths and lawns and other places where they are unwelcome, they can be gathered up and stored in containers (a wired rectangle is quite sufficient) where they will eventually rot down into compost. To burn the fallen leaves, as so many 'tidy' gardeners do, is a wanton waste and is to be deprecated.

Whether newly introduced trees and shrubs should be pruned or no is a matter of some controversy. In my opinion, the decisive factor is the size of the plant and the way it has been grown. If it comes from a pot, there should have been no root disturbance and the plant should be able to grow away without any check. Similarly, a small plant taken from the open ground should have not suffered any gross damage and should be only very slightly checked. With larger plants, with the exception of plants such as rhododendrons, which have a very dense, shallow root-ball which can generally be lifted nearly intact, there is almost certain to be some damage to the roots. This means that the ratio between the aerial and the subterranean parts of the plant has been altered. Under these circumstances, there is an obvious argument in favour of reducing the aerial portion of the plant, so that the curtailed roots do not have to supply an excessive aerial portion. To offset this argument, it must be remembered that if the aerial parts are pruned, the plant will have to develop latent buds; a feat which presumably entails the expense of additional energy and it may well be best, unless the roots have been very badly damaged, to leave the plant unpruned for the first season and to prune it slightly in its second season. The matter could best be decided by comparative trials, but what may be effective for one soil and position may be less so for another and it is probably not possible to be dogmatic. As in so many other aspects of gardening, empiricism is the best solution.

Acer - Berberis

ACER

We had better, I think, begin with the acers, although the claim of *Abies forrestii* to admission is not easily refuted. This attractive conifer has reddish young branches, leaves that are dark green above and white on the underside and, when large enough, purple-blue cones; like so many conifers it is of interest at most seasons. However, with the exception of *Pseudolarix*, I am omitting conifers on the ground that their virtues are generally recognized. In most species the attraction lies only in the foliage and it is only rarely that the flowers or fruits are attractive. This is not very logical, but will help to keep the book to manageable proportions.

For some unfortunate reason the *Acer* genus is chiefly known in gardens through the unspeakable sycamore, *Acer pseudo-platanus*. This has the advantage of being very quick-growing and, as anyone within a hundred yards of an established specimen is only too ruefully aware, of coming very easily from seed. This more or less exhausts its merits and its excessive distribution must have done the genus considerable harm among gardeners.

The genus is found over most of the temperate regions of the northern hemisphere, with the greatest concentration in North America and eastern Asia. Unless there are some species still to be introduced to cultivation, there are not a great number in Europe nor western Asia, nor the Himalayas, and it is in China, Japan and North America that there is a great proliferation of species. The genus comprises many large forest trees, as well as small trees and shrubs. Its most characteristic feature is the fruit, which consists of a pair of nutlets enclosed in a winged case, known botanically as a samara; an agreeable name which might well be used more extensively than it is at present. The vast majority of the species are deciduous; the only evergreen species in cultivation, so far as I know, is *A. syriacum*, though *A. fargesii* is described as semi-evergreen in favourable situations. A few species have attractive flowers, but most of the plants owe their attractiveness to their foliage, and a few to their handsome bark. Very many turn the most gorgeous colours in the autumn and a surprisingly large number also have very attractive young foliage.

Except for the various cultivars, which require to be grafted, seed is the best method of propagation. By no means all acers show the same freedom of germination as the sycamore, and sometimes seed is slow to germinate and germination is not very good. There seems no good reason why they should not be propagated as cuttings, but I have not heard of this being done very extensively. Their rate of growth varies considerably; some grow fairly rapidly, while others, notably *A. griseum*, are extremely slow. There are a very large number of species in cultivation, though not all that are described in gardening dictionaries are easily obtainable.

Acer argutum is, unlike the majority of species, unisexual and there seems no record of hermaphrodite plants being known. As a result it seems to be very rare in cultivation. It makes a deciduous tree up to 25 feet and does not appear to be very rapid in its growth. The bare wood, particularly the younger growths, is an attractive purple in colour. In April, before the leaves have emerged, the greenish-yellow flowers are produced in clusters, each flower on a slender stalk, which elongates as the fruits mature. The leaves are pale green, with veins that appear whitish on the underside, up to 4 inches long and as wide, and markedly 5-lobed with double-toothed edges. The leaves are not dissimilar in shape to the better-known *A. palmatum*. In the autumn they turn a good golden-yellow before falling.

It can be imagined that this is a very attractive small tree with attractive young wood, flowers, leaves and autumn colour and, owing to its modest dimensions, suitable for small gardens, which most of us have to make do with in these days. It is a native of Japan and not, I understand, unduly rare there, so that further importation of seeds should not be very difficult.

The plant was introduced to this country in 1881 by Messrs. Veitch. It had been collected between 1877 and 1879 by Charles Maries, who seems to have been a good and successful collector, but who remains rather a mysterious figure. He appears to have collected very successfully in Japan, but far less so in China. James Veitch in *Hortus Veitchii* writes rather condescendingly of him: 'Maries had enthusiasm, but lacked "staying power": he was musical, much to the delight of the Japanese peasants, and doubtless this must often have helped the work.' Later when writing of E. H. Wilson he says that he was: 'a contrast to his predecessor, Charles Maries, who, when in the Ichang region of the Yangtze valley in 1879 could have sent many plants, subsequently found by Wilson. . . . Maries was *difficile*: and the natives, naturally resenting this, destroyed the collection, and he returned to the coast reporting the people hostile.' One certainly gathers the impression that he was not the easiest man to get on with and on his return from collecting for Veitch he was soon recommended by Sir Joseph Hooker to superintend the gardens of the Maharajah of Durbhungah and he remained in India for the rest of his life. Messrs. Veitch, although extremely enterprising, and all gardeners must for ever be grateful to them, were not, it is reported, the most generous of patrons and one has a sneaking suspicion that it was about money that Maries may have proved *difficile*. Bean suggests that both this species and the following appreciate some shade around the roots.

Acer capillipes is the first of the snake-barked maples and one of the most pleasant. Although it can reach heights of 30 or 40 feet, it is usually somewhat smaller. The 3-lobed leaves are a pleasant red colour as they emerge, up to 5 inches long and 3 inches across, with the central lobe considerably larger than the two lateral ones. Both the petiole and the main veins are red in colour. The flowers are not very spectacular, being greenish-white, and tend to be hidden under the leaves in drooping racemes. In favourable situations the leaves turn a rich crimson in the autumn. As the plant ages the striation of the bark tends to become obscured; a phenomenon that may be noted in many of these snake-barked plants. However, it remains for at least five years and is constantly being added to as fresh new wood is produced. The plant is again a native of Japan and was introduced to cultivation by Professor Sargent of the Arnold Arboretum, who did a great deal of work on the trees of Japan.

It is probably convenient to deal with all the snake-barked maples together and the next, in alphabetic order, is *A. davidii*. This is a more vigorous species, capable of reaching 50 feet in height. Unlike the majority of acers, it has entire leaves, ovate in shape, up to 8 inches long and 4 inches across. They are reddish when they unfurl and have some reddish down on the underside. The flowers are unisexual, but both male and female flowers are produced on the same plant; they are yellowish in colour and not particularly decorative. The leaves should turn gold, crimson and purple in the autumn. The striated bark is very handsome, one of the best in the group. The plant comes from Central China and was introduced by Maries in 1879. It was not recognized and was distributed as *Acer* species, always a safe way of getting round any trouble. It was reintroduced by Wilson in 1902.

Acer grosseri itself is very little known, while the variety *hersii*, sometimes given separate specific rank, is popular and easily obtainable, although it was not discovered before 1919 and not received in England until 1924. The type of *A. grosseri* is a shrub rather than a tree and does not exceed 20 feet in height, whereas the variety *hersii* tends to be tree-like in habit, and will reach 30 feet. The leaves are more or less oval in shape and shallowly 3-lobed and the striation of the bark survives for many years. In favourable situations the leaves turn a rich crimson in the autumn. The plant appears to grow quite rapidly.

Acer pennsylvanicum is the only North American in this series and, owing to its provenance, has been known for considerably longer in gardens than the Chinese and Japanese plants. It was introduced into cultivation in this country as long ago as 1755 and it received its name from Linnaeus himself. Unlike the Oriental species, the striation is not visible on the young wood, but develops when it is over two years old. Although trees taller than 30 feet have been known, it rarely exceeds 20 feet in cultivation. The leaves are 7 inches long and as much across, circular at the base and 3-lobed at the apex. They have a pinkish tinge when young and turn a good golden colour in the autumn. In 1904 the well-known Berlin nurseryman, Späth, put into commerce his variety of this, *erythrocladum*, in which the year-old shoots were bright crimson, thereby making the plant very conspicuous in the winter with its crimson young wood and striated bark; I do not know if it is still available, but it is not in any catalogue that I have seen. The yellow flowers, which are quite sizeable, are born on pendant racemes up to 6 inches long in May.

A related species from Japan, introduced by Maries in 1879, is *A. crataegifolium*, but it has few attractions apart from its bark. There was a cultivar, given the name 'Veitchii', in which the leaves were variegated with pink and white, but it appears to have been lost.

Another of Maries's introductions was *A. rufinerve*. This introduction also dates from about 1879, but a variegated form was exhibited by Standish and Noble in 1869 and there seems no record as to who was responsible for its introduction. Since the specific name was given by von Siebold, it is probable that he may have introduced it before Maries did. The type is very near *A. pennsylvanicum*, but differs in its smaller leaves, which do not exceed 5 inches in length and which are sometimes 5-lobed. The flowers are borne on erect, not pendulous racemes. The young fruit is covered with reddish down, as are the undersides of the leaves for most of the season. The petioles and midribs are red in colour and the young shoots are bluish-white in the winter. The tree can reach a height of 40 feet, but is not particularly rapid in growth. I would say this was probably the best of the snake-bark maples, particularly if you have a form in which the leaves turn bright crimson before falling.

Acer tegmentosum, a native of Korea and Manchuria, also has striated bark, but otherwise appears to be little known and would probably prove very difficult to obtain.

We can now return to the maples whose charms do not include striated bark. *A. circinatum* is a low, thicket-making shrub, although if trained as a tree with a single trunk it can reach 30 feet. The leaves are nearly circular in general shape but are somewhat shallowly 7- or 9-lobed. The flowers appear in April and are very striking, remarkably so indeed in a genus not notable for floral beauty. They appear in clusters, each flower being about ½ inch across, with red-purple sepals and white petals. When this display is complete, a second one starts with the development of the young fruits which are red in colour. In suitable situations the leaves will turn red and orange before falling.

This is one of numerous plants from western North America for which we must thank the enterprise of the Royal Horticultural Society in sending David Douglas to North America and also, of course, the enterprise of the great collector himself. When one reads his journal one is continually amazed not only at his enthusiasm, but at his refusal to be discouraged when time and time again his collections were destroyed. His various expeditions transformed the garden scene in many ways, and also the landscape in those parts where the Douglas fir has been used in forestry. He introduced this maple in 1826.

Acer fargesii is a slightly tender tree that is partially evergreen in favourable localities. Its leaves are distinct in being entire and oblong-lanceolate in shape. They can reach a length of 4 inches and are then about 1¼ inches across. Both the young leaves and the young shoots are a vivid pink, fading to a pale green as they age. The flowers are red and so are the fruits, although neither are very large. The flower panicles are about 2 inches long, while the fruits are eventually about 1½ inches across. However, coming after the pink shades of the young leaves and the young shoots the plant gives a continuous display of colour throughout the spring and summer. It is not, apparently, particularly brilliant in the autumn.

This plant is yet another of Messrs. Veitch's introductions (under the name of *A. laevigatum fargesii*), which was brought into commerce in 1902. It was collected in Hupeh and Szechwan by E. H. Wilson, a name we shall continually find among the introducers of Chinese shrubs and trees. Wilson was to make four great journeys in Central China, between 1899 and 1911, working either for Messrs. Veitch or for the Arnold Arboretum and its director, Professor Sargent. It would seem probable that his collections have transformed our gardens more than those of any other collector. We tend to associate him with trees and shrubs, forgetting that he was also responsible for the introduction of such popular plants as *Lilium regale*, *L. sargentiae* and *L. willmottiae* as well as a number of primulas (including the very popular *P. pulverulenta*), *Meconopsis integrifolia* and *Thalictrum dipterocarpum*, to name but some of the most popular.

To take another example, one associates George Forrest with the introduction of rhododendrons, but here again we find that Wilson was responsible for the introduction of a large number including such indispensable species as *augustinii*, *auriculatum*, *discolor*, *moupinense*, *orbiculare*, *souliei* and *williamsianum*, to name only the most popular. He was an extremely erudite man with a wide knowledge of all branches of natural history, allied to a fine physique and considerable patience. Although he appeared to get on well with the Chinese, he did not win their confidence in the same way that Forrest did and he does not appear to have had a very high opinion of them. In a tribute to him after his tragic death in a motor accident in 1930, E. H. M. Cox wrote: 'Keenness . . . was one of the outstanding things about him. Courteous though he was, there was a directness in his dealings with people and plants that did not always suit the dilettante. He hated wasting time. He liked a plain question and a plain answer.' His collecting was not confined to China: he also collected in Japan and in Formosa and he travelled to most parts of the globe, but it is chiefly with Chinese plants that he was associated, and when botanists decided to honour him by naming a genus after so distinguished a collector, the name they chose was, appropriately, *Sinowilsonia*.

Perhaps as a result of spending so much time alone, he appears to have been somewhat austere and uncommunicative and does not seem to have had many intimate friends, although his admirers could be numbered in scores. In spite of the fact that he collected and introduced herbaceous plants and lilies (and indeed wrote a monograph on Asian lilies) his main interests undoubtedly lay in woody plants. It is significant that in an article he wrote on his visit to Formosa in the *New Flora and Silva*, Volume 2, he mentions a large number of trees and shrubs, but otherwise only two lilies and one herbaceous plant. Moreover, the lilies and woody plants are given their Latin names, while the herbaceous plant is referred to simply as 'an Edelweiss'.

Wilson's original journeys to China were done at the behest of Messrs. Veitch and took place between 1899 and 1902 and between 1903 and 1905. His later journeys were financed by Harvard University and the Arnold Arboretum at Boston, an institute of which he was Keeper at the time of his death. I make no apology for this brief outline of his career, as his collections must be regarded as among the most important ever made for gardeners and we shall be meeting his name continually throughout this book.

To get back to our maples, the next species that the gardener in search of an acer for more than one season should consider, is *A. ginnala*. This is rather a large shrub than a small tree, although it can, of course, be trained on a stem. It has dark green, 3-lobed leaves, which are heart-shaped at the base. They are not large, being about 3 inches long and 2 inches across; the central lobe is, by far, the largest. The petioles and midrib are reddish in colour, which adds slightly to its attractions. It is grown mainly for its brilliant red autumn colour, which appears to be fairly reliable in its appearance, and also for its whitish flowers. These are not particularly conspicuous, but they have a delightful fragrance which can perfume the air around during the month of May. The plant is a native of northern China and Japan and also of Manchuria. It was distributed by Regel from the St. Petersburg Botanic Gardens in 1860. Its introducer to St. Petersburg does not seem to be known.

Acer griseum is the first of the species we have been discussing which belongs to the section Negundo. In this section the leaves are not lobed, but are compound, being composed of a number of leaflets. In the case of *A. griseum*, the leaf is composed of 3 leaflets, of which the central one is slightly larger than the two lateral ones: it may reach a length of 2½ inches and a width of 1 inch. All the leaflets are an elongated oval in shape. The young leaves are pinkish in colour, fading to a medium green and generally colouring red or orange in the autumn. During the summer the bark peels away in large flakes to reveal a bright orange new bark underneath, which makes a very striking feature. The plant is extremely slow-growing and, although it is said to make a tree up to 40 feet high,[1] there can be very few of such dimensions in this country. Plants 15 years old are only about 10 feet high. The plant is thus very suitable for small gardens. This is another of Wilson's plants and was introduced to commerce by Messrs. Veitch.

Another trifoliate maple is *A. henryi*. This is again a small tree, not exceeding 30 feet in height. The greenish flowers appear in early May, before the leaves unfurl. The latter are borne on longish petioles and consist of 3 leaflets, oval but elongated into a long point, which gives the plant a very elegant appearance. The immature fruits are quite a brilliant red and the leaves generally turn a rich crimson in the autumn.

This was also one of Wilson's introductions, but its discovery was due to Dr. Augustine Henry, in whose honour it was named. Dr. Henry was a keen botanist who worked in the Chinese Imperial Maritime Customs Office and travelled in many parts of China that few Europeans had previously visited. Although he introduced few plants himself, he was instrumental, through Wilson, in bringing many hitherto unknown

[1] Wilson records a tree in China 60 feet high with a girth of 7 feet.

plants into cultivation. Wilson's first action on landing in China was to visit Dr. Henry in Yunnan and it was Henry who indicated to the inexperienced Wilson the best areas to visit. In 1882 he had been transferred from Shanghai to Ichang, 1,000 miles up the Yangtze, and it was in the mountains around the Ichang gorges that Henry started to botanize, sending a large number of herbarium specimens to Kew Gardens. He remained in the Customs service in various parts of China until 1900 and then returned to Europe to study forestry. With H. J. Elwes he wrote the monumental *Trees of Great Britain and Ireland* and eventually was appointed Professor of Forestry at the College of Science of Dublin. Someone who knew him in his old age described him to me as being a very lovable but formidable old man.

Acer japonicum is a rather small, bushy tree, which rarely exceeds 30 feet in height, although plants up to 50 feet have been known. The leaves are roundish, but shallowly lobed (except in the variety *aconitifolium*, which has the leaf divided into numerous, thin, deep lobes), and are up to 5 inches long and wide. The purplish-red flowers appear in April before the leaves have unfurled and are attractive with their long stalks. The leaves of the type turn a rich crimson in the autumn. This autumn colour is lacking in the variety *aureum*, which has rich golden-yellow leaves that maintain their colour throughout the summer. As the name implies the plant is native to Japan and was introduced in 1864, presumably by von Siebold.

Acer platanoides, the Norway maple, makes a large tree, easily reaching 60 feet in height and is very rapid in growth. The leaves are 5-lobed and heart-shaped at the base, up to 7 inches across in large specimens and about 5 inches long. The greenish-yellow flowers appear before the leaves in great quantity in April, while the leaves themselves will generally colour well in shades of red and yellow. This is naturalized in many places in this country, although not truly native, but it is native to many parts of Europe from Norway southwards. There are several cultivars known, among the most notable being 'Schwedleri', which has crimson young growth and purplish flowers. The leaves eventually fade to a dark green and may colour in the autumn. An opposite sequence appears in 'Reitenbachii', in which the leaves turn red in late summer. 'Goldsworth Purple' (also known as 'Nigrum' and 'Crimson King') has rather heavy, dark purple leaves which keep their colour throughout the season, and also has purple flowers. 'Drummondii' has leaves with a white variegation. Although the cultivars with coloured leaves are not quite so rapid in growth as the type, they are still among the fastest growing of trees and the type or any of the cultivars can be recommended for anyone wanting a sizeable and attractive tree in a short time.

A well-flowered specimen is, in my opinion, one of the most attractive of early flowering trees.

Acer palmatum is the popular Japanese maple, usually seen as a large shrub, but in theory capable of reaching heights between 20 and 40 feet. It is rather intolerant of alkaline soil. Wilson found plants in Central China and it may, like so many plants that have long been cultivated in Japan, have originated thence. The Japanese cultivars have been known in this country since 1820 and they are all characterized by graceful, deeply lobed leaves. For our purposes the best are those known as 'Osakazuki' and 'Senkaki'.

'Osakazuki' is one of the more vigorous cultivars of the variety *heptalobum*. The young leaves and twigs emerge in various shades of pink and this colour is also to be noted in the immature fruit, after the leaves have become green. In suitable situations the leaves turn the most vivid scarlet of all trees in the autumn and there are few more colourful spectacles than 'Osakazuki' at its autumnal best. In excessively windy situations, the leaves sometimes fall before they colour and they appear to do best in soils that retain moisture for a long time.

By contrast 'Senkaki' grows very slowly and never, apparently, makes a very large specimen. This too has pinkish young growth and fairly brilliant autumn colour, although far inferior to 'Osakazuki'. Its main attraction lies in the coral-red year-old bark, which makes this a most attractive plant during the winter months. Almost all the cultivars of the 7-lobed variety have pinkish young growth and good autumn colour, but the two described are the most satisfactory.

Acer rubrum is a North American tree, which can reach up to 80 feet in height. It has rather attractive 3- or 5-lobed leaves which are up to 6 inches long and 5 inches across; dark green on the upper surface, but an attractive downy blue-grey on the underside. The flowers appear in late March, before the leaves, but they are a brilliant red in colour. At a later date the immature fruits acquire a dull red hue, which makes them conspicuous. In its native land it colours brilliantly in the autumn, but does not make a very satisfactory display in this country, unless the cultivar 'Sanguineum' can be obtained.

Somewhat similar, but with greenish-yellow flowers, is *A. saccharinum* (syn. *A. dasycarpum*), which has a silver underside to the leaves, which are very attractive when swayed by the breeze. This is a fast-growing tree and one which generally colours well to gold or red in the autumn. It has a very graceful habit, with the younger growths being pendulous. The leaves are larger than those of *A. rubrum* and more deeply lobed, and in mild seasons it is in flower in February. As a result of its early flowering, seeds are rarely set in this country, but, if they are, they are ripe by the end of May and will generally germinate immediately. It can reach a height of 90 feet.

A complete contrast is *A. tartaricum*, which is a shrub up to 30 feet in its natural habitat, but generally less. Young plants resemble many other maples in their leaf-shape, but once the plant is mature it produces leaves that are unlobed or nearly so, broadly oval in shape with a rounded base. Again, unlike most maples, the flower spikes, which do not appear until late May or June, are erect, not pendulous, and some 3 inches long. The flowers are greenish-white in colour. The fruit, which has a samara about an inch long, is a showy red in the autumn, while the leaves turn golden in colour before they fall. Similar in its erect racemes and red fruits is *A. spicatum* from North America, but this has lobed leaves and generally a more brilliant autumn colour. It is not at all easy to obtain, whereas *A. tartaricum* is generally available.

AESCULUS

Although most of the horse chestnuts and buckeyes are agreeable trees and shrubs with their digitate leaves and handsome panicles of flowers, there is only one species which I feel merits inclusion here and even so the point may be felt to be stretched rather to include it.

Aesculus californica is generally a moderately-sized shrub, from 10 to 15 feet high, but spreading rather more, although it can be trained as a tree, when it may attain a height of 30 feet. It is not a very rapid grower. Its leaves are the smallest in the genus, and are composed of five or seven oblong-oval leaflets, which end in a point. Each leaflet is from 2–4 inches long and of a rather curious metallic grey-green colour, which makes the plant conspicuous when not in flower. The white, pink-tinged flowers appear in terminal panicles between the end of June and August and are very fragrant. Very often the top flower of the panicle opens long before the others and may even have set a fruit, before the latter open. This is an attractive shrub or small tree and, in spite of its Californian provenance, appears perfectly hardy.

This is yet one more plant available due to the enterprise of Messrs. Veitch and their collectors, the man in this case being William Lobb. Very little is known of this enterprising Cornishman, who collected assiduously in South America, as well as in California, where he died in 1863. A very large number of attractive plants were first introduced by him, including such treasures as *Embothrium coccineum* and *Lapageria rosea*. His younger brother, Thomas Lobb, was also employed by Messrs Veitch and collected in Malaya and the East Indies. *A. californica* was introduced about 1850 and was first recorded as flowering in 1858.

28

ALNUS

The alders are useful plants for ground that tends to become waterlogged or for any cold and dank place. Where conditions are more promising, there are certainly better plants to be had. However, for an unpromising situation there is much to be said for growing the form of *Alnus incana* called *ramulis coccineis*. This can make a tree up to 60 feet in height and is distinguished from the type by the young wood being reddish in colour, while the male catkins, which usually open in February, are quite a bright red. There is also a variety, *aurea*, in which the young shoots are yellow and so are the leaves, which retain their colour throughout the season. If you have a situation which only an alder will tolerate, you will get more pleasure out of these varieties than of any others, but it would be misleading to claim unusual beauty for either of them.

AMELANCHIER

A genus of the rose family, with which it is difficult to go wrong. They all cover themselves in spring with a mass of white flowers, which may, or may not, be followed by berries that turn red and then purple and finally they tend to make a splendid display of autumn colour. Some of the species are merely shrubby, while others make small trees from 20 to 30 feet high. Most of the species come from the northern parts of North America, but in Europe there is the large-flowered *Amelanchier vulgaris*, while China is the home of *A. asiatica*. The most commonly grown species is known as *A. canadensis*, but may be *A. laevis*. *A. laevis* is slightly more desirable, in that the young leaves are bronzy-purple in colour, while those of *A. canadensis* are green and covered with white hairs. Otherwise there is little to distinguish them. They both flower in April, before the leaves have fully expanded, and both colour red and gold in the autumn.

Amelanchier asiatica has a somewhat more graceful habit, flowers in May, when the leaves are fully expanded, and will often flower again, though less copiously in September. It is not quite so reliable in its autumn colour.

Among the shrubby species, the European *A. ovalis* (syn. *A. vulgaris*) has the largest individual flowers, but does not always thrive so well as some of the North American suckering species, such as *A. oblongifolia* and *A. stolonifera*.

All these species will grow practically anywhere, although one would expect *A. canadensis* to be less vigorous on chalky soils.

There is a somewhat deplorable attitude in gardeners to be rather supercilious about plants that are easily grown, however beautiful they may be. This attitude is often to be found with regard to amelanchiers. Why anyone should sneer at a plant that gives so much pleasure I cannot imagine. They are certainly more attractive than many plants which are more difficult to grow, and give of their attractions over a longer period.

I appear to have omitted to mention the hybrid between *A. canadensis* and *A. laevis*, called *A.* × *grandiflora*. This has the purple young growth of *A. laevis*, but the young leaves are downy, as in *A. canadensis*. The flowers are somewhat larger than those of either of its parents and this is probably the best plant to obtain.

AMORPHA

A North American genus of the *Leguminosae*, the flowers of which are very small, and consist only of a standard petal, with no keel, but crowded in very dense spikes, so that the form of the individual flower is not noticed. Only one species will fit our requirements and that is *Amorpha canescens*. It is only the base that is woody; the growths elongate every spring and die down each winter. The stems and leaves are thickly covered with grey down, which gives the plant a striking appearance. These stems reach from 2–4 feet in height. As they mature, the spikes of flower buds appear in the leaf axils and eventually a large leafy panicle of flowers is formed, consisting of an immense number of small, purplish-blue flowers. In exceptional seasons this panicle can be 18 inches long, but is usually from 6–10 inches. The individual spikes are from 3–6 inches long. The pinnate leaves are only about 3 inches long, but are composed of up to 20 pairs of leaflets, each leaflet being minute. As can be imagined from this description, this is a striking plant at all times during the summer. It used to be thought that its presence indicated that there was lead in the soil and its popular name is the Lead Plant.

ARBUTUS

The strawberry trees are ornamental through their showy fruits and attractive peeling bark. Less so perhaps through their flowers, although they are far from inconspicuous. From this point of view the best-known species, *Arbutus unedo*, is the least decorative, but even so it is an extremely attractive tree and one which will thrive on chalky soils, which very few of the *Ericaceae* do. Although very rewarding, it should be emphasized that arbutus species are rather a long-term investment. Large plants resent root disturbance, so that only small plants should be brought into the garden, and growth is not very rapid at first. Left to themselves they tend to grow as shrubs and some pruning is necessary to induce the formation of a single trunk. All the species are evergreen and all have small urn-shaped flowers with a puckered mouth. In most of the species they are in erect panicles, but in *A. unedo* they are drooping.

There are three species and a hybrid in cultivation, but one species is rather rare. This is *A. andrachne*, a native of eastern Europe and Asia Minor. No one seems to have suggested that it is not perfectly hardy, but I would expect some damage to the leaves in a bad winter. The oval leaves are up to 4 inches long and 2 inches across, dark shining green on the upper side and paler below. The mature branches and the trunk are reddish-brown. The flowers appear in terminal panicles about 3 inches long and are composed of small, dull white, urn-shaped flowers produced in late March and early April, which are followed in the autumn by red 'strawberries'. The plant is not known to exceed 20 feet in this country and is usually much less. In Greece it grows on acid soil, while *A. unedo* is found on calcareous soil.

Where these soils adjoin there occurs the hybrid between the two species, to which the name *A.* × *andrachnoides* has been given. Under this name are a number of plants differing somewhat in size of leaf and vigour, but fairly obviously intermediate between the two species. It can make a tree up to 30 feet in height, but is generally only half this measurement. The flowers are in terminal panicles and may be produced either in late autumn, as on *A. unedo*, or in spring, as is the case with *A. andrachne*. The fruits are ripe in the autumn following the flowering. Formerly there were several selected clones, which were given Latin names such as 'Magnifica' and 'Photinaefolia'. These had particularly large leaves and large flower trusses, but they had to be grafted on to stocks of *A. unedo*, and this has now proved uneconomic so that these clones are probably no longer available.

Arbutus unedo itself is the strawberry tree and is found in southern Europe and also in south-west Eire. This is a smallish tree or large bush, rarely more than 30 feet high, and frequently considerably less. It is easily distinguished from the other common species by the hairiness of the young growths. The leaves tend to be obovate, reaching a length of 4 inches, but with a width of not more than 1½ inches. The flowers are produced in drooping racemes, deep pink in the variety *rubra*, otherwise white, and appear between October and December. The fruits ripen at the same time as the succeeding crop of flowers is emerging. The variety *rubra* has very attractive flowers, but only makes a somewhat low, spreading bush, so that neither the flowers nor the handsome reddish bark can be appreciated as they should be.

A much larger plant than any of the European species is the Californian *A. menziesii*, the madrona. This can reach 100 feet in its native land, but the largest British plant is 50 feet high and most do not exceed 30 feet. Unlike the other species, this will grow quite rapidly, once it has become established, and appears to be perfectly hardy in spite of its provenance. The bark peels yearly to disclose wood of a striking cinnamon colour, which on its own would be sufficient to make this a tree worth growing. Add to this a profusion of elongated oval leaves, up to 6 inches long and 3 inches across, which are a shining dark green on the upper side and a pale glaucous blue underneath and you have something more. But this is not all; in May every branch will produce a pyramidal panicle of white flowers, each panicle up to 9 inches long and 6 inches across and the flowers are followed by red fruits about the size of a pea. It will be appreciated, therefore, that the plant is continually attractive and you may well wonder why it is seen so rarely. The only explanation would seem to lie in the fact that only small pot-grown plants will move successfully, so that one must be prepared to wait some five or seven years before enjoying the plant's full beauty. Once one has passed this proving period, the plant will continue to increase in size and attractiveness for the rest of your life, so it is a worthwhile long-term investment.

The madrona was introduced by David Douglas in 1827 and is named in honour of Archibald Menzies, an enthusiastic amateur naturalist who was the physician on Vancouver's expeditions.

ARCTOSTAPHYLOS

A genus of ericaceous shrubs requiring peaty, acid soils. They are evergreen and the species to be described here are tall shrubs in this country, although *Arctostaphylos manzanita* can become a tree 25 feet high in its native California. I mention these plants as they have been in cultivation, but I would not like to say where they can be obtained at the present day. They would be useful for their early flowers, handsome bark and reasonably decorative fruits.

Arctostaphylos manzanita is a tallish, branching shrub, rarely more than 8 feet high in this country, but up to 25 feet in California. It is curious in that the young shoots, flower buds and leaf stalks are covered with a thick felt. The older bark peels to reveal chocolate-brown wood which is rather striking. The leaves are oval to heart-shaped, up to $2\frac{1}{2}$ inches long and $1\frac{3}{4}$ inches across, dull grey when young, becoming glaucous as they age. The flowers, which are similar to those of the arbutus and pieris in shape, are produced in terminal panicles in March and April; they are a good deep pink in colour. They are followed by reddish-brown berries about $\frac{1}{2}$ inch across. This is a striking plant with its

Acer davidii is one of the
snake-bark maples

Many Acers, such as this
ahogany-like *Acer griseum*,
have attractive bark

Arbutus × *andrachnoides*
has lily of the valley-
like flowers

Its handsome bark is
cinnamon-coloured
when mature

Arbutus unedo has strawberry-like fruits and is popularly known as
the Strawberry Tree

Berberis aristata has large
yellow flowers which
are followed by bloom-
covered red fruits

The gleaming white
bark of *Betula ermanii* is
particularly welcome in
winter

Clematis tangutica has handsome yellow flowers

Its very ornamental seedheads are decorative and long-lasting

Clerodendron fargesii has purplish young growth and white fragrant flowers

The flowers are followed in good seasons by blue fruits

Crataegus orientalis.
The various *Crataegus* species are valuable both for their flowers and also for their fruits and autumn foliage

The attractive white
bracts of *Cornus kousa* are
followed by strawberry-
like fruits

Cornus mas has pale
yellow flowers and its
foliage may colour well
in the autumn

Hippophaë rhamnoides has silver leaves and orange fruits which the birds will ignore

Malus 'Red Sentinel'. Most *Malus* species have brilliant fruits as well as beautiful flowers

The early-flowering
Rhododendron 'Shilsonii'
has brilliant red flowers
followed by glaucous
blue young growth

Rhododendron makinoi
produces its shell-pink
flowers in May and its
handsome new growth
in July and August

Rosa moyesii and its
hybrids have very
attractive flowers. This
variety is 'Geranium'

These are followed by
large bright scarlet heps

The young emerging
shoots of *Sorbus aria*

Sorbus intermedia. Most
of the *Sorbus* species
have brilliant fruits

Stachyurus praecox produces its catkin-like flowers very early in the year

In the autumn the leaves colour well

The white flowers of
Stewartia sinensis

Later the leaves colour
and the old bark flakes
away to reveal a pale
pink trunk

Viburnum opulus 'Xanthocarpum'. Our native Guelder Rose is difficult to
top as a flowering shrub
It has attractive fruits, especially this variety with its yellow berries

conspicuous bark, greyish foliage and pink flowers. It is said to require a sunny position and to be impatient of root disturbance. Plants should be put in their permanent positions when very small.

Arctostaphylos patula, another Californian species, is of recent introduction. It makes a branching shrub from 3–5 feet high with rather striking smooth, bright red bark. The leaves are nearly round, 1¾ inches long and 1½ inches across, and are bright green, sometimes with a faintly glaucous tinge. The pink flowers are produced in quite large, loose panicles from March to May and are followed by blackish berries. The Royal Horticultural Society's *Dictionary of Gardening* says that this is: 'one of the finest species in cultivation'. Presumably it has not been found very easy to propagate. Both these Californians are regarded as quite hardy, although I have no reports of what may happen in very severe winters.

BERBERIS

A large genus of generally medium-sized shrubs with a rather curious distribution. Like several other genera, there is a distribution across the north temperate zones from North America through Europe and Asia to China and Japan, but also, somewhat unusually, there are a number of species found in the temperate parts of South America, in Chile and Argentina. Moreover, the closely related genus of *Mahonia* (distinguished principally from *Berberis* by their evergreen pinnate leaves, but *Mahonia* and *Berberis* will hybridize) is also found in the Tropics. Although, owing to the large number of species, it is convenient to hive off *Mahonia*, botanists will tell you that *Berberis* do not in reality have simple leaves in tufts, as appearances suggest, but that each leaf is the terminal leaflet of a pinnate leaf, of which the side leaflets are suppressed, while the tuft is in reality a branch in which the internodes are suppressed. Similarly the spines, which are usually in groups of three, are also metamorphosed, pinnate leaves. Occasionally a berberis will produce a pinnate leaf, which goes some way towards proving the botanists' argument.

From our point of view, the attraction of berberis, apart from the flowers, lies in their colourful fruits and, sometimes, in brilliant autumn leaf colour. This excludes all the evergreen species, which have blue-black berries that are not very conspicuous. Similarly all the South American species, although they contain those species with the most attractive flowers, tend to have rather dull berries and are either evergreen or, when deciduous (*B. chillanensis* and *B. montana*), the autumn colour is not noteworthy. Occasionally the popular *B. darwinii* will cover itself with bunches of purplish berries, looking like miniature grape clusters, and will then look quite effective. Such a phenomenon is not of yearly occurrence and, as a general rule, *B. darwinii* is grown entirely for its splendid flowers.

Even when one has excluded all the evergreen species and all those from South America, one is still left with far too many. Moreover, they all tend to look rather similar with yellow flowers. However, the type of inflorescence will give some help in identification, and the leaf size and shape vary. As a general rule berberis appear fairly indifferent to the type of soil they are offered, but a few will not be happy in rather shallow, chalky soils. They like plenty of light. As a general rule, the leaves are obovate in shape and they will not be described in the following accounts, unless they differ from this typical shape. On the other hand, their dimensions will be given, as these are sometimes helpful in distinguishing the species. The plants I list have been rather arbitrarily selected and many equally valuable species may have been omitted.

Berberis aemulans may well be only a form of the better-known *B. diaphana*. It is, however, preferable to this species, owing to its plum-red young shoots which give the shrub some interest, even in the winter. It is a vigorously growing shrub, up to 6 feet in height. The leaves are up to 2 inches long and ¾ inch across. The flowers appear in summer in clusters of 3–6 and are a good bright yellow, and are followed by orange-red berries. The leaves often turn red before falling. This is yet another of Wilson's introductions.

Berberis angulosa is a Himalayan plant, up to 4 feet in height with rather leathery, glossy, dark green leaves up to 1½ inches long. The flowers are produced singly from the leaf axils on slender stalks up to 1 inch long and are large for the genus, up to ¾ inch across and orange-yellow in colour. The berries are also quite large and reddish in colour. The flowers appear in June or July. A similar species, but much larger and with a glaucous underside to the leaf, was introduced by Ludlow and Sherriff in 1938 and given the name *B. ludlowii*.

Berberis aristata[1] makes a spreading shrub up to 10 feet high and 15 feet across and so must be allowed plenty of room. It is not always completely deciduous; young plants are liable to retain most of their leaves through the winter and, in old plants, vigorous new growths from the root may keep their leaves. These may be up to 4 inches long and are grouped in tufts of from three to seven. From each tuft in early summer a drooping raceme about 4 inches long bears a large number of bright golden-yellow flowers, followed by red berries covered with a bluish-white bloom which is very effective. Occasionally the flowers show a reddish tinge. Apparently it is not as common in cultivation as its ap-

---

[1] The plant usually supplied under this name is, apparently, *B. glaucocarpa*.

pearance in catalogues suggests, *B. floribunda* being often sent out under this name. This is very similar but has leaves only up to 2 inches long, the flowers are smaller and the berries less pruinose. Another similar species is *B. chitria*. This can be most easily distinguished by the two-year-old wood, which is grey in *B. aristata* and reddish-brown in *B. chitria*. The flowers in *B. chitria* are produced in a panicle, not a raceme, and do not appear until late June or July; both species are equally desirable.

Berberis beaniana, yet another Wilson plant, is a shrub up to 8 feet in height with deep yellow flowers in June and purple berries in the autumn. It appears, like so many berrying plants, to fruit with more vigour if several plants are put together to allow cross-fertilization. The flowers are in dense panicles that may contain 25 florets, each one only ¼ inch across. It is unusual in its purple fruits, which are covered with a mauve bloom making a striking autumn display. The leaves are up to 2 inches long, but generally less.

Berberis dasystachya is easily distinguished by its nearly circular leaves tapered to a stalk. The leaves themselves are up to 2½ inches long and slightly less wide, and the stalks are from 1–1½ inches long. The flowers appear in late April and May in densely packed racemes and are extremely fragrant. Reginald Farrer, who introduced the plant, compares the scent to that of *Lilium auratum*. It makes a large arching shrub up to 12 feet high, but considerably wider. The flowers are pale yellow in colour and are packed on to slender racemes, to be followed by coral-red berries. Unfortunately, like so many of the rarer berberis, seed is not easy to come by and the plant is hard to propagate by other means. *B. kansuensis* is very similar, but, if anything, preferable, as it has reddish young shoots, which keep their colour for the first winter, and slightly larger flowers.

One is always rather surprised to find Farrer's name as an introducer of a shrub; his name is so associated with alpines that one forgets his wider interests. It is to him that we owe *Buddleia alternifolia* and on his last voyage, when he had E. H. M. Cox with him, he sent back seeds of several berberis, rhododendrons and of *Magnolia rostrata*. He also, through his vivid writings, may indirectly have helped other plant collectors. His descriptions were so vivid that he may well have encouraged innumerable gardeners to subscribe to the work of such men as Forrest and Kingdon-Ward. He had an extremely sharp tongue and made many enemies, but few could doubt his devotion to plants or fail to admire his descriptions; although occasionally his prose was slightly of the kind a gardener might term *purpurascens*, that was at least preferable to the colourless, pedestrian stuff which is all that most of us can produce. If you compare his descriptions of plant collecting in China in *On the Eaves of the World* with Wilson's *A Naturalist in Western China*, one cannot fail to be struck, not only with Farrer's far greater readability, but also with the fact that you get a much more vivid impression of the terrain and its inhabitants, although Wilson will give you more information about the plants themselves. If Farrer was not interested in a plant he ignored it and his interests were fairly circumscribed; everything was grist to Wilson's mill.

Berberis dictyophylla is a graceful shrub up to 6 feet in height with arching growths that give a fountain-like effect. The growths from the root are reddish in colour, covered with a whitish bloom to start with (this bloom is lacking in the variety *epruinosa*). The leaves are very small, usually less than an inch long, green above, but white on the underside, produced in tufts at interval along the branches. The small pale yellow flowers appear in May and are followed by red fruits, which are covered with a white bloom at first. The foliage turns a good red fairly consistently before falling. According to the author on the genus in the Royal Horticultural Society's *Dictionary of Gardening*, the true species is rare in cultivation and most plants with this label would be more suitably ascribed to *B. approximata*, now given specific rank, but at one time regarded merely as a variety. It is distinguished from the true species by its smaller leaves and by the presence of bloom on the berries.

This is the first plant we have met with, so far, whose introduction is due to the remarkable French missionaries, who travelled around so much of China in the nineteenth century, at a time when there were few other Europeans in the interior. Two of them are associated in this plant. It was discovered by Delavay in Yunnan in 1886, but it was some years later when Farges sent seed to the great French nurseryman Maurice de Vilmorin. He distributed plants in 1897. All these missionaries, David, Delavay, Farges and Soulié, botanized and collected herbarium specimens, but they did not introduce so many plants as the more professional collectors. This is, after all, only to be expected. Botany could be for them only a spare time recreation and, although they could often, doubtless, collect seeds, they might have to wait a very long time before they could be despatched to Europe and many seeds must, therefore, have lost their viability. This probably accounts for the fact that of the original 37 seeds of *Davidia involucrata* that Père Farges sent to Vilmorin, only one germinated.

Berberis francisci-ferdinandii, a rather off-putting name, makes a fairly tall shrub, up to 10 feet high and rather more across. The young shoots are purplish in colour for the first year. The leaves are shortly stalked and may reach a length of 2½ inches. The yellow flowers open in June, are very small but are borne in great numbers on drooping racemes that may be 5 inches long. They are followed by brilliant red berries, looking like miniature bunches of scarlet grapes. This is yet one more Wilson introduction.

Berberis jamesiana is a fairly tall shrub, reaching to 9 feet or more, with purple young shoots and leaves in clusters, each leaf up to 2¼ inches long and 1½ inches across. The yellow flowers open in late June and are arranged in racemes up to 4 inches long. These are followed by coral-coloured translucent berries, which are quite outstanding. Moreover, the foliage turns a good red before it falls and, all in all, this is one of the most rewarding of this baffling genus.

The plant was discovered and introduced by George Forrest on his third expedition which lasted from 1912 to 1914. It would be difficult to decide whether gardeners owe more to Forrest than to Wilson or vice versa, and remarkably unprofitable. Both were collectors of the highest order. Forrest appears to have got on remarkably well with the Chinese and was able to train them to help in his collecting. Unfortunately for us he died on his last expedition and we are deprived of his own account of his wonderful work. It would surely have been worth reading. He is most renowned for the amazing number of rhododendron species he introduced to cultivation for the first time, but he enriched all branches of the garden.

Berberis koreana is somewhat less vigorous, reaching only to about 6 feet with comparatively large leaves up to 2½ inches long and 1¾ inches across, which colour well in the autumn. In some forms the spines are as much as ¼ inch across and, since the young shoots are reddish, they are quite conspicuous on these. The yellow flowers appear in May on slender racemes up to 4 inches long and are followed by bright red, rather waxy berries, which will hang on the bush for a long time if the birds allow.

Berberis morrisonensis is found on Mount Morrison in Formosa at great heights. Although it is reported as growing up to 6 feet in the wild, it rarely exceeds 3 feet in cultivation and makes a useful compact shrub for the front of shrubberies. The young shoots are often, but not invariably, red in colour. The leaves are in tufts, each leaf up to an inch in length. In June the pale yellow flowers emerge in clusters and are followed by bright red translucent berries. Before they fall the leaves turn many brilliant shades of gold and scarlet.

It was apparently first collected by an amateur, a Mr. W. Price, in 1912, but its introduction into commerce was due to Wilson, who collected it for the Arnold Arboretum in 1918.

Berberis poiretii is another of these Chinese barberries with pendulous

branches, yellow flowers in racemes and brilliant berries. As it is cultivated in Japan in gardens, it has been in cultivation for longer than most
of the Chinese species, being introduced about 1860. The flowers emerge
at the end of May. The plant is of a very graceful habit and will not
exceed 6 feet in height. Yet another of these is *B. prattii* (originally
distributed as *B. polyantha*) which is distinguished by its very profuse
panicles of flowers, up to 4 inches long and 1½ inches across, which may
bear 50 florets and which are followed by large clusters of red berries.
This can reach a height of 10 feet. The species was discovered by
A. E. Pratt in 1899 and introduced by Wilson five years later.

Berberis replicata is one of the evergreen berberis. It is not very tall, up
to 5 feet in height and grows rather slowly. The young shoots are quite a
conspicuous yellow. The leaves are linear, with recurved edges, so that
they appear very narrow. They are up to 2 inches long, tipped with a
spine, dark green on the upper side and whitish below. The flowers are
a good bright yellow, a ¼ inch across, which is quite large for a
berberis, in clusters of up to 10, each flower on a separate stalk about
½ inch long. In mild seasons they may appear in February, but more
usually in April. They are followed by berries which turn first red and
then a dark purple. Introduced by Forrest in 1917, this is one of the most
striking of the evergreen berberis and the only one with ornamental fruit.

Berberis telomaica is outstanding among the barberries for its glaucous,
blue-green leaves, which make it a unique foliage plant. Both the pale
yellow flowers and the red fruit are also covered in a white bloom,
which permeates the whole plant. The flowers are solitary or in clusters
and open about June. The plant can reach a height of 6 feet, but spreads
more widely. It is sometimes very slow to get away, after being moved,
and some patience may be necessary for the first year or so. Once
established it will grow vigorously. I would doubt if it would thrive in
chalky soils, although as a general rule berberis are very tolerant of all
soil conditions. The plant was discovered by Kingdon-Ward in south-
east Tibet and was introduced in 1927. Kingdon-Ward can be mentioned
in the same breath as Wilson and Forrest as a great collector; as well as
visiting China, he explored in Burma and Tibet and so greatly extended
the range of available plants. Moreover, he was a highly literate explorer
and has chronicled his journeys in a very attractive manner.

Berberis thunbergii is one of the better-known species, with its neat
habit and small rounded leaves. The purple-leaved form, *B. t. atropurpurea*, is perhaps even more popular than the type. It is capable of reaching a height of 8 feet, but is usually considerably less, as it tends to spread
rather than to ascend. The flowers have red sepals and the yellow petals
are flushed with red, but they are produced singly in the leaf-axils and

are not very conspicuous. On the other hand, the berries are very brilliant and the green-leaved form turns a brilliant crimson in the autumn.

Berberis vernae is an attractive shrub up to 10 feet in height, with long narrow leaves, up to 1¾ inches long and ½ inch across. It has densely crowded, racemose inflorescences of a very bright yellow, which open in May. They are followed by salmon-coloured berries. The young shoots are reddish in colour and quite attractive in the winter. The plant was discovered by William Purdom in Kansu in 1910, but its introduction appears to be due to Wilson. Purdom seems to have been a very unfortunate collector. Even when, as in the case of *Viburnum farreri* (syn. *V. fragrans*), he introduced a valuable plant, it was neglected and it was not even named, until Farrer praised it in his writings. According to Farrer he was a perfect travelling companion and he has never been given the credit he would appear to have deserved.

Although not outstandingly attractive, *B. virescens* deserves a mention for the brilliant orange-red of the young growths, which are quite outstanding in winter. It will grow to about 9 feet in height and has, generally, good autumn colour. The flowers are greenish-yellow and not very conspicuous; the red berries are also not among the most exciting in the genus. This was discovered and introduced by that prodigy of energy Sir Joseph Hooker, the mere enumeration of whose activities tends to make normal mortals feel slightly fatigued. The first scientific collecting of plants in the Himalayas was only an episode in his crowded life, which enriched not only botany but most gardeners as well.

Our own native *B. vulgaris* is not to be despised with its profusion of yellow flowers in May and its marvellous display of scarlet berries in the autumn. Moreover, the birds do not find the berries very palatable, so that they remain for some time on the bushes. The leaves do not colour, but apart from that, there is little to say that the Oriental species are superior either in flowers or in fruit. There is also a good purple-leaved form, known as *B. v. purpurifolia*.

Berberis wilsonae is a rather low shrub, sometimes partially evergreen, with brilliant coral-red berries and good autumn colour. It is a pleasant enough shrub in its way, but when crossed with one of the species with long racemes of flowers (probably *B. aggregata*) it has given rise to the hybrid known as *B. × rubrostilla*. This has extremely large fruits, over ½ inch long, of a beautiful translucent red. There are various forms, differing in the colour of the berries. *B. wilsonae*, named in honour of Mrs. Wilson, was introduced about 1904, while *B. × rubrostilla* appeared at the Royal Horticultural Society's Garden at Wisley and was first exhibited in 1916. The cross was not made deliberately, which is why no one is quite sure of the pollen parent. Subsequent crosses were made deliberately with B. *aggregata*, so that this is the probable parentage of most modern forms of this hybrid.

Berberis yunnanensis is a dense, rounded shrub of from 3–6 feet in height, with nearly circular leaves up to 1½ inches long and 1 inch across. It is noteworthy for the size of its flowers, which are ¾ inch across, produced in clusters of from 3–8 flowers. They are a rather disappointing pale yellow. The bright red berries are also large, ½ inch long, and make a brave display, which is enhanced by the brilliant crimson of the autumnal foliage.

The plant was discovered by Père Delavay in 1885 and he may well have sent seed to Vilmorin. In any case the plant reached England via France in 1904.

It may seem otiose to state that this is a very confusing genus and it is by no means easy to make a choice of the best varieties. If it can be obtained, there is much to be said for B. *dasystachya* on account of its fragrant flowers. Both B. *beaniana* and B. *vernae* have deeper yellow flowers than the majority, and even more brilliant are the flowers of B. *aristata*. B. *beaniana* is also exceptional in its purple berries, while the bluish bloom on the berries of B. *aristata* also makes them different from the majority of species. The foliage of B. *telomaica* is very striking, but the flowers and fruits are less interesting than those of many others. For autumn colour B. *morrisonensis* is probably the first choice, but here the selection is very wide. For a really brilliant display B. *prattii* is noteworthy, but it is not too easy to obtain and one may well have to make do with B. *aggregata*, which has panicles only some 1½ inches long, as opposed to the 4-inch long panicles of B. *prattii*, and which tends, therefore, to be rather less effective.

❧ Betula – Cotoneaster

BETULA

A genus of deciduous trees and large shrubs found throughout the north temperate zones, the birches (*Betula*) attract attention through their graceful habit and often through their attractive bark. The leaves will occasionally turn golden in the autumn, but birches are not generally notable for their autumn display. Although they make handsome trees in quite a short time, they are not particularly suitable for small gardens if many other plants are to be grown. This is because they have a very wide-ranging, extensive root system and take the nourishment from the soil over a far wider range than the spread of their branches would suggest. However, this extensive root system ensures that the plants will grow well even in rather poor, thin soils. In large demesnes, where space is available, they are very useful for their colourful bark and graceful branchlets.

Betula albo-sinensis has a rather inappropriate name. It will make, eventually, a tree up to 60 feet or more high, with a trunk of more than 6 feet in girth. The leaves are oval, with a pointed end and rounded base and are 3 inches long and 1½ inches across. The plant's main attraction is the brilliant 'orange-red bark, which on exfoliating exposes the glaucous waxy bloom of the layer below', as Wilson, its introducer wrote. There is a variety, *septentrionalis*, with the bark either orange-brown, orange-yellow or orange-grey, which Wilson thought even more attractive.

Betula ermanii shows a curious divergence between the colour of the bark on the branches and on the trunk. The trunk is a very fine creamy-white, while the branches are orange-brown. This makes, as one might imagine, a very splendid display in winter. The leaves are broadly ovate, tapering to a point and with a heart-shaped base; they reach a length of 3 inches and a width of 2 inches. In its native lands of Manchuria and Korea it makes a tree up to 100 feet high. Like so many plants from these regions, it is not acclimatized to the English winter and is liable to start into growth, whenever there is a mild spell in the winter and subsequently be damaged by frost. It is best, therefore, to obtain the Japanese form, *B. e. nipponica* (syn. *B. e. subcordata*), which starts later into growth and is only distinguished from the type by slight botanical differences that do not concern the gardener.

Betula jacquemontii is a Himalayan plant, close to the better-known *B. utilis*, but far hardier and a better garden plant. It can make a tree up to 60 feet high and has exceptionally brilliant white bark. The leaves can attain a length of 3 inches and a width of 2 inches. If one has plenty of room one could find room for the North American *B. lutea*, which has the peeled bark an unusual shade of yellow-brown and also has unusually large leaves, up to 4½ inches long. Our own native birch, whatever it may be called now—it appears to fluctuate between *B. pendula* and *B. verrucosa*—takes a lot of beating if an agreeably barked tree is required. The two pendulous forms 'Tristis' and 'Youngii' are particularly attractive. The variety *dalecarlica*, the Swedish birch, with laciniate leaves, is another attractive form, but appears to be rather a poor doer. Where it will thrive, this is probably the most attractive of all the white-barked birches, as the laciniate, lobed leaves give an additional attraction, which most birches lack.

CALLICARPA

A genus of mainly tropical shrubs, of which there are three hardy species. I would be a little doubtful about growing two of them in the north of the country. The third species, *Callicarpa dichotoma*, is native to north China and Korea, and should be completely impervious to any frosts that might occur in the winter, but would be tender with regard to late spring frosts. All the hardy species are rather low-growing shrubs, with pinkish flowers in late summer and masses of small violet or lilac berries in October. At the time that the berries colour, the leaves will turn delicate shades of pink.

The tallest of the hardy plants seems to alternate its name between *C. bodinieri giraldii* and *C. giraldiana*. This can reach a height of 9 feet, although it seems comparatively rarely that it exceeds 6 feet. The leaves are lanceolate, up to 5 inches long and half as wide and are downy on both surfaces. The lilac flowers open in July and are borne in axillary clusters, that may be as much as 1½ inches across, and are followed three months later by masses of pale lilac berries. Although birds will attack callicarpa berries, they usually leave them to the last, so that, even in bird-infested gardens, some enjoyment can be confidently looked for.

The plant is native to China and, from its name, one would expect it to have been discovered by the Italian missionary Padre Giraldi, but its discovery is attributed to Augustine Henry in 1887 and its introduction twenty years later to Wilson.

Callicarpa dichotoma was introduced to cultivation in 1857 by Fortune (under the name *C. purpurea*). It has a wide range, and plants from the northern extremes should be reliably hardy. It makes a small shrub, rarely much more than 4 feet high, with oval leaves up to 3 inches long, axillary clusters of deep pink flowers, which open in July and, eventually, dark lilac berries. Although it has been so long in cultivation, it is rather a scarce plant and the first introductions did not prove very hardy. Later introductions appear to be more satisfactory.

The species most frequently seen in gardens is *C. japonica*. This will reach a height of 5 feet and has leaves similar to those of *C. giraldiana* but somewhat narrower, and glabrous. The Chinese form of this, *C. j. angustata* (syn. *C. j. longifolia*), has leaves that are only about an inch across, but may be 9 inches long. The pale pink flowers open in August in clusters about an inch across and are followed by the abundant small violet berries, which make this one of the most attractive of berrying shrubs. The plant was diagnosed by Thunberg in the late eighteenth century and introduced to cultivation in 1845, presumably by von Siebold. However, the Chinese plant, according to Loudon's *Hortus Britannicus*, was in cultivation as *C. longifolia* in 1825 (he also records *C. purpurea* as being in cultivation in 1822, but this was probably not *C. dichotoma* as its provenance is said to be the East Indies).

CAMELLIA

The small-flowered *Camellia cuspidata* deserves mention here, not only for its profusion of small white flowers, which appear in April, but also for its copper-coloured young growth, which makes it attractive in June and early July. This attractive young growth is also found in the charming hybrid 'Cornish Snow' (*saluenensis* × *cuspidata*) which has larger flowers, more profusely borne. Neither of these plants make very large shrubs; they rarely exceed 6 feet in height, and they have shining, evergreen leaves, ovate in shape, tapering to a point and rounded at the base. Like all camellias they prefer a humus-rich soil, which should be slightly acid and should not be exposed to prolonged drought. *C. cuspidata* was introduced by Messrs. Veitch from Wilson's collecting and first distributed in 1912.

CARYA

The hickories are extremely handsome trees, related to the walnuts. They all have very large pinnate leaves, which turn a good golden colour before falling, while the trunks are also rather striking. Although perfectly hardy, they are rarely seen. This is because they can only be moved successfully when very small plants and are best grown from seed and planted out in their permanent positions as seedlings. The first root to be produced by the seedling develops into a tap root and plants always grow better if this is not damaged. W. J. Bean wrote: 'A young tree in deep loam, undisturbed, and with its tap root preserved, will be a better tree in 10 years than another treated in the ordinary way will be in twenty'. The majority of the species are natives of eastern North America, but two species have been discovered in east Asia. So far as I know only *Carya cordiformis* and *C. pecan* are currently in commerce, but it should be possible to obtain seeds of other species from America.

Like all members of the walnut family, they like a rich deep soil and would be no good on shallow soils, although the actual soil reaction does not appear to be important. The walnut family has a reputation for being slow growing, which does not seem to be justified. In the right soil these trees appear to grow quite rapidly and to make sizeable specimens in from seven to ten years. Seedlings do not make a great deal of top growth for the first two or three years, but tend to accelerate markedly as they age. Of the species to be described here, *C. myristicaeformis* does appear to be rather a slow grower, the others are quite rapid.

Carya cordiformis (syn. *C. amara*) has been known in English gardens, according to Aiton's *Index Kewensis*, since 1766. It will, eventually, make a large tree up to 100 feet in height. It has brownish bark, which exfoliates like a birch or *Acer griseum*, and the winter buds are covered with bright yellow scales, so that the tree is quite striking in the winter. The pinnate leaves are composed of 5 or 7 (rarely 9) leaflets. Each leaflet may be up to 6 inches long, except the lowest pair, which is always smaller. The whole leaf can attain a length of 15 inches, although this is unusual, and 10 inches can be considered a good size. The individual leaflets are an elongated oval, tapered at each end and toothed, up to 6 inches long and $2\frac{1}{2}$ inches across. When the plant is sufficiently large it will produce male and female inflorescences. The females are inconspicuous, but the male flowers appear in bunches of catkins some 3 inches long and are moderately attractive. The leaves turn a good, clear yellow in the autumn. This has proved to be the best species for gardens in this country.

Carya myristicaeformis, 'perhaps the most beautiful of the hickories' according to Professor Sargent, is a native of the south-eastern United States and is often found growing on limestone formations. Although discovered by Michaux in 1802, it was not brought into cultivation in this country until 1911, presumably through Professor Sargent and the Arnold Arboretum. It will eventually make a tree up to 80 feet high, but is slow-growing in its early stages. The young wood is covered with yellowish scales. The leaves are up to 14 inches long, made up of from 5 to 11 leaflets. The terminal leaflet is much larger than the others and of a more oval shape. The side ones tend to be lanceolate and about 3 inches long, while the terminal leaflet is obovate and up to 5 inches long. The underside of the leaves are covered with silvery scales, which gives the plant its distinct attraction. In spite of its southern habitat it appears to be quite hardy. All these trees come into leaf rather late in the season and so are unlikely to be damaged by late frosts, except in very unusual seasons.

Carya ovata makes a tree up to 120 feet high, with very characteristic grey bark, which flakes away from the trunk in pieces over a foot in length. This flaking is similar to that observed in the planes, except that in this carya, the flake is attached to the trunk at its centre, before it becomes detached. This has been known in English gardens since 1629, but has never become common, although it makes a very handsome tree. The leaves of mature trees are up to 14 inches long, but can be twice this size on young vigorous trees. The leaf is composed of 5 leaflets, of which the top 3 are larger and more rounded than the bottom pair and on young trees the terminal leaflet alone may be a foot in length and 5 inches across. The tree colours a good golden-yellow in the autumn.

Carya tomentosa has the delightful name of the Mocker Nut, and is rare in cultivation, although it has been grown over here since 1766. It is similar in many respects to *C. ovata*, from which it is easily distinguished by the fact that the leaf of *C. ovata* has only 5 leaflets, while that of *C. tomentosa* has either 7 or 9, and even more by the fact that the leaf of *C. tomentosa* is delightfully fragrant and can scent the air in favourable conditions, such as an early summer morning while the dew is still on the ground. *C. tomentosa* also lacks the shaggy bark of *C. ovata*. On young plants the leaves can attain a length of 20 inches and the terminal leaflet can be 8 inches long. The winter buds are large, nearly an inch long and $\frac{1}{2}$ inch across and the young shoots are covered with down. In the autumn the leaves turn a very fine yellow and the tree is most spectacular.

Although the pecan nut, *C. pecan* (syn. *C. olivaeformis*), is available commercially, it never seems to have proved very satisfactory in our climate, owing to the fact that it comes so late into growth that the young wood never ripens satisfactorily. This is a pity as it has very attractive leaves composed of from 11–15 scimitar-shaped leaflets, which may each be 6 inches long, so that the whole leaf is extremely large.

CASTANOPSIS

Castanopsis chrysophylla is an evergreen tree, capable of reaching over 100 feet in its native California, but rarely more than 30 feet in this country. The leaves are a lance-shaped oval, up to 4 inches long and 1 inch across, dark glossy green on the surface, but a wonderful golden colour on the underside. The plant is monoecious, with the male flowers in erect catkins up to 1½ inches long, but quite conspicuous, with their yellow stamens. The female flowers eventually produce a burr, similar in appearance to that of the sweet chestnut (*Castanea sativa*). The plant was seen on several occasions by Douglas, but he failed to introduce it and it was not until 1844 that it arrived in this country. The fruit will ripen in the British Isles, but takes two years to do so; the nut is edible, but not outstandingly delicious. Acid soil is essential for its success and according to W. J. Bean: 'it is fatal to expose the trunk of this tree to full sunlight and its lower branches should not be cut away'. This is really rather a pity as the most outstanding feature of the plant is the golden underside of the leaves and these could best be observed by standing underneath the branches. If it is dangerous to expose the trunk to bright sunlight, it would be best perhaps placed in a somewhat shaded position; say in the lee of a larger tree that could protect the trunk from the midday sun. It would also, presumably, grow satisfactorily if planted in woodland. It does not appear to be a very rapid grower in our climate.

CATALPA

A genus of deciduous trees with very bushy heads and large handsome leaves, followed by pyramidal panicles of trumpet-shaped flowers. The plants are rapid growers, but not very long-lived and should be expected to deteriorate after 40 or 50 years. The very bushy top is due to the fact that the new growths never form a terminal bud, as do most trees, but two or three lateral buds, so that each growth will produce two or three branchlets the succeeding year. In order to get a proper trunk, it is necessary to train up a single leader for some years, pinching out all lateral growths until the desired height is reached, after which it can be allowed to branch freely. The trees have an exotic appearance, with their large, ovate leaves and heads of flowers in August, but, personally, I always have the feeling that there is something slightly disappointing in them. Next year, one feels, there will be a really splendid display, but next year, like tomorrow, never comes and the display always falls short of being as impressive as the size of the tree would seem to warrant.

For our purpose only one plant is really suitable and that is the cultivar 'Aurea' of *Catalpa bignonioides*. *C. bignonioides* itself is the species most frequently seen and the one that seems best adapted to the British climate. It is easily distinguished from other species in cultivation by the vile smell that the leaves give out when crushed. These leaves, ovate with a heart-shaped base, are very large in young specimens, and up to 10 inches long and 8 inches across on mature trees. In the cultivar 'Aurea' these leaves are a rich yellow, which intensifies somewhat as the season advances. The flowers, like those of the type, are white with yellow and purple spots, each flower about 1½ inches long, gathered in a pyramidal panicle that may be 10 inches long and wide.

A plant that is sometimes offered as *C. ovata purpurea* and sometimes as *C. × hybrida* 'Purpurea' has somewhat larger leaves, which may be 3-lobed, and the young wood and the unfolding leaves are of so dark a purple as to appear almost black. This purple colouring eventually fades out and the leaves are a dark green for the latter half of the season. The flowers are not dissimilar from those of *C. bignonioides*, but are slightly smaller. Both these species make trees from 20–40 feet high. After a hot summer all catalpas will produce their long, thin, cylindrical seed capsules, which may be as much as 2 feet long and which can look very effective.

Catalpa bignonioides is native to the eastern United States and has been known in Great Britain since 1726; *C. ovata*, although native to China, has long been cultivated in Japan. Engelbert Kaempfer mentioned it in his book about Japan, *Amoenitates Exotici*, published in 1694, and it was from Japan that Siebold introduced it to Europe in 1849. Owing to his medical skill, Siebold was allowed to travel in many parts of Japan that were otherwise closed to foreigners in the early nineteenth century, and he took full advantage of his opportunities. The high opinion that the Japanese had of him was shared by Siebold himself and he was rather unpopular with his fellow botanists, who regarded him as conceited and overbearing. This may well have been true, but it is undeniable that European gardeners have to thank him for many Japanese plants, although, like Robert Fortune, his main importations were garden plants rather than native wildings.

CLADRASTIS

Cladrastis lutea (syn. *C. tinctoria*), known as the Yellow Wood, is a deciduous tree, usually around 40 feet in height, with large pinnate leaves and panicles of white, pea-shaped flowers. The leaves may reach a length of 12 inches and are composed of 7 or 9 leaflets. These are broadly oval in shape and vary in size; the largest is the terminal leaflet, which may be 4½ inches long and 3 inches across, while the basal pair will be only 1½ inches long and ¾ inch across. They turn bright gold in the autumn. The white pea-shaped flowers, produced in June, are individually about 1½ inches long and are produced in drooping panicles over a foot in length. They are not produced very freely after wet summers.

Cladrastis sinensis, with bluish flowers in erect panicles, produced in July, is a more reliable flowerer, but lacks the handsome autumn colour of the American species. It might be admitted here, as the leaves, which are very large and composed of 11 or 13 leaflets, each of which is from 3–5 inches long, are an attraction in themselves. The plants are not rapid growers and do not flower until about 10 feet high and 15 years old, so far as I can make out. It comes into leaf very late indeed; probably the last of all deciduous trees to come into leaf. The underside of the leaves has a pleasant glaucous hue.

CLEMATIS

There is a group of Asiatic clematis, flowering from midsummer on-wards, all with yellow flowers which are followed by very picturesque seedheads. Each seed has a long feathery style, so that the plant is covered after flowering with these feathery conglomerations. Our own Travellers' Joy also has these attractive fruits, but lacks any beauty of flower.

The first of these clematis to flower is also the best. This is *C. tangutica*, which will start into blossom in late June and continue for at least six weeks. This means that at one period both flowers and fruiting heads can be seen together. The leaves are pinnate or doubly pinnate up to 8 inches long. The yellow flowers are up to 4 inches across in the best clones, but usually somewhat less and are shaped like a lamp-shade. This will be followed by *C. serratifolia*, with biternate leaves, but otherwise similar to *C. tangutica*. The flowers are smaller, but borne in greater profusion. They tend to appear in August and September.

Last of these clematis to flower is *C. orientalis*, which is found over most of Asia and is, accordingly, very variable. This will flower from August to October. The most popular form is that sent back by Ludlow and Sherriff under their number 13342. This has remarkably thick petals, looking like lemon peel. It is not, however, a particularly good colour, but a rather insipid pale yellow and there are other forms about with larger flowers of a better colour. The best forms have purple stamens like those of *C. serratifolia*. Owing to its late flowering, *C.*

orientalis gives a shorter display of seedheads than the other two species. The yellow clematis appreciate shade around their roots, but have to get into the sunshine before they produce flowers. They are fairly vigorous climbers, usually up to about 15 feet, but since they flower on the current year's growth, they can be pruned back every spring. All these species are very close to each other and *C. tangutica* may well prove to be a variety of *C. orientalis*. *C. serratifolia* remains distinct through its biternate, as opposed to pinnate, leaves, although the lower pinnae in *C. orientalis* are occasionally trifoliate.

CLERODENDRON

Either two species, or one species and its variety, according to whether you follow Dode or Rehder, can be included here. These are *Clerodendron trichotomum* and *C. fargesii* (syn. *C. trichotomum fargesii*). Both species make large bushes or small trees, up to about 20 feet high and have oval, taper-pointed leaves 9 inches long and 3 inches wide. These leaves are a dark purple on their first unfurling. In August and September they produce heads of fragrant white flowers, the whole inflorescence is about 6 inches across and each flower is about 1 inch in width. In *C. trichotomum* the calyx is purple, while in *C. fargesii* it is green. The flowers should be followed by pea-sized blue berries; a pale blue in *C. fargesii*, but dark blue turning eventually to black in *C. trichotomum*. *C. fargesii* is said to fruit more freely, but in my own experience, berries are very rarely produced, only abundantly in a hot summer and when more than one plant is present. The plants are liable to produce suckers, which can be detached and planted separately and which come into flower in a remarkably short space of time. They are vigorous growers, but may lose some of their young wood in hard winters, although they are never killed back completely. *C. fargesii* is said to be more resistant than *C. trichotomum*. This tree is native to China and Japan and was sent from the latter country in 1800. *C. fargesii* was sent to Vilmorin by Père Farges in 1898.

CORNUS

A genus that is being rapidly reconstituted and split into two or more genera, but which will be treated here as in the Royal Horticultural Society's *Dictionary of Gardening*. As it exists today it contains many plants that appear to be very different in habit and in their attractions. They range in dimensions from quite small shrubs to sizeable trees. The flowers tend to be small and insignificant, although in the case of *Cornus mas* and *C. officinalis* they are produced in such profusion that they are very effective. In some species the flowers are surrounded by large conspicuous bracts, with a petal-like appearance and these are very ornamental flowering trees. There are also two species with brightly coloured bark.

Cornus alba makes a very vigorous, suckering shrub, which should be given ample room to expand, as otherwise it will strangle everything within reach. It reaches about 10 feet in height, but as its main attraction is the brilliant red bark of the year-old shoots it is often cut back every spring, to encourage the further growth of the young wood. A large number of forms with variegated leaves have been selected, which give the plant attraction during the summer. It can produce rather inconspicuous flowers that should be followed by very pale blue berries, but these are not very freely produced in this country. The type has rich red bark, while that of *C. a. sibirica* is somewhat paler. The best variegated forms are 'Gouchaltii' with a yellow margin and pink markings, 'Spaethii' with the leaves more golden-yellow than green, and *C. a. sibirica* 'Variegata' with white margins to the leaves. 'Spaethii' is probably the best form to obtain, as it keeps its good colour throughout the season. *C. alba* has no objection to moist conditions and is often planted around ponds.

Cornus capitata (syn. *Benthamia fragifera*) is very different and, were it only reliably hardy, would be a must for every garden. It is an evergreen tree, up to 30 or 40 feet high, but considerably more across. The leaves are oval-lanceolate up to 5 inches long and 1½ inches across and a dull green in colour. The inconspicuous flowers are surrounded by large pale yellow bracts which give the impression of a large flower some 4 inches in diameter. They are followed by strawberry-like fruits which give a second attraction to the plant. The bracts are at their best in late June, while the fruits are ripe in October. The plant requires acid soil conditions. Although there are a few good trees in sheltered spots in Sussex, Hampshire and Dorset, this is really only safe in the West Country and Ireland. Where it does well there are few more effective trees. The plant is native to China and the Himalayas and was introduced from these mountains in 1825, but I have not found out who was responsible for its introduction.

Cornus florida also has its flowers surrounded by ornamental bracts, which are white in the type, but a rich pink in the variety *rubra*. It makes a large bush, or small tree from 10–20 feet in height and is deciduous. Most years the leaves will turn various shades of red in the autumn. This also requires acid soil, but is quite impervious to winter cold. It does, however, require rather special summer conditions to ripen its wood satisfactorily and does not seem to do well east of Sussex. It starts rather early into growth and is then susceptible to frost damage, so it is not a plant for everyone. Where it can be grown, it is extremely lovely. The variety *rubra* appears to do rather better than the normal white form. The leaves are oval, tapering to a point at either end, up to 6 inches long and 3 inches across. Like other species with coloured bracts around the inflorescence, the buds are visible at the end of the season.

Cornus kousa will eventually make a much larger specimen than *C. florida*, up to 20 feet in the typical form, but up to 30 feet in the variety *chinensis*, which has proved far more satisfactory in gardens. The oval leaves are 3 inches long and 1¾ inches across with a wavy margin, so that, although the individual leaves are not particularly striking, the general effect of a well-grown specimen is very elegant. It comes into flower later than *C. florida*, usually in mid-June and early July. The type, which comes from Japan, tends to flower earlier than the Chinese variety. In the best forms the bracts are up to 3 inches long in the variety *chinensis*, about 2 inches long in the type; in each case they are a creamy-white; some forms turn to pink as they fade. Notionally they are followed by fleshy, strawberry-like fruits, but these are not invariably produced. It may well be that they are produced more freely if more than one plant is present, but this is not essential. I have seen an isolated tree fruiting. There is great variation in the size and width of the bracts and few plants are more striking than a well-flowered specimen of a good form, while that of an indifferent form is considerably less effective, although all forms improve as they age. The tree is also extremely effective when well fruited, although the display is liable to be rather short-lived, as the birds think highly of the fruits. The Japanese type plant was introduced in 1875 while the Chinese form was found by Augustine Henry and introduced by Wilson in 1907.

The plant appears to be perfectly hardy and is much easier to grow than *C. florida*. It grows moderately rapidly, but will not flower until it is about 10 years old and does not give of its best until it is considerably older. The waiting time can be reduced by buying moderately sized specimens, which will generally move without difficulty.[1]

Cornus mas is one of the most reliable and prettiest of winter-flowering shrubs. It is a vigorous, quick-growing shrub or small tree, up to 25 feet. Again it will not flower as a young plant and you may have to have it in the garden for five years before you see any flowers, but once it starts it flowers profusely and will continue to do so with unfailing regularity. Unless the weather is exceptionally cold, it is in flower in February, when the stems will be wreathed with heads of individually tiny golden-

[1] Some clones also show brilliant autumn colour.

yellow flowers. These may be followed by dark red cherry-like fruits; the plant was at one time cultivated as a fruit tree and known as the Cornelian cherry, but, unless the lower branches have been cut away, the fruits are liable to be hidden under the foliage. The plant has no reputation for autumn colour, but a plant in my garden after some years of no display suddenly turned purple and crimson one autumn and continued to do so, year after year.

There are various cultivars with variegated leaves, of which 'Elegantissima', with the leaves suffused with gold and pink, is one of the handsomest of variegated shrubs. It is slower-growing and far less vigorous than the plain-leaved type. 'Aurea' with yellowish leaves and 'Variegata' with white margins to the leaves, are slightly more vigorous, although less striking than 'Elegantissima'.

The Japanese version of this plant, *C. officinalis*, has a taller, more fastigiate habit and rather brighter yellow flowers. I have no knowledge of how the leaves behave in autumn.

Cornus stolonifera is very close to *C. alba* and has the same attractive red bark. It spreads rapidly by stolons, which throw up suckers and can only be used safely where there is ample space. The variety *flaviramea* has the bark a bright yellow, which is effective in winter. The plants make thickets some 8 feet high. The small flowers are followed by white berries. The plant was introduced by Messrs. Veitch who received seeds from the Rocky Mountains in the 1860s and distributed them under the name of *C. capitata*, which must have caused considerable confusion to the recipients. The Royal Horticultural Society's *Dictionary of Gardening* gives 1656 as the year of introduction, but this seems improbable, as it is not mentioned in Sweet's *Hortus Britannicus* of 1830. Although its winter bark is attractive, it does not really deserve mention here as its foliage is of only moderate attraction and the white berries, although effective, are not borne very profusely.

COTINUS

Formerly included in *Rhus* this comprises from the garden point of view two deciduous shrubs that owe their main attractions to their seedheads and to their brilliant autumn colour.

Cotinus americanus (syn. *Rhus cotinoides*) makes a small tree up to 30 feet high in its native America, where it is rare. In this country it barely exceeds 15 feet. It is dioecious and the male plant has the more vigorous habit. The inflorescence ends in thread-like hairs, but is not so handsome as that of the next species. On the other hand, the autumn colour is particularly gorgeous in its shades of orange and purple. Excessively rich conditions seem to inhibit the autumn colour and it should be grown in rather poor soil. Although discovered in 1819 it did not reach cultivation in this country until 1882, when Professor Sargent sent plants to Kew. The leaves are obovate, tapering to the petiole, about 5 inches long and 2½ inches across and are coloured purplish when young.

Cotinus coggygria (syn. *Rhus cotinus*) is rather more satisfactory. Its popular names of smoke-tree or wig-tree give an idea of its extraordinary plume-like inflorescences. This smoke-like appearance is not due to the styles as is the case with the clematis, but to thread-like growths emanating from the inflorescence. This is usually effective from July onwards. The stalked leaves are nearly circular and may be 3 inches in diameter, although they are usually somewhat less and they emerge quite late in the season. In the autumn they tend to turn various shades; some turn red, others turn gold. The variety *atropurpureus* has green leaves, but a purplish inflorescence, and the leaves turn scarlet in the autumn. The cultivar 'Foliis Purpureis' has dark purple leaves and young growth, and the normal grey inflorescence; the leaves turn a very brilliant crimson in the autumn, even on soils which do not normally produce good autumn colour. 'Rubrifolius' has wine-red leaves and a purplish inflorescence. The type and its cultivars are all very effective from July until the leaves fall and they will thrive in the poorest soils.

COTONEASTER

A very confusing genus of the rose family. It is allied to the hawthorns and the pyracanthas. Easily distinguished from crataegus by their entire leaves and lack of thorns, less easily distinguished from pyracantha, but this latter genus is invariably evergreen, cotoneaster is more generally deciduous. The flowers are produced singly, or in small groups, or in large corymbs; they are not very large and are white or occasionally pale pink. They are followed by berries, generally red in colour, but sometimes yellow or black. These fruits are very often the most effective display on the plant's part, but for so many gardeners, this means that the display is only momentary. Wilson wrote a small book about the Arnold Arboretum and when he came to describe the berrying shrubs he headed his chapter 'Food for Feathered Friends'. This at least faced up to the basic problems, but not all gardeners would put the R in the final word, and if your avian population is excessive, you may find that cotoneasters are not worth the space they take up.

As a general rule they are not very tall, but they tend to spread in a fashion more than middle-aged and take up quite a lot of lateral space. They are all good hardy shrubs with no fads about soil and little about aspect, except that they do require some light and will grow unhappily in heavy shade. They are easily propagated by means of cuttings or from seed, but the latter may not always come true, as they are somewhat promiscuous and liable to hybridize. The list that follows is somewhat selective and many, doubtless admirable, species may have been omitted.

Cotoneaster bullatus makes a fairly tall shrub, up to 12 feet or more and has oblong-ovate leaves which in the best form, the variety *floribundus* (*macrophyllus*), may be 6 inches long and 3 inches across. The leaves have a slightly swollen (bullate) appearance in the sections between the principal veins, which makes the species reasonably easy to identify. The flowers appear in clusters of up to 30 flowers; they open a few at a time with rosy-pink petals, which fall very quickly, so that the plant is not particularly ornamental in flower. The berries are a brilliant sealing-wax red and are very handsome and the leaves often colour well, before falling. The type was introduced by Vilmorin in 1898, presumably from Delavay's seed, while the larger variety was introduced by Wilson.

Cotoneaster conspicuus is a small-leaved evergreen with arching branches. It is an admirable shrub for training over banks or allowed to fall down some walling. The more prostrate forms are sometimes given the varietal name *decorus*. The leaves are roughly oval and measure about ¼ inch in each direction; they are thickly set on the branches, dark green on the upper side, covered with whitish wool on the underside. The erect form will reach up to 5 feet or even higher, but spreads far more laterally. In late May and early June, flowers appear singly in every leaf axil. They are large for the genus, up to ½ inch in diameter and are white with conspicuous purple anthers. A well-flowered specimen is easily among the most effective of the genus. The flowers are followed by scarlet berries of the same size as the flowers. Given the right position, this is one of the very best cotoneasters and there are few more decorative shrubs for trailing down slopes. The plant was introduced from south-east Tibet by Kingdon-Ward in 1925 and has become popular very rapidly.

Cotoneaster frigidus will make a large shrub up to 20 feet high, but is perhaps more effective if kept to one stem when young, and trained as a small tree. The rather dirty white flowers do not usually appear before early July and are in flat corymbs, not unlike those of the mountain ash; they are some 3 inches across. They are followed by berries about the size of a pea which are borne in great profusion. Wilson's feathered friends do not find them particularly attractive and they are usually left until December, while in some places they may hang on the tree until February. The leaves are a very elongated oval, up to 5 inches long and 2 inches across and, when young, are very woolly on the underside. The species has proved a useful parent. The hybrid 'Cornubia', of which the other parent is unknown, is not dissimilar in appearance, but has larger corymbs of flowers and subsequently a display of berries that make it outstanding. Crossed with the prostrate evergreen *C. dammeri*, the plant known as *C.* × *hybridus pendulus* makes either a vigorous arching evergreen or, if trained as a tree, a delightful pendulous specimen with corymbs of flowers and brilliant red berries.

Cotoneaster harrovianus is another evergreen species with arching stems that reach a height of 6 feet, but which spread considerably farther sideways. The oval leaves are somewhat leathery in texture, a shining dark green on the upper side, while the underside is covered with yellowish down for the first season. They grow up to $2\frac{1}{2}$ inches long and 1 inch across. The flowers are produced profusely in terminal and axillary corymbs, each about $1\frac{1}{2}$ inches across and are white with conspicuous reddish anthers. They appear late in the season, with the result that the red berries are not fully coloured until the end of the year. This is the best evergreen cotoneaster for floral display. It was discovered in Yunnan by Augustine Henry, introduced by Wilson and named by him in honour of George Harrow, the foreman at Veitch's nursery and the man responsible for the successful rearing of all his various introductions. He used to sow half the seed immediately on receipt and the rest at what he considered would be a suitable season.

Cotoneaster hupehensis is a deciduous arching shrub reaching to about 6 feet, with the usual ovate leaves with a greyish downy underside and a dark green upper side. The flowers are produced in clusters of about 10 in great profusion on the upper side of the shoots and are quite sizeable. They appear at the end of May and the beginning of June and are followed by bright red berries. It is fairly close to *C. frigidus*, but rather more handsome in its flowers, although the fruiting corymbs are not so large.

Cotoneaster lacteus is an evergreen, with obovate leaves about 2 inches long and 1 inch across and milky-white flowers in early July. The leaves have the underside covered with thick white down, which becomes yellowish with age. The plant grows from 10–12 feet high and is rather more in width. The young shoots are covered with down. The flowers are produced on quite long-stalked corymbs, which are some 3 inches wide and which open in late June or early July. As a result of this late flowering, the fruit does not ripen properly until late October or November and will hang until March. Very similar, but flowering a month later, is *C. serotinus*. If allowed, the fruits of this hang until April. Both these late-flowering cotoneasters are Forrest introductions. They are both fairly free flowering and if your garden is situated in a relatively bird-free district, they are very valuable for the long time that the berries hang on the trees.

Cotoneaster multiflorus must have the most curious distribution of any plant. It has been found in various parts of China, but a variety that is barely distinguishable is found in the Sierra Nevada in Spain (*C. m. granatensis*). There has never been any suggestion that the Spanish plant is anything but a native of the region, but I search my brains in vain to find any other similar phenomenon. The nearest approximation I can think of comes with the genus *Pelargonium*, which is exclusively southern African with the exception of *P. endlicherianum*, which is native to Asia Minor. But in this case the disjunct plant is a separate species, not identical with an African one. Anyway, this plant with its curious distribution is a graceful deciduous shrub, that can be trained as a small tree with good effect. It will reach up to 12 feet in height and has long, slender arching branches with roundish leaves, up to 2½ inches long and 1½ inches across. The white flowers are produced in clusters of from 3–15 in great profusion in late May and early June and are followed by berries that are bright red by August. The original plants were introduced in 1837, but subsequently Wilson found a form, which he named variety *calocarpus*, which has leaves that are longer and less rounded and larger fruits and which appears to be an improvement on the type. This plant, together with the evergreen *C. conspicuus*, is the best of the genus for its floral display, and is superior to *conspicuus* in the number of its fruits. However, there is no real rivalry between the plants, as their mode of growth is so distinct.

Cotoneaster rotundifolius is best described as a semi-evergreen. Most of the leaves tend to persist throughout the winter, but have fallen before the new leaves start to unfurl. In some ways it resembles the well-known *C. horizontalis*, with its rather stiff, horizontal branches wreathed with small circular leaves. It does, however, have a marked upright habit and can reach a height of 8 feet. The pink-flushed flowers are large for the genus, up to ½ inch across and are either produced singly or occasionally in pairs over the plant. They are followed by rosy-red berries, which the birds are liable to leave alone for as long as any other food is available.

Cotoneaster salicifolius is a variable shrub, that is usually evergreen, but may shed all its leaves in very cold winters. Most forms grow up to 15 feet high, but the variety *rugosus* only reaches to 10 feet and may be less. The leaves tend to be lanceolate, with a slight tendency to becoming oval; they reach a length of 3½ inches but are only about ½ inch across. The upper side is somewhat wrinkled. The flower buds are covered with down and the flowers themselves are inconspicuous and a rather dirty white. They appear in late June. The berries are small, but very brilliant. Wilson's variety *floccosus* has more slender branchlets and the underside of the leaves thickly covered with white down. The flower corymbs are somewhat smaller, but the fruits tend to be more brilliant. The variety *rugosus* has more ovate leaves, up to 1¾ inches across, larger flowers and larger berries, which are coral-red in colour. There is a handsome yellow-fruited variant of the type, known appropriately as 'Fructu-luteo'.

Cotoneaster turbinatus is a graceful evergreen with the young shoots and the underside of the new leaves thickly covered with white down. The leaves are a narrow oval, pointed at each end, 2½ inches long and an inch across and a very dark green in colour. The rather small white flowers have pink anthers and appear in rounded corymbs at the end of July, about the same time as those of *C. serotinus*. The deep red fruits are shaped like a top and are ripe by October. The plant is a vigorous grower and can easily reach to 12 feet. It was introduced from China, presumably through one of the famous French missionaries, though which one does not seem to be recorded, and first raised by Vilmorin. Its introduction to England was in 1910.

Cotoneaster wardii, as its name implies, was discovered and collected by Kingdon-Ward, who found it in Tibet in 1913. It is a moderately sized evergreen with ovate leaves up to 1¾ inches long and 1 inch across, a shining dark green on the upper side and a rather brilliant silver on the underside. The flowers are white or pale pink, produced in small corymbs and opening in June. They are followed by orange-red berries, while at the same time the 18-month-old leaves tend to turn orange, so that the shrub is very conspicuous in the autumn. Apparently many plants distributed as *C. wardii* should more correctly be known as *C. franchetii sternianus*, but since *C. wardii* and *C. franchetii* are very hard to distinguish in any case, it probably does not much matter.

Cotoneaster × *watereri* is probably *frigidus* × *henryanus*. It appeared as a *frigidus* seedling in the well-known Bagshot nursery and was named in 1928. It is generally evergreen, with leaves up to 3 inches long and tapered at either end and it fruits with more abandon than most of the species or other *frigidus* hybrids. It is a vigorous plant which might well reach 20 feet. The flowers, which appear in June, are nothing outstanding, but it is arguably the most brilliant fruiting species in the genus.

As can be seen, the choice is very large, but a few observations may help one somewhat in making a selection. Birds will first attack the fruits of *C. frigidus* and its hybrids, so that where they are a menace, it is unlikely that *C. frigidus* or any of its hybrids will prove very satisfactory. This leaves the late flowerers, *C. lacteus*, *C. serotinus* and *C. turbinatus*, together with the floribund *C. multiflorus* as the best of the berriers. In its way *C. conspicuus* is also handsome in fruit, but it is perhaps to be regarded as primarily a flowering shrub with handsome fruit. *C. bullatus* has the advantage of good autumnal foliage, as well as shining fruits and rather handsome leaves, but against this must be set its inconspicuous and ephemeral flowers. *C. harrovianus* is very handsome in flower and its late ripening berries are useful, where they are spared, while *C. rotundifolius* has not only handsome flowers, but fruits that the birds will neglect for as long as they can. I suppose, if one is going to be honest about such matters, none of the cotoneasters, with the exception of *C. conspicuus*, is worth garden space if one is not going to have much time to enjoy the berries. Like most of the sorbus, the flowers, although pleasant enough, would not justify giving up much space in the garden and by and large the species take up a lot of room. Where the fruits can be enjoyed, the position is very different and they will then well repay their growers.

❧ Crataegus – Hamamelis

CRATAEGUS

The hawthorns are among the most neglected of garden trees. There are a very large number of species named, although many of these are barely distinct; at one time there were over 900 differentiated in the United States alone. It is, indeed, in North America that the majority of species occur; there are a certain number of species in Europe and Asia Minor, but comparatively few in the rest of Asia. For the most part they are small trees or large shrubs, armed with thorns and with leaves either toothed or lobed or both; the majority of species have lobed leaves and the amount of lobing is often diagnostic. The flowers are produced in corymbs and are white or cream, except in the case of *Crataegus oxyacantha*, where pink and red forms have occurred, as well as forms with double flowers. There is also a reported red form of our other native May, *C. monogyna*, but this is probably a mis-attribution. The flowers are followed, in the autumn, by haws which vary considerably in size and colour. Indeed, in order to give some coherence to this section, I propose listing the various species under the colour of their haws. With one or two possible exceptions all the species are hardy and all indifferent as to the type of soil provided. Most of the species, in addition to their handsome flowers and fruits, also have brilliant autumn leaf colours.

Although not all the most desirable species are available, a very large number are and it seems a great pity that this splendid genus should be so little known. There are not many plants that have so many attractions and are so easy to grow. They are also rapid growers and soon make an attractive specimen. The seeds take two years to germinate, although this could probably be speeded up through refrigeration; nevertheless seed is the best method of increase, as cuttings are not always easy to root. The list that ensues is by no means exhaustive, but contains what I would imagine to be the best.

(a) Species and cultivars with blue or black haws

Crataegus brachyacantha does not, I fear, appear in cultivation at the present time, but since it appears to be a very desirable acquisition to our gardens, it is described here in the hope that it will soon be reintroduced. In its native haunts, which are the southern central states of the United States, the plant can reach 40 feet or more, but it is unlikely to do that in this country and probably only half that height can be relied upon. The leaves are entire, toothed and ovate in shape, 2 inches long and half as wide. The small flowers appear in June and the petals turn orange before falling. The haws are bright blue, covered at first with a blue-white bloom and are about ½ inch in diameter. The thorns are from ½–1 inch long, which seems quite considerable for a plant put in the *Brachyacanthae* or short-thorned section. The species would appear to be unique in its bright blue berries. It was introduced to this country in 1900 and it may be that, owing to its southerly provenance, it did not fruit very well over here. *C. apiifolia*, which has an even more southerly origin, only succeeds in the milder counties. It grows quite well, but will not bear fruit. On the other hand, as we shall see, *C. saligna* from Colorado, behaves well in our climate.

Crataegus chlorosarca is handsome in a leafless state, owing to the deep purplish-brown tinge of the year-old growths. It has quite large leaves that may reach a length of 4 inches and are nearly as broad at the base. Indeed, the leaves are basically triangular in shape but, since they are shallowly lobed, this basic shape is not immediately apparent. The flowers, which appear in May, are quite large and produced in smallish corymbs about 2 inches across. The fruit is a very dark purple, nearly black. The plant is one of the few Oriental thorns, being native to Manchuria and Japan, and is practically thornless. This is the feature that distinguishes it most clearly from the allied *C. dsungarica*, which has small spines about ½ inch long. The leaves are somewhat smaller, the flowers and corymbs somewhat larger. This also comes from Manchuria and northern China and is probably a geographical form (ecotype) of the preceding species.

On the other hand *C. saligna* is an attractive small tree, with inch-long thorns, shallowly lobed leaves about 2 inches long, white flowers in early June and small haws that turn first red and then a shining blue-black. Although a native of Colorado, it comes from quite high up in the mountains and appears to be perfectly hardy.

(b) Species and cultivars with yellow haws

Crataegus altaica is a small tree from the Altai mountains in central Asia, as its name suggests. The leaves are basically triangular in shape, but very deeply lobed with from 5–11 lobes, the basal ones being nearly pinnate. They reach up to 4 inches in length and are nearly as wide at the base. The white flowers are sizeable for the genus, about ¾ inch across and are produced in corymbs 3 inches across in some profusion in May. The fruit is bright yellow and appears transparent, unlike the majority of haws. The leaves are liable to colour well in the autumn. This is one of the most delightful of the genus and should be better known. It is one of the thorns to which the name of *C. korolkowii* has been given, but this has also been applied to the plant now known as *C. pinnatifida major*, and the name *korolkowii* is best discarded. Incidentally, as far as I can see, *C. wattiana* is indistinguishable from *C. altaica*.

Crataegus azarolus might well come in this section, although the colour of the haws varies from white, through yellow and orange to red. However, an orange-yellow appears to be the most frequent. This makes a nearly spineless tree, that can reach 30 feet, but rarely does. The leaves are very deeply lobed but the lobes are few in number, usually 3 or 5. The leaves are small, not exceeding 3 inches in length. The white flowers are about the same size as our May, with purple anthers, and appear in dense-flowered corymbs in June. The fruit may be an inch in diameter and is globe-shaped. The haws have an apple-like flavour and they were once cultivated in parts of south-east Europe. The plant itself is a native of Asia Minor and North Africa, although the African form was once considered a separate species and called *C. sinaica*. It differs from the Asian form in its entirely glabrous leaves; those of the type are downy on the underside.

Crataegus flava is the only North American species with yellow fruits in cultivation, but it is not one of the more attractive species. The leaves are diamond-shaped, up to 2½ inches long and 1½ inches across, and toothed at the edges. The white flowers are the same size as our own hawthorn, but are borne in few-flowered corymbs, so that they are not very conspicuous. Nor are the greenish-yellow pear-shaped haws. However, there now appears to be a new collection in which the haws are orange-yellow and this may well prove more attractive. Our own native *C. monogyna* has a yellow-fruited form known either as 'Aurea' or 'Fructu-luteo' and the same can be said of the normally red-hawed *C. punctata*. In this case the variety is known as 'Xanthocarpa', although occasionally the name 'Aurea' is used again. *C. monogyna* is surely too well known to require any description, but *C. punctata* will be described, among the red-hawed plants.

Most of the yellow-fruited hawthorns are unarmed or only very slightly thorny and this character is found in our next species. This has a multiplicity of names of which the earliest would appear to be *C. stipulacea*, although, since the authority for it is, nominally at least, the nineteenth-century nurseryman from Hackney, Conrad Loddiges, it may not be thought to be a very cogent authority. However, he was probably advised by some respectable botanist of the period and this name would appear to be botanically correct. In any case it would seem to be preferable to Stapf's name of *C. pubescens stipulacea*, which suggests that this rather distinct plant is only a variety of *C. pubescens* (whatever that may be) and, if one is unwilling to accept Loddiges's name, the best alternative would seem to be de Candolle's *C. mexicana*, which indicates its unusual provenance.

There are not many Mexican plants that are hardy in Great Britain and not many hawthorns in Mexico, so this plant is remarkable, quite apart from its attractiveness. It has entire, toothed leaves, roughly diamond-shaped, up to 4 inches long and 2 inches across. These are dark green on the upper surface, but downy below. At the base of the leaf stalk are a pair of very large stipules, which give the plant its name. In June appear the heads of quite large flowers, which are followed by yellow haws about ¾ inch long, which persist on the tree for a long time, if allowed. The leaves do not colour, but remain on the tree until after Christmas, so that, in the early winter, one gets the impression of an evergreen thorn. The plant is not very large, up to 20 feet high and is slower growing than most of the genus. Seeds were sent to Loddiges by a Mr. A. Lambert in 1824 so, for a Mexican plant, it has a long history in cultivation. It is one of the parents of the red-hawed *C.* × *carrierei*, to which we shall shortly be getting.

Perhaps the nicest of the yellow-fruited thorns and, to my mind, one of the best of all the thorns, is *C. tanacetifolia*. Its only fault is that it is somewhat slow-growing. It can reach a height of 35 feet and trunks 5 feet across have been recorded, but such trees are rare. The new growth and the leaves are covered in white down, which persists for more than a year on the wood. The leaves are not large, up to 2 inches long and the same across, and are so deeply lobed that they could well be termed pinnatifid. The botanist Persoon considered that they resembled those of the tansy (*Tanacetum*), and named the plant accordingly, but the resemblance is purely fanciful. In late June the large fragrant flowers appear in clusters of from 6–8 blossoms, each one an inch in diameter, and these are followed by large yellow haws, sometimes flushed with red. Each haw is subtended by one or more bracts that are so laciniate as to have a mossy appearance.

These haws have an apple-like perfume and, so I am told, flavour. The plant resembles in many ways *C. orientalis*, but this latter species lacks the moss-like bracts underneath the fruit and the haws are not yellow, but coral-red. Both plants seem to come from south-east Europe and Asia Minor, and the statement in the Royal Horticultural Society's *Dictionary of Gardening* that *C. orientalis* comes from the Orient is misleading. To most of us, surely, the Orient suggests China and Japan.

(c) Species and cultivars with orange haws

There are so many species with haws in varying shades of red, that it seems worth while separating the few in which the haws are orange or coral.

Crataegus aprica is the plant one is most likely to receive as *C. flava*. It makes a small tree, up to 20 feet high. The branches are armed with thorns up to $1\frac{1}{2}$ inches long and tend to grow in a zigzag manner. The leaves are small, roughly diamond-shaped, up to 2 inches in each direction. The white flowers are each about $\frac{3}{4}$ inch across and are produced in numerous small corymbs, and are followed by orange fruits. The plant flowers with some large show and is well worth having. The leaves turn deep purple in the autumn.

Crataegus calpodendron (syn. *C. tomentosa*) is one of the very best of all the genus. It is not very large, seldom exceeding 15 feet in height. The bark and the thorns are of a distinctive grey character. The leaves are more or less oval, up to 5 inches long and 3 inches across, which is large for the genus. The lower part of the leaf is entire, but the top is either deeply toothed or shallowly lobed. The flowers appear in June and are, individually, of the same size as our own may, but are produced in much larger corymbs, so that this is one of the handsomest of the genus in flower. The orange fruit is always borne erect, so that in some ways the fruits suggest those of a sorbus. They are a matt orange in colour. This is one of the best species for autumn leaf colour; the leaves turn either a brilliant orange or scarlet before falling.

The plant was introduced in 1765 by the famous firm of Lee and Kennedy. Presumably seed was sent to them by a correspondent, but they were responsible for several introductions and no one quite knows how they obtained some of their plants.

Crataegus × carrierei (also known as *C. lavallei*) is a hybrid of dubious parentage. M. Carrière, after whom it is named, said that it came from seed of *C. stipulacea*, and both *C. crus-galli* and *C. punctata* have been suggested for the pollen parent. Whatever its parentage it makes a tree up to 20 feet high with large ovate toothed leaves up to $4\frac{1}{2}$ inches long and $2\frac{1}{2}$ inches across; dark green and glossy above, downy on the underside.

The large flowers appear in June and are followed by orange-red haws, which are speckled with brown. As in the case of *C. stipulacea*, the leaves will remain green until December or later. If allowed, the fruits will hang until March. This is a really splendid tree with good flowers and fruit and the leaves are also handsome.

Crataegus orientalis, which has already been mentioned, makes a tree up to 20 feet high and is practically devoid of thorns. The young growths are downy and so are the young leaves, which eventually become dark green on the upper side, while the underside remains grey and downy. The leaves are not large, basically triangular and measuring 2 inches in each direction, but very deeply lobed into from 5–9 lobes. The quite large white flowers appear in June in moderately sized corymbs and are followed by slightly downy coral-red haws, which are rather large. This is a very attractive plant which sometimes colours well in the autumn; in other districts it fails to do this. There is a variety *sanguinea* with rather dull purplish-red berries, which is far less attractive.

Crataegus submollis is a pleasant tree in many ways, but the orange fruits fall early in the season and the plant is bare by October. It can reach 30 feet, and has lobed leaves about 3 inches long. The large white flowers appear in June.

(d) Species and cultivars with red haws

Most of the hawthorns come into this section and it is not always easy to distinguish some of them with much success.

Crataegus arkansana is closely related to *C. mollis*, but is less vigorous and holds its fruits longer. It will make a tree up to 20 feet, with shallowly lobed leaves and is quite heavily armed. The large flowers, an inch across, appear in June and the large red fruits do not ripen until October. They are an inch across and slightly longer. The leaves turn a rich yellow in autumn. Fairly similar is *C. arnoldiana* with thorns up to 3 inches long and pendulous haws looking like cherries.

Crataegus mollis itself might well come in here. This makes a fairly large tree up to 40 feet and has attractive grey bark. It is heavily armed with thorns averaging a length of 1½ inches. The leaves are up to 4½ inches long and as much across, shallowly lobed in from 9–15 lobes. The large flowers appear in sizeable corymbs and are followed by large fruits, which, unfortunately, do not persist for long and have usually all fallen by the 1st October. Quite often the leaves will colour well after the haws have fallen.

Crataegus coccinea has diamond-shaped, toothed leaves up to 3 inches long and 2 inches across. The white flowers are about the same size as our own hawthorn and appear in May. The fruit is pendulous and red, not scarlet, although it is called the Scarlet Haw in its native America. Closely allied is *C. coccinioides* which is slightly preferable, owing to its reddish young growth and its more reliable autumn leaf colour. The fruits hang until November.

Crataegus crus-galli is a much better plant. It makes a flat-topped tree, which can reach 30 feet, but is usually considerably less. The branches, which tend to grow horizontally, are clothed with obovate leaves, toothed only on the upper half, up to 4 inches long and 1½ inches across. There are forms known as *C. c. pyracanthifolia* and *C. c. salicifolia* with even narrower leaves. The white, pink-anthered flowers are about ¾ inch across and appear in June to be followed in October by rather small, deep red haws, which can hang on the tree until the following March. The leaves turn a brilliant scarlet before falling and this display is fairly reliable. The plant has very large thorns, up to 3 inches long and eventually somewhat longer and branched. This is one of the best of all small trees, handsome in habit, in flower and in its combined autumn splendours, while the fruit is handsome during the winter if the birds will allow.

Crataegus × dippeliana (syn. *C. leeana*) is a hybrid of some red-berried thorn with *C. tanacetifolia*, and occurred in Lee's Hammersmith nursery in 1830. The leaves are very similar to those of *C. tanacetifolia*, but the flowers are considerably larger, while the fruit is smaller and a rather dull red.

Crataegus durobrivensis makes a shrub from 10–15 feet high with broadly ovate leaves, entire in the lower portion, but toothed and shallowly lobed in the upper half. They reach a length of 3 inches and are slightly less wide. The flowers are among the largest of the genus and appear in May. The moderately sized, shining crimson fruits will hang until mid-winter, if allowed. Sargent considered this to be among the most ornamental crataegi of the northern United States.

Crataegus heterophylla is a rather rare tree from Armenia. It can reach up to 20 feet and is particularly interesting from the fact that it carries two different types of leaves. Those on non-flowering shoots are quite large, up to 3 inches long and 2½ inches across, with the upper portion deeply lobed, while the lower half is entire, lozenge-shaped and tapered to the petiole. These large leaves also have stipules at their base. The leaves on the flowering shoots are much smaller, only 1½ inches long and ¾ inch across, oval in shape, sometimes entire, sometimes toothed at the apex and sometimes 3-lobed at the apex. These leaves have no stipules. The white flowers, borne in corymbs that are 3 inches across, are borne abundantly in late May and early June. The haws are rather long and slender and are a good bright red. A splendid plant and it is a pity that it is not easy to obtain. It is practically without thorns.

Crataegus × *grignonensis* is another *stipulacea* hybrid; it is thought that the other parent is *C. crus-galli*. The plant is practically thornless and makes a tree up to 20 feet. The obovate leaves are about 3 inches long and 2 inches across, deeply lobed on young wood, but eventually becoming entire. The large flowers are produced in some abundance in May and give way to globe-shaped, bright red hanging haws. Like *stipulacea* itself the leaves remain green until December and the berries will also hang for a very long period if conditions allow.

Crataegus macracantha is something of a curiosity. It has the worst spines of all thorns; they can reach a length of 5 inches and are produced in great numbers. The leaves, which colour well in the autumn, are obovate, sometimes lobed in the upper part, up to 4 inches long and 3 inches wide, quite sizeable. The plant itself rarely exceeds 15 feet. The white, yellow-anthered flowers are of normal size and appear in early June. The bright crimson haws are among the showiest in this section. However, in spite of its charming fruits, this would not be anyone's first choice in the genus, unless a very fiercely armed tree were required.

Crataegus missouriensis comes from the southern United States, but appears to be perfectly hardy. It is a small tree or shrub, usually not more than 10 feet high, with leaves and young stems covered with white down. This soon falls from the upper part of the leaves, but persists on the underside. The leaves are oval or obovate, 3 inches long and about 2 inches across on very short petioles. The flowers are quite sizeable, produced in May in few-flowered clusters, and are followed by scarlet, rather small, pear-shaped haws. This is a useful plant where space is at a premium and it is effective in the spring, when the downy leaves emerge, when it flowers and when it fruits.

Crataegus phaenopyrum (syn. *C. cordatum*), the Washington thorn, is notable for its very late flowering. It does not come into bloom until July. The leaves are roughly heart-shaped, 3 inches long and 2 inches across on inch-long petioles. The tree grows fairly rapidly and can reach 30 feet in height. The late flowers are individually rather small, but produced in numerous corymbs that are 3 inches across and the fruit is also small, but a good scarlet, and not much liked by the birds. The berries can persist on the tree until the spring, but I personally found that the birds were usually able to nerve themselves to eat them by early December. However, at that time I gardened in a particularly bird-infested region and doubtless they would have survived longer in less 'favoured' districts. The leaves should turn scarlet and orange before falling, but sometimes this display is not so brilliant as the literature would suggest. The autumnal colouring appears to depend a lot on the type of summer experienced and if it is rather wet the leaves do not always colour well. In spite of their lateness the flowers are not among the best in the genus, but a well-flowered specimen is still rather striking.

Crataegus pinnatifida is a tree from north-east Asia which can reach 20 feet and is nearly unarmed. In northern China it is represented by its variety *major*, which is in all ways a better plant and which is the plant to be described here. It has very large leaves, up to 6 inches long and as much across at the base. They are roughly triangular in shape, but at the base on each side there is a pinnatifid lobe, while the terminal portion of the leaf is less deeply lobed. These leaves are borne on petioles which may be over 2 inches long, at the base of which are toothed stipules more than an inch across. The leaves are a dark green with the midrib and principal veins tinged with red; the young wood also has this red colouring. The moderately sized flowers appear in early June in 3-inch corymbs and are followed by deep red pendulous fruits, the size of small cherries. The leaves also colour well in the autumn. This is an outstanding plant with its large leaves borne on long stalks and its autumn display is among the best.

Crataegus prunifolia has not been found in the wild, although it has been in cultivation for some time and it has been suggested that it is a hybrid between *C. crus-galli* and *C. macracantha*. This may well be so, although it appears to come true from seed, which one would not expect a hybrid to do. It makes a tree up to 20 feet high with spreading, pendulous branches which may reach the ground. It bears spines up to 3 inches long. The leaves are oval in shape, toothed at the margin, shining green on the upper surface, pale and slightly downy on the underside. They may reach a length of $3\frac{1}{2}$ inches and a width of $2\frac{1}{2}$ inches. The flowers are large for the genus and produced in June in rounded clusters about 3 inches in diameter. They are produced in great profusion and are followed by rich red haws, which fall with the leaves some time in October. The leaves also turn a very brilliant crimson in the autumn and altogether this is one of the very best of thorns.

The same might be said of *C. punctata*, which is one of the larger species capable of making a tree up to 35 feet high, with a rounded head which may be more than 35 feet in diameter. The plant is armed with spines up to 3 inches long and has egg-shaped leaves up to 4 inches long and $2\frac{3}{4}$ inches across. The largish flowers open in early June in corymbs that may be 4 inches across and this is one of the most conspicuous in flower. The crimson fruits can be an inch in diameter and are marked with pale dots, which give the plant its specific name. Forms have been selected with deeper red fruits, and also fruits striped with yellow. The yellow-hawed form has already been mentioned. The leaves also colour well in the autumn, but fall with the fruits at the end of October. The plant can always be distinguished by the parallel veins on the leaf.

The best known of the genus are the coloured cultivars of *C. oxyacantha*. This is rather a case of familiarity breeding indifference. They are so well known that we tend to forget how handsome they are. The double-flowered forms give a brilliant floral display and the leaves will colour in the autumn, but the single scarlet and pink forms will also have red haws, which are not the best in the genus, but which are by no means un-attractive. Why these colour breaks should have occurred only in this species it is difficult to say. The plant is separated, somewhat dubiously, from our other native thorn, *C. monogyna*, by the fact that this latter has only one style and the haw contains only one seed, while *C. oxyacantha* has 2 or 3 styles and the haws contain 2 or 3 fruits. Presumably the fact that both species, though predominantly *C. monogyna*, are used for hedging and so thousands of seedlings have been raised, is the reason why variants have been noticed here; in the other species far fewer plants have been raised. However, the occurrence of pink and red forms exclusively in *C. oxyacantha* is still rather strange. There is a reputed double red form of *C. monogyna* called 'Sesteriana', but since it is double, it is not possible to prove that it is a form of *monogyna* and it is more probably *oxyacantha*. No single-coloured forms of *monogyna* have been recorded, nor have any double-flowered forms.

Although it is just possible to make a satisfactory selection of cotoneaster species, there are so many handsome crataegus that selection becomes rather a matter of space available than anything else. I think my own selection would be *CC. altaica, calpodendron, orientalis* and *pinnatifida major*, with *tanacetifolia* as a possible alternative to *altaica*. However, this list leaves out a lot of very desirable plants and I should mention that there are many other species in cultivation which have not been referred to in this selective list. I think the ones I have mentioned are the best, but you might not agree.

DAPHNE

Most daphnes have their sweetly scented flowers followed by berries, but comparatively few appear to be borne with any consistency in our climate. The species that do fruit fairly consistently are *Daphne alpina* and *D. mezereum*.

Daphne alpina is not one of the showiest species, but makes a small gnarled deciduous shrub, usually about 12 inches high. It has narrow, lanceolate, grey-green leaves which are about an inch long, and heads of small white fragrant flowers in late May and early June. They are followed by orange berries which are translucent.

Daphne mezereum is well known, not only for its fragrant purple flowers very early in the year, but even more for its maddening temperament. Plants appear to be thriving and then will suddenly collapse and die for no ascertainable reason. At any rate, that is the present condition of affairs, although it may be rectified some day. Usually a rather short shrub, it can sometimes reach as high as 7 feet. The purple flowers open before the leaves unfurl, in February in mild seasons, otherwise in March. In early July the berries turn red, if they have not been removed before ripening by greenfinches, who have recently developed a perverse taste for the unripe fruit. There is an albino form with yellow berries, which is somewhat more vigorous and less temperamental. Plants come easily from seed, if this can be procured. It is not a rapid grower and probably short-lived in any case. Although it can reach up to 7 feet in gardens, plants in the wild are rarely more than 2 feet high. It has one of the pleasantest perfumes of all shrubs.

Another daphne which occasionally sets fruit over here is the yellow-flowered *D. giraldii*. This is a deciduous shrub about 2 feet high with clusters of yellow flowers in early June followed by small, bright red berries. The plant, a native of China, was discovered by Père Giraldi and introduced by Purdom in 1911. Although it may bear these berry-like fruits, they do not persist for long, as they are very attractive to the feathered songsters of the grove. They appear to be least attracted to the yellow berries of the white form of *mezereum* and I have seen this plant looking very effective in August.

DAVIDIA

Davidia involucrata is a splendid deciduous tree, capable of growing as high as 60 feet. It is a rapid grower and will probably start flowering some eight years after young plants have been purchased or in about ten years from seed. The leaves are rather like those of a lime tree, more or less heart-shaped, but pointed at the apex. They can attain a length of 6 inches and a width of 4 inches. The young leaves have quite a pronounced perfume. The flowers themselves are not particularly conspicuous, as they consist of little more than a mass of red or white stamens, but they are subtended by two very large white bracts, which give the plant its popular name of the Handkerchief Tree. The lower of the two bracts may be 8 inches long and 4 inches across, while the upper one is about half these dimensions. They appear in late May and early June and persist for two or three weeks. The fruits that follow are quite attractive, being pear-shaped, green with a purple bloom, about 1½ inches long and 1 inch across. Very often the leaves turn a good golden-yellow in the autumn, but this appears to depend somewhat on the district and cannot always be assured. The tree discovered by Abbé David had leaves that were white-felted on the underside, but the original introduction by Père Farges had leaves that were glabrous underneath. This form has been given the name *D. i. vilmoriniana*.

The plant was discovered by David in 1867, but seed did not reach Europe until 1897, when Père Farges sent 37 seeds to Vilmorin. Of these seeds only one germinated and that one took two years to do so. In the warm climate of Vilmorin's nursery, the plant flowered for the first time in 1906, seven years after germination. However, in 1901 Wilson sent plenty of seed to Veitch which germinated well, and the first plants from his sendings flowered in 1911. This was also the glabrous-leaved form. On his second tour during 1903–5, Wilson sent back seed of the hairy-leaved form, which he regarded as a better plant. It appears to be a little longer coming to flowering size, requiring at least 12 years. For all its exotic appearance, this tree is bone hardy and fairly indifferent to soil re-action, although it likes a good depth and so would not thrive on shallow soils.

DIERVILLA

This genus is chiefly known in gardens through its Chinese and Japanese species, which have been hived off into the separate genus of *Weigela*. With these we have nothing to do, but there is a little-known species from the south-eastern United States, which has considerable charm as a foliage plant, and has flowers, which are individually not very showy, but which are produced with some abundance and at a time of the year when there are few flowering shrubs about. This is *Diervilla sessilifolia*, a suckering shrub that rarely exceeds 3 feet in height, but which can reach twice this height if left unpruned. It will spread considerably laterally.

The leaves are ovate-lanceolate and can reach a length of 7 inches, although 4 inches is the usual length, and such leaves are about 1¼ inches across at their base. As the specific epithet implies they are stalkless. They emerge a very attractive bronzy-purple, and this colour returns to the mature leaves when grown in full light. The flowers appear from late June until August, in quite large terminal clusters, and rather smaller axillary ones. The individual flowers are not more than ½ inch long, and look rather like small honeysuckle flowers. They are a pale butter-yellow in colour and look well against the coppery leaves. Since the flowers appear on the current year's growth, the plant can be cut hard back in spring, when it will produce a very large number of shoots which will subse-quently flower. On the other hand, the leaves seem to have a better colour on older wood. Although stemming from a well-explored area it does not seem to have been introduced to cultivation before 1902.

DIPTERONIA

A genus of only two species, related to the maples and indigenous to China. The only species in cultivation is *Dipteronia sinensis*, a deciduous tree never exceeding 30 feet in height. It has large pinnate leaves, up to a foot long, composed of from 7–11 leaflets, ovate-lanceolate in shape, each to 4 inches long and 1¼ inches across. Each leaflet is coarsely toothed. The flowers are individually inconspicuous, although borne on erect pyramids that may be 12 inches long. They are greenish-white with more conspicuous white stamens. Although the flowers are very small, they are produced in some profusion and are not so negligible as descriptions suggest. They are followed by clusters of winged seeds which are a good red in colour. Apart from its handsome leaves, it is these profusely borne red samaras that give the plant its second attraction, although, as we have said, the flowers should not be ignored altogether. The plant appears perfectly hardy and will succeed in most soils. It is yet one more Wilson plant.

ELAEAGNUS

I should perhaps issue a warning note, as the elaeagnus are plants for which I have particular affection and I may well be too promotional. The genus is distributed from southern Europe eastwards to Asia, and in the United States. The plants have little floral beauty, in that the flowers are rather small, but they are produced in great numbers and are usually deliciously fragrant. They are followed by berries of various colours, but these are not formed with much abundance unless more than one plant is present. The leaves of many of the species are silvery, either permanently or in the juvenile state.

Elaeagnus angustifolia is the only European species and it is not common, although it becomes plentiful as soon as one gets to Asia Minor. It makes a small deciduous tree, up to 20 feet high and is most remarkable for its silvery leaves and young stems. As the leaves age, they tend to lose their silveriness on the upper surface, but retain it on the underside. When the plant is mature its attractiveness is enhanced by the dark smooth bark on the branches, which have the appearance of polished walnut. The small, fragrant, tubular flowers are produced in June in the leaf axils of the current year's growth. They are silvery on the outside and yellow inside and are followed by small oval yellow berries with silvery scales on them. In warm climates this is one of the loveliest of trees in the spring and is extremely handsome in this country, although it does not seem to get the gleaming quality that wild trees do in southern Turkey. The individual leaves are oblong, up to 3 inches long, but only ½ inch across. The young growths keep their silvery scales until their second season, so that the plant is quite striking in the winter. In spite of its Mediterranean provenance it appears to be perfectly hardy. There is a more easterly form, *E. a. orientalis*, which has larger oval leaves, 3 inches long and 1 inch across, but otherwise differs little.

Elaeagnus argentea (syn. *E. commutata*) is a stoloniferous, deciduous shrub, rarely more than 7 feet high, although it can reach 12 feet, and is not a very rapid grower. The young shoots are covered with reddish scales, but the oval leaves, which may be 3½ inches long and 1½ inches across, are a shining silver on both sides and look extremely striking. I know few plants with such metallic-looking foliage. The flowers are produced in May in the leaf axils of young twigs and resemble those of the last species, although they are very slightly larger. The small egg-shaped berries are also silvery in colour, so that the plant gives a continuous display of different shades of silver throughout its leafage. This is the only North American species of the genus.

Elaeagnus macrophylla is a spreading evergreen shrub, which may reach up to 12 feet in height, but tends to grow outwards rather than upwards. The leaves are nearly circular, up to 4½ inches long and 3 inches across. The young leaves are a gleaming silver on both surfaces, the mature leaves preserve this silver on the underside, but become a dark green on the upper surface. The silvery flowers appear in the leaf axils in October and early November and, although they are not very showy, they are deliciously fragrant and they come at a time when any flowers are welcome. They are followed by small red berries, but these are not produced with much freedom in our climate. Even so the shrub is very handsome in the spring when the silvery new growths and leaves are appearing and it is handsome at all times. The late flowers add to the plant's charms. The plant is native to Korea and Japan and was introduced from the latter country by Maries in 1879.

Elaeagnus multiflora has the most conspicuous flowers and fruits of the cultivated species. It is a deciduous shrub, semi-evergreen in mild localities. It can reach heights of 10 feet, but is usually less and like so many of the genus tends to spread outwards rather than upwards. The elongated oval leaves are up to 2½ inches long and 1½ inches across; a fairly light green above and silvery on the underside. The yellow flowers are produced in the axils of the new shoots and open in April and May. Although small, they are very profuse and since they appear before the leaves are fully expanded, they show up more than do most of the others. They are followed by orange berries which are ripe in July, but which the birds delight in, so that one cannot usually enjoy them for long. This is a pity as the branches wreathed with small pendulous orange spheres make a delightful picture. Even a single plant will fruit well, but the most abundant display is produced where two or more plants are grown, making cross fertilization possible.

Like the last species it was introduced from Japan, although it is also found in China. In Japan it is cultivated for its fruit, which have a tart but agreeable flavour, and there makes a small tree up to 20 feet high. It would obviously make a rather attractive tree and it might be worth anyone's while to try and train it as one.

Elaeagnus umbellata, a deciduous plant, has a very wide range of distribution, from the Himalayas, through China, to Japan and so is a variable plant. The chief variation appears to be in the flowering time. It is fairly close to *E. multiflora*, but flowers later, in May and June, the flowers are creamy-white rather than yellow and it makes a larger plant, up to 18 feet high and more across. The leaves are a brighter green, longer and narrower, and up to 4 inches long and 1½ inches across. The berries are silvery at first, but ripen to a dark red. Cross fertilization appears to be essential to getting a good set of fruit. This is one of the most rapid growers of the genus. Indeed, the whole genus seems to bear an undeserved reputation for being slow growing. My own experience is that they take a little time to establish themselves, but will then grow with great vigour. They do not appear to be at all fussy about soil provided there is plenty of it. *E. argentea* is the slowest of the genus, but even this is not so slow-growing as many other shrubs.

ENKIANTHUS

A distinctive genus of ericaceous shrubs, with the leaves situated in whorls at intervals along the branches, thereby giving the plant a distinctive appearance, that is reminiscent of many Oriental paintings. The pendulous flowers are generally grouped in umbels and are urn-shaped, sometimes with a pinched-in apex. Sometimes the umbel is elongated into a raceme and it is often found that this occurs as the plants gain vigour. Like most ericaceous plants they will only do on acid soil and cannot be grown on the chalk. The best of the genus from the flowering point of view is *Enkianthus quinqueflorus* with large pink flowers emerging from large pink bracts, but unfortunately this is a native of southern China, including Hong Kong, and cannot be regarded as hardy. Even on the West coast it is doubtful.

The species that are hardy will generally colour very brilliantly in the autumn and it is this autumn colour which brings them in here. Although produced fairly consistently, there are some districts where the phenomenon fails to occur. The plants do best in sunlight or dappled shade and dislike excessive shade. All the species are deciduous and all have narrow oval leaves. None of them makes very large plants.

Enkianthus campanulatus can be any height from 4–10 feet, but the latter height is rather exceptional. The leaves are up to 2½ inches long and 1 inch across and, like all the genus, are produced in whorls at the end of the twigs. The pale yellow, red-veined flowers are produced either in an umbel or a raceme from the terminal buds and appear in May. They are bell-shaped and not over ½ inch long. The leaves turn gold and red in the autumn. The variety *E. c. palibinii*, which has now been given specific rank, is distinct in its dark red flowers and a line of reddish down on the midrib on the underside of the leaf. The plant is a native of Japan and was brought to Messrs. Veitch by Maries in 1880.

Enkianthus cernuus, an attractive small Japanese shrub, has been in cultivation since 1900, but no one appears to know by whom it was introduced. It makes a plant up to 10 feet high, usually somewhat less. It has rather small leaves, up to 1½ inches long and ¾ inch across and racemes of white bell-shaped flowers in May. The flowers have a fringed mouth, which distinguishes them from other species. The variety *E. c. rubens*, which is preferable to the type, has deep red flowers and is a very handsome shrub. It also has red-coloured seed capsules. Both the type and its variety should have orange and crimson leaves in the autumn.

Enkianthus sinohimalaicus (syn. *E. chinensis*, *E. deflexus*) is the largest species in cultivation. Its correct name is anyone's guess. Anyway, it is the Chinese form of the Himalayan tree which is known as *himalaicus* and *deflexus* and was introduced by Wilson in 1908. The Himalayan plants are not reliably hardy, while the Chinese plants appear quite satisfactory. This plant can reach 20 feet in height and can be grown as a small tree. The leaves reach a length of 3 inches and a width of 1¾ inches, which is large for the genus. The young growths are red and the leaves often have red petioles. The flowers appear in June and there are occasionally as many as 20 blossoms in a raceme. Each flower is bell-shaped, over ½ inch long and yellowish-red with darker veins. The leaves should turn crimson in the autumn.

Enkianthus perulatus has been in cultivation longer than any other hardy species (*E. quinqueflorus* first flowered in this country in 1814). It was introduced by Standish and Noble in 1869, yet it is still the least well known. It is a small shrub, not more than 6 feet high, with leaves up to 2 inches long and ¾ inch across. These leaves always have a reddish tinge which turns to a rich crimson in the autumn and this can be expected to occur with unfailing regularity. The white flowers come in terminal clusters and in rather small numbers, although heads of 10 flowers are not unknown. They are urceolate in shape, urn-shaped with a puckered edge, and are rather small, less than ½ inch long.

None of the enkianthus can be regarded as very rapid growers, even the most vigorous, *E. sinohimalaicus*, will make little more than 6 inches of growth each year, although it may be more vigorous as a young plant. This, combined with their naturally small dimensions, makes them admirable plants for small gardens, where their elegant habit can be most appreciated.

EUCRYPHIA

A small genus of shrubs and trees with a curious distribution. Four species are generally recognized, of which two come from Chile, one from Tasmania and one from the Australian mainland, in New South Wales, where it is found in a somewhat restricted locality. With the exception of *Eucryphia glutinosa*, the plants are evergreen and, in general, somewhat tender. They all bear handsome large white flowers which occur late in the season. For our purposes only one species need be considered and that is *E. glutinosa*. Although generally deciduous, it usually manages to preserve a few leaves throughout the winter and the amount of these depends on the mildness of the climate. It can, apparently, make a small tree up to 25 feet high, but is generally seen as a shrub of from 5–10 feet in height. The pinnate leaves, which are a dark glossy green, are composed of 3 or 5 leaflets; each leaflet is ovate, about 2 inches long and 1 inch across and the whole leaf may be about 6 or 8 inches long. The 4-petalled white flowers are produced singly or in pairs from the ends of the branches and in the terminal leaf axils in July and August. The leaves turn orange and red before falling in the autumn.

Like so many Chilean shrubs, this seems to grow best with its roots in the shade and its branches in the sun, and a cool root run seems essential. The plant was collected for Messrs. Veitch by Richard Pearce, who introduced the plant in 1859. It is not clear why Lobb had missed it earlier. The plant was for long known as *E. pinnatifolia*. It is the hardiest of the species, but, even so, would need a sheltered position in the Midlands and the North. All the species are very attractive flowering plants, but only our species has the additional attraction of good autumn colour. Lime-free soil is essential for this plant.

FOTHERGILLA

The name commemorates Dr. John Fothergill, an eighteenth-century gardener, who was indirectly responsible not only for the introduction of many North American plants into gardens, but also for the introduction of many alpines.

Fothergilla is a member of the hamamelis family and produces its flowers before the leaves have unfurled, although by no means so early in the year as the hamamelis do. Late April and May is when the flowers appear and it is only in May that the leaves start to unfurl. The flowers themselves are devoid of petals, but have conspicuous bunches of stamens, which give the plant an interesting, though by no means riotous, appearance in the spring. However, the plants are mainly grown for the brilliant crimson of the leaves in the autumn. They are not nearly so effective as their Asiatic relative, *Parrotia persica*, but they make smaller plants and so are more suitable for small gardens or restricted spaces. They are often planted in marshy ground, where they survive but do not look particularly happy, and they require acid soil. They grow somewhat slowly. Three species are in cultivation.

Fothergilla gardenii is a very small shrub, usually less than 3 feet high. It bears its masses of white stamens, which are 1½ inches long, while the inflorescence is an inch across, in April and May, and these are followed by oval leaves with a heart-shaped base, which reach up to 2½ inches long and 1¾ inches across. These generally turn a good crimson in the autumn, but some clones appear to be unsatisfactory. The flowers are fragrant.

In respect of autumn colour *F. major* is more reliable; it also makes a larger plant, from 6–10 feet high and as much across. The stamens have a pinkish tinge, while the more rounded leaves are up to 4 inches long and 3 inches across. The autumn colour tends to be orange rather than crimson. The plant has a rather odd history in English gardens. It was in cultivation in 1780, but apparently was lost subsequently and had to be reintroduced from the Arnold Arboretum in 1902. Eight years later came *F. monticola*, which makes a more spreading shrub, and which is slightly less tall; usually not more than 6 feet high. The inflorescence is also somewhat more conspicuous, as the stamens may be 2 inches long and more across. The autumn tints are red and crimson and, if only one species were to be grown, this is probably the best.

FRAXINUS

The ashes are a rather remarkable genus, divided as they are between the Ornus section, which has showy panicles of flowers and the Fraxinaster, to which our native Ash, *Fraxinus excelsior*, belongs and in which the flowers are devoid of any petals and are quite inconspicuous. It is difficult to believe that they belong to the same species and I well remember when I first saw the Manna Ash, *F. ornus*, growing wild in Greece, I mistook the plant for a rather handsome elder (*Sambucus*). Most of the species with which we shall be concerned here belong to the Ornus group, but there is a cultivar of our common ash with yellow bark which deserves inclusion. The dimensions of the plants range from large trees to comparatively small shrubs. Almost all the species have pinnate leaves and they all have characteristic seed-capsules, known as 'keys'. This is an elongated membrane, at the end of which the seeds develop, singly in some cases, in others in pairs. These keys are usually from 1-1¼ inches long and sometimes make a distinctive feature. Many of the species colour well in the autumn, usually some form of purple, but this feature is somewhat unreliable, although some species are more consistent than others. The rate of growth seems to correlate rather conveniently with the tree's ultimate dimensions. Large trees make fairly rapid growth, but the smaller species are rather slow.

Fraxinus bungeana is one of the smaller species, a shrub rather than a tree, not exceeding 15 feet, and usually considerably less. It has small leaves for the genus, not more than 6 inches long, composed of 5 or 7 obovate leaflets, each one of which is about 1½ inches long and ¾ inch across. The handsome white flowers are produced in large terminal panicles in May and give place to quite showy keys about an inch in length, but only ¼ inch in width. The leaves may turn golden before falling. This is a delightful, unusual shrub for the small garden and has just been reintroduced to cultivation.

Fraxinus chinensis is a moderately sized tree, capable of reaching a height of 50 feet; the variety *rhynchophylla* appears to do better than the type in this country. The species has quite large leaves, very large in juvenile specimens, composed of 7 or 9 leaflets. The terminal one is always the largest and on young plants may be more than 6 inches long, and is large even on mature plants, often over 4 inches long. The lateral leaflets are also quite sizeable and the plant gives a very frondose appearance when in full leaf. The panicles of white flowers open in June and the leaves may turn a good purple in the autumn. The variety *rhynchophylla*, which is sometimes regarded as a separate species and given the varietal name as a specific one, is characterized by the great size of the terminal leaflet, often 7 inches long, with the result that the individual leaves are a foot in length, and by its greater vigour. It is distinguished from the type by its large terminal leaflet and by the fact that the leaf usually consists of only 5 leaflets. The plant belongs to a subgroup, Ornaster, in which the flowers have a coloured calyx but no petals. The plant does not usually come into flower until it is quite sizeable.

Fraxinus dipetala, a native of California, was discovered by Douglas in 1830 but not introduced into this country until 1879, when Sargent sent plants from the Arnold Arboretum. It is a shrubby plant, about 10 feet high, with leaves from 2–5 inches long, usually composed of 5 leaflets, but sometimes of 3, 7 or 9. The flowers appear in 4-inch long panicles on the second-year wood in June and are cream-coloured. This habit of flowering on the two-year-old wood has given the plant the name of the fringe-flowered ash, and it does somewhat resemble the fringe tree (*Chionanthus*). Unfortunately, it is somewhat tender and should only be tried in the south and west of the British Isles.

Fraxinus excelsior aurea is a variety of our common ash, with yellow one-year-old wood which becomes progressively darker as it ages, but which preserves some yellow colour for three or four years. The plant is thus ornamental in the winter and, if it is required to grow a common ash, this is the form to acquire. The leaves turn a rather brilliant yellow before falling. Eventually this will make a tree of the largest size, over 100 feet in height and it is remarkably esurient, so it is really only suitable for parks or for very large gardens.

Fraxinus longicuspis is a small Japanese tree, usually from 20–30 feet high, but capable of reaching 50 feet. The leaves are about 6 inches long and are usually made up of 5 leaflets. They frequently turn a rich purple in the autumn. The white flowers are borne on long terminal and axillary panicles in June. This is one of the most attractive of the Ornus group. Although the autumn colour cannot be relied upon, it gives an additional charm when it does occur. Unfortunately, the plant is rare in cultivation and I have no idea where it can be obtained.

Fraxinus mariesii is so outstandingly handsome a tree, that I wonder why I trouble to describe any other ashes. This is easily the most desirable. It is a small tree, not exceeding 20 feet and usually somewhat less. The leaves are up to 7 inches long, composed of 3 or 5 leaflets, which are ovate in shape, up to 3½ inches long and half as wide, dull green in colour with a purple flush at the base. Similarly the main leaf stalk is purplish in colour and deep purple at the base. In June the creamy-white flowers appear in terminal and axillary panicles that may be 6 inches long. They are followed by the keys which turn dark purple by early August. The leaves themselves may turn purple before falling, but this is a bonus that cannot be relied upon. The plant is not a rapid grower and is ideal for small gardens. No one has ever suggested that this plant is at all difficult to grow and it is hard to understand why such an outstanding small tree should not only be barely known to gardeners, but also extremely difficult to obtain. It is listed in one very comprehensive catalogue but, at the moment that I write, the nurserymen concerned are unable to supply it; it is to be hoped that it will soon become available again.

This is one of the few plants, other than *Primula obconica*, that Maries introduced from China, which he did in 1878 and it has been named after him. One could wish for no better memorial.

Fraxinus ornus itself can make a tree up to 60 feet high, but comes into flower while still a shrub. It is very luxuriantly leafy, with leaves up to 8 inches long, composed of from 5–9 ovate leaflets, each one up to 4 inches long and 1½ inches across. The white flowers appear in May at the same time as the leaves in numerous panicles, each up to 4 inches long, but larger in warmer climates. The leaves often turn a good yellow in the autumn. This is a handsome tree, even when not in flower, owing to its abundant foliage. The plant is native to south-east Europe and Asia Minor, where it often grows out of limestone cliffs. A preparation called Manna Sugar is obtained from the sap and gives the plant its name of the manna ash.

Fraxinus spaethiana is a Japanese Ornus, with remarkably large leaves, often 18 inches long, usually composed of 7 or 9 leaflets, which can be individually 9 inches long and 3½ inches across. The base of the main leaf-stalk is reddish-brown in colour and swollen to a remarkable degree at the point where it clasps the main stem. This monstrous base of the petiole makes this species easy to recognize. The cream-coloured flowers appear in terminal and axillary panicles of some size in June. The colour of the leaves has a yellowish effect, although this is only apparent *en masse* and is not easily perceptible if a single leaf is examined. The leaves usually turn a good golden colour before falling. The plant can eventually make a tree from 40–60 feet high, but it is not a particularly rapid grower.

The plant came into European cultivation in 1873, being introduced, as the name would suggest, by the well-known nursery firm of Späth. The person responsible for its introduction does not seem to be known. The plant is striking and attractive in appearance and can be thoroughly recommended where an ornamental, moderately sized tree is required.

GAULTHERIA

A large genus of evergreen, ericaceous shrubs with a strange distribution. The genus is found in North America, but not in Europe, Africa nor western Asia; however, it reappears in the Himalayas, and spreads eastwards to China and Japan and southwards to the Malay Archipelago and thence to Australasia. Indeed, in many ways its distribution parallels that of rhododendron, except that there are some European and west Asian representatives of that genus, and it does not go farther south than northern Australia, while gaultheria goes as far south as New Zealand. The plants are related to arctostaphylos and vaccinium, having urceolate corollas and fleshy berries, which the birds find very attractive. Many of the species are prostrate shrubs, suitable for the rock garden, while others will reach heights of from 3–6 feet. The most attractive species are of somewhat dubious hardiness, while the indubitably hardy species are somewhat second-rate. In most of the species the calyx becomes fleshy as the fruits enlarge.

Gaultheria cuneata is a low shrub, growing from 12–18 inches high, but spreading in its habit. The leaves are ovoid in shape, a dark shining green, about 1 inch long and $\frac{1}{2}$ inch across. The flowers are produced in axillary racemes, about $1\frac{1}{2}$ inches long from June onwards and are white in colour. So are the berries which follow and which start ripening in August and persist until November. The berries are ornamental and the plant is a good ground cover in shade; it requires rather moist conditions. Wilson introduced it in 1909.

Rather similar in habit and much easier to obtain is the Japanese *G. miqueliana*. This is somewhat lower, usually less than a foot in height, has slightly larger and rounder leaves, the racemes are slightly longer and the berries may be either white or pink.

Quite close to this last species in some ways is *G. fragrantissima*. This is a larger plant, making either a large shrub or a small tree, up to 15 feet. The leathery ovate leaves may reach 4 inches long and 2 inches across. The flowers are produced in axillary racemes from the previous year's growth and these racemes may be 3 inches long and are thickly set with small white or pale pink drooping, fragrant flowers. The flowers appear in April and the dark blue berries follow about July. The plant is found on most of the Indian mountains and also in Burma and Ceylon. At the moment it is only suitable for mild localities, but one cannot help feeling that with so wide a distribution, it should not be impossible to find plants in colder districts, which might prove more suitable for our gardens. It is one of the pleasantest of the species.

Gaultheria hookeri is another Himalayan species, but somewhat hardier than the last named. It makes a spreading shrub from 3–6 feet in height, with relatively small, narrow leaves, up to 2 inches long and $\frac{3}{4}$ inch across. The racemes are up to 2 inches long and the fruits are purplish, but covered with a blue bloom.

A plant of recent introduction is *G. semi-infera*, which is a shrub of great promise. We do not yet know its ultimate dimensions, but it is probably not more than 4 feet high. Young plants are procumbent, but older plants are said to be more erect. The leaves are elliptic in shape and about $1\frac{1}{2}$ inches long and $\frac{1}{2}$ inch across. The white flowers, which open in June, are quite large and grouped in few-flowered racemes. They are followed by dark blue berries about the size of small grapes. These latter are most attractive and the plant would seem to have great possibilities both for its flowers and fruit.

Gaultheria shallon, although far from being the most attractive, is interesting, however, as one of the parents of the bigeneric hybrid with *Pernettya mucronata* which has been called × *Gaulthettya wisleyensis*. It does not seem to be known with any certainty whether the plant was raised at the Royal Horticultural Society's Garden at Wisley or no. The plant is a bushy shrub around 3 or 4 feet high, with oval leaves up to 2½ inches long and half as wide, and with terminal and axillary racemes of lily-of-the-valley-like flowers in late May and early June. The purple berries are produced in considerable abundance in the autumn and the plant is attractive, although rather slow growing. *G. shallon* itself is one of Douglas's introductions.

Gaultheria veitchiana makes a dense rounded shrub, from 1-3 feet high, which spreads by stolons. The oblong leaves, which taper at the base, are dark green and wrinkled, up to 3 inches long and half as broad. The flowers appear in axillary racemes and are small and white like so many of the genus. The fruit is dark blue. The flowers appear in May and the fruits are ripe in late August. For some reason a synonym of this plant is *G. fragrantissima hirsuta*, although it could scarcely be more distinct from *G. fragrantissima*. That plant is tender, whereas *G. veitchiana* is perfectly hardy. The Indian species makes a large shrub or small tree, while this Chinese species makes, as I have said, a low rounded plant. It was introduced by Wilson in 1907.

Gaultheria wardii makes a rather lanky shrub from 3-4 feet high. The leathery leaves are elliptic in shape, up to 3½ inches long, but not more than 1¼ inches across. The flowers appear in late May and June from the terminal axils of the preceding year's growth and are in short racemes, but a good pure white and produced fairly abundantly. The blue berries are covered with a white bloom to give what is invariably described as a milky effect. The plant is liable to be damaged in severe winters and is only reliable near the coast or in the south-west of the British Isles. It was discovered by Kingdon-Ward in Tibet in 1924, growing in full sun.

Like so many ericaceous plants, gaultherias need acid soil and prefer this to be of a peaty nature. They also generally appreciate rather moist conditions, and the prostrate species appear to thrive in shade. They would not be my first choice, but it would be silly to deny their charm for many people.

The well-known *Ginkgo biloba* merits a brief mention. The kidney-shaped leaves resemble the individual pinnae of a maidenhair fern and give the tree a very airy and graceful appearance. They can be relied upon to turn a rich gold in the autumn. The plants are not very rapid growers and are very long-lived. They are dioecious, and the male plants tend to be more upright and fastigiate than the females, but this is not invariable. The ginkgo is the sole survivor of a genus which is chiefly known from fossils and seems to owe its survival to the fact that the Chinese used to plant it by their temples. It has never been found in the wild.

GLEDITSCHIA

This is a small genus of deciduous trees, sometimes known as the honey locusts. Their main attraction lies in their large, pinnately divided feathery leaves, which can usually be relied upon to turn a good, clear yellow in the autumn. They are members of the *Leguminosae*, the pea family, but their flowers are very distinct from the majority of such plants as we know them, whether they be the typical pea-shaped flowers of the *Papilionidae* or the symmetrical flowers of the *Caesalpinioidae*, or the staminate flowers of the *Mimosoidae*. The flowers of gleditschia presumably belong to the *Caesalpinioidae*, but they are very small and inconspicuous, greenish in colour and borne on short racemes. However, in favourable seasons, these minute flowers can give place to extremely large pods, which give the tree a distinctive character in the autumn. Unfortunately they cannot be relied upon in this country. In some species the flowers are hermaphrodite, while in others male and female flowers are borne on separate racemes.

A less attractive feature of the genus is the fact that not only the branches, but also the trunk, are armed with stout spines, which are often branched. The genus is mainly confined to eastern Asia but has outliers in Persia and in eastern North America. Its absence in western North America is rather strange. The species to be described are hardy, although young plants sometimes continue in growth for so long that part is not ripened by the time that winter sets in. As the plants age, they seem to correct this tendency. Plants do better in the southern half of the country and even better on the Continent where hot summers are more usual. Under these conditions, they appear impervious to the coldest winters. Out of a number of species in cultivation I am describing the three that seem to be the most reliable.

Gleditschia caspica is the only Persian species, being found, as its name suggests, around the Caspian Sea. It makes a tree around 30 feet high, with its trunk 'excessively armed', to quote W. J. Bean, with branching spines that may be at least 6 inches long and are sometimes more. The leaves are up to 10 inches long and are bipinnate on the more vigorous growths, simply pinnate on the others. Each pinnate division is composed of some 20 leaflets, ovate in shape, up to 2 inches long and ¾ inch across (larger in very warm districts). The small flowers are perfect (it seems slightly odd that hermaphrodite flowers should be described as perfect, while such a condition in mammals would be regarded as far from that condition). The pods are curved and may reach a length of 8 inches, while they are an inch or so wide.

I have said that young plants of gleditschias are liable to be rather tender, but this stricture does not seem to apply to G. *japonica*. This is a slow-growing tree, that can reach up to 60 feet in its native Japan, but which has not got anywhere near these dimensions in this country. Like all the species, the trunk and branches are covered with branched spines. The young shoots are a pleasant purple-brown in colour. The leaves of young trees suggest a maidenhair fern. They are up to 12 inches long, either pinnate or bipinnate, every pinnate section being composed of about 20 leaflets, each one about ½ inch long. Apparently in Japan the leaves change in appearance as the plants age and the leaflets are then very much larger. As a foliage tree, this must be given a very high place.

Gleditschia triacanthos, from central North America, has been cultivated in this country since 1700 and appears to grow the best. In the wild it can make a tree up to 140 feet high, but the largest British tree is half that size, which is still pretty sizeable. Although the spines are less thickly set than in the two preceding species, they make up for that by sometimes attaining a length of 12 inches. The leaves are bipinnate on the main growths, pinnate on the lateral twigs. Each pinnate division is composed of from 14–32 leaflets, which are lance-shaped, up to 1½ inches long but only ½ inch across. The full leaf may be 8 inches long. The flowers are unisexual, but both sexes are produced on the same plant. The pods, when formed, can be 18 inches long and, to quote the master again, 'a tree well-laden with dry pods rattling with every fitful movement of the air, makes rather a weird sound in the dusk'. There is a spineless variety of this plant, G. *t. inermis*, and a cultivar called 'Sunburst' in which the emerging leaves are bright yellow. They do not maintain this yellow colour for long, but this is certainly a desirable form to obtain.

GYMNOCLADUS

This is related to the gleditschias and consists of only two species, one Chinese and one North American. The Chinese species sounds very attractive, but is tender and not in commerce, so the genus is represented in our gardens by the North American *Gymnocladus dioica* (syn. *G. canadensis*). As its name suggests, different sexes are borne on different plants, so that two would be necessary if fertile seeds were required. Since its attraction lies entirely in its foliage, with its changing colours, the fact that one tree alone will be sterile is of little importance. The plant is a deciduous tree that can reach 110 feet in height in its native United States, but has not been recorded taller than 60 feet in this country. The leaves are pinkish when unfurling and turn a good yellow in the autumn. They are bipinnate and extremely large, reaching up to 3 feet in length and 2 feet across, which makes them among the largest of all hardy trees. The individual leaflets are ovate in shape, up to 2½ inches long and half as wide. It is completely hardy so far as winter frost is concerned, but ripens its wood more satisfactorily after a hot summer. Owing to the fact that some of the new growth may not be adequately ripened, the actual rate of increase of the tree is not commensurate with the actual growth rate and is slower than it would be in districts with a Continental climate. The tree presents a curious spectacle in the late autumn, when the leaflets have dropped from the tree, but the common stalks still persist, to fall about a fortnight later. Although the plant must be regarded as rather a long-term investment, it is so very attractive throughout the whole time that it is carrying its enormous leaves, that it is well worth having.

HALIMODENDRON

A monotypic genus, the only species being *Halimodendron argenteum* (syn. *H. halodendron*), a native of Siberia, where salt deposits are found. This makes a shrub up to 6 feet high, deciduous, with pinnate leaves, comprised of only 4 leaflets and with a spine in place of the expected terminal leaflet. The leaflets are long and narrow, each about 1½ inches long and ¼ inch across and they, together with the young wood, are covered with a grey, persistent down. In June and July, the quite large, pea-shaped flowers are produced in few-flowered racemes from the old wood. They are purplish-pink in colour and are followed by inflated pods. The plant is attractive, with its silvery-grey foliage, as well as its rosy-purple flowers. It dislikes damp in the winter and it is suggested that it not only fares better, but also looks more attractive, if grafted on to 4-foot standards of *Caragana arborescens*, when it will make a graceful, slightly pendulous small tree. Owing to its normal wild habitat it is a very suitable plant for seaside gardens as it is quite impervious to driving salt.

HAMAMELIS

Although grown for their abundant, fragrant early flowers, the two Asiatic species, *Hamamelis japonica* and *H. mollis*, usually have their leaves turn an agreeable golden colour in the autumn. The North American *H. virginiana* also colours well, but carries its flowers at the same time, so that it really only has the one season of attraction. The two Asiatic species are similar, but each have their own characteristics. The leaves of *H. mollis* tend to be larger and rounder than those of *H. japonica* and are borne on shorter petioles. The petals of *H. japonica* are very wavy, while those of *H. mollis* are nearly straight. There tends to be more variation in colour in the Japanese plant, ranging from red to bright yellow and to pale yellow, while *H. mollis* seems to be either the typical golden-yellow or, as in the variety *pallida*, a delightful sulphur colour. The pale yellow, rather tree-like variety *zuccariniana* of *H. japonica* seems to be the best for autumn colour, the leaves often turning orange and looking very brilliant. By and large *H. mollis* tends to give a more brilliant floral display, but the plant can often become rather gaunt with a lot of bare wood at the base, while the Japanese plant is inclined to remain clothed to its base.

Neither of the species can be regarded as rapid growing, but they are long lived and certainly the best shrubs for winter ornament. They are untouched by the most severe frosts; even if these occur while they are in flower, it is only the flowers that are actually expanded that will be damaged. The unopened buds will come out as soon as the frosts cease. In mild districts *H. mollis* will start into flower in December, some two or three weeks earlier than *H. japonica*. Both, however, are at their best in late January and February. They will grow in alkaline soil, but not if it is excessively chalky and they certainly appear to do better if the soil is neutral or slightly acid. The various forms of *H. japonica* cannot be relied upon to come true from seed and are grafted on to *H. virginiana*, so that any suckers should be removed. There seems to be general agreement that all the hamamelis are very fragrant, but their fragrance is a dead spot in my nose and I have never been able to appreciate it.

❧ Hippophaë – Prinsepia

HIPPOPHAË

The sea buckthorn, *Hippophaë rhamnoides*, is a berrying shrub that can be grown even by the most bird-infested gardeners. Why a shrub should trouble to produce brightly coloured berries, which are presumably intended to attract birds, and then fill the berries with an acrid juice which makes them unpalatable, is one of the questions one would like evolutionists to consider. As gardeners we can only rejoice. However, there is no unalloyed benefit to be found in plants and hippophaë makes up for its reliable berrying by being dioecious, so it is necessary to have at least two plants and it is really better to have four in the ratio of three ladies to one gentleman. This more or less means that the plant is only suitable for the larger garden.

The sea buckthorn is a spreading shrub, occasionally of tree-like proportions and then reaching a height of 30 feet. Generally it is not more than 10 feet high. A member of the elaeagnus family, it is native to most of Europe, including Great Britain, and often colonizes sand dunes. The underside of the linear leaves and the young wood are covered with silvery scales, which gives the plant an attractive appearance in the summer. The orange berries are ripe by September and persist until February, when they start to fall. The plant is deciduous and so makes a very brilliant winter display, while the silver leaves make it agreeable also in the spring and summer. The plants will stand any amount of wind, sea spray and other hazards and, where room allows, must be regarded as one of the most ornamental of shrubs. If large quantities are being grown the ration of six females to a male is perfectly satisfactory. The pollination is done by the wind, so if there is a prevailing wind, the male should be sited accordingly; otherwise the gentleman is best placed in the centre of the ladies, where its bare winter condition can pass unregarded. For a small garden there seems to be no reason why a male branch should not be grafted on to a female plant, but I have not heard of this being done.

HYDRANGEA

The majority of this genus are only attractive through their flowers, but there are a couple of species which merit inclusion here.

Hydrangea quercifolia is a native of the south-eastern United States. It is a deciduous shrub, up to 6 feet high, with large leaves, shaped, as the specific name suggests, like those of an oak. These may be 8 inches long and 6 inches across. The panicle of flowers, of which the outer florets are large and sterile, while the inner fertile flowers are small but very numerous, may be as much as 8 inches long. It is a creamy-white to start with, becoming pale purple as it ages. The flowers come at irregular intervals from June onwards. In the autumn the leaves turn brilliant shades of orange and scarlet. Unfortunately the plant is somewhat tender and requires a warm, sheltered position and an acid soil. It also appears to do best when growing in dappled shade. Where it can be accommodated, it is a splendid plant with handsome leaves, striking flowers and a very brilliant autumnal display.

Hydrangea radiata (syn. *H. nivea*) is one of those rather tiresome plants whose main attraction, apart from their flowers, lies in the underside of the leaves. This is perfectly satisfactory when dealing with trees, but with plants such as this which make a shrub from 3–6 feet high, it is necessary to have some wall or bank on which to place them, so that these undersides can be seen. *H. radiata* is deciduous, and the leaves are oval in shape, up to 6 inches long and 3 inches across, tapered at both ends. They are dark green above and snowy white on the underside, which is densely covered with a felt-like tomentum. The plant flowers in July with flattish corymbs, up to 8 inches across. The outside of this corymb contains a few large sterile florets, but the main inflorescence is made up of a great number of very small, perfect flowers. The colour is a rather shining white. Unlike the last species, this seems quite hardy, although it is found in North and South Carolina. Very severe winters are liable to damage all the putatively hardy hydrangea species, but the damage is rarely fatal.

HYPERICUM

There are three species of the St. John's Wort which have berry-like fruits and these are so similar in many ways that they may well be considered together. They comprise our native tutsan, *Hypericum androsaemum*, the Canary Island *H. elatum* and the mid and southern European *H. hircinum*. This last is evergreen, the other two are partially so; that is to say they will keep some leaves throughout the winter. *H. androsaemum* reaches up to 3 feet high and has ovate leaves that may be 4 inches long and 2 inches across. The flowers appear in clusters at the ends of the branches, and are ¾ inch across of a rather pale yellow colour. The berry-like fruits are first red and then darken to become nearly black. All these berrying hypericums flower rather sparsely over a fairly long period, so that it is possible to have both fruits and flowers on the same plant. *H. hircinum* generally starts flowering in May, *H. androsaemum* in June and *H. elatum* in July. *H. hircinum* has the largest and best coloured flowers of the three, but the least ornamental berries, and it has the further disadvantage of giving out a revolting smell of goats when bruised in any way. The species most usually seen is *H. elatum*, generally in the form known as 'Elstead Variety' which has rosy-pink fruits. This can continue flowering until mid-September, while the other two species will have stopped by August. Some forms of *H. elatum* grow up to 5 feet high in their native Canary Isles, and similar heights are sometimes recorded over here, but in general it may be reckoned on not exceeding 3 feet. Incidentally there appears to be a misprint in Bean's classic four volumes of *Trees and Shrubs Hardy in the British Isles*. He gives the flowering times of *H. hircinum* as from early August till October. It is so rarely that one catches this Homer nodding, that it seems necessary to point out when he does, as he is so generally correct that one is liable to credit all his statements (another classic error is the location of *Erica arborea alpina* in the 'Mountains around Cuenca', probably the only place in Central Spain where it is not found, as they are exclusively limestone and carry no ericaceous plants). Some writers have suggested that *H. elatum* needs a sheltered position, but my experience does not bear this out. One would expect a plant from the Canary Isles to be somewhat frost tender, but it grows high up in the hills, where frosts are far from unknown.

ILEX

The hollies are thought of as purely berrying shrubs, so much so that it is quite hard to find any description of the flowers. Unfortunately most of the species are dioecious, so that it is necessary to have plants of each sex, in order to obtain fruit. Apart from the space that this entails, this is not necessarily a bad thing, as the male flowers are often produced in great profusion and are more ornamental than their small dimensions would suggest. In the case of *Ilex latifolia* they are a conspicuous yellow colour and appear in June. This plant has very handsome leaves up to 8 inches long and 3 inches across, which are devoid of spines and it has the usual red berries, which are produced abundantly in favourable situations. The plant is not reliably hardy and can only be cultivated successfully from Sussex westwards.

There is a group of deciduous hollies, which were once put in a separate genus, Prinos, which have the advantage of being monoecious, so that one plant will bear fruit. Of these the best from our point of view is *I. verticillata*, a native of North America. It is a spreading shrub that rarely exceeds 8 feet in height. The leaves are more or less lance-shaped, to 3 inches long and 1 inch across, purplish on emergence and retaining a slight tinge of this colour throughout the summer. The white flowers are noticeable, without being very ornate, but the red berries are extremely ornamental. They colour before the leaves fall and, if the beaks permit, will persist throughout most of the winter. Apart from their monoecious condition, the deciduous hollies are more rapid growers than the evergreen species, which move very slowly in their young stages and take at least ten years to reach flowering and fruiting size.

An evergreen holly which might be noted by those on the lookout for something unusual is *I. pedunculosa*. This can reach from 20–30 feet high and has unarmed, ovate leaves 3 inches long and 1¼ inches wide, of a good dark glossy green. The flowers appear in June in axillary cymes and are followed by the berries which, very unusually in this genus, are borne on stalks that are 1½ inches long. Incidentally, those who describe plants are sometimes rather elusive about the hollies. I get the impression that the flowers of *I. pedunculosa* are perfect and that one tree should produce fruits, but nowhere is this stated in so many words in the works that I have consulted. The plant is a native of Japan, but the variety *continentalis* from the Chinese mainland is barely different. It merely appears to be rather more robust and to have much larger leaves, up to 5 inches long. Sargent introduced the Japanese plant and—need we say it? Wilson introduced the Chinese form.

KOELREUTERIA

Why this superb tree is not in every garden I cannot think as it is perfectly hardy, easily available, moderate in price and of moderate dimensions. This *éloge* is directed at *Koelreuteria paniculata*, but can apply equally to the other species in cultivation, *K. apiculata*. The genus is named in honour of the botanist J. G. Koelreuter, who conducted some of the earliest experiments in hybridization. *K. paniculata* makes a small tree, usually about 20 feet high, but twice this height has been recorded in this country and up to 60 feet on the Continent. It has large pinnate leaves, up to 18 inches long, with the individual leaflets up to 4 inches, and these may be pinnately lobed themselves. They suggest a handsome fern frond. When they first emerge they are quite a distinct pink in colour, and then turn a pinkish-bronze and eventually green. In the autumn they become a good gold

89

before the fall. In July and August mature trees produce large terminal panicles, often over a foot in length, of golden-yellow flowers. These are followed by conspicuous inflated fruits that are 2 inches long. Once established the plant grows vigorously in its young stages, but does not flower as soon as *K. apiculata*. Since the flowers appear at the top of the tree, it should be sited so that it can be looked down upon, or viewed from some little distance, otherwise the flowers may be wasted.

Koelreuteria apiculata makes a smaller plant, usually not more than 20 feet high, but with a disproportionately thick trunk; it may be 3 feet across. Unlike the simply pinnate leaves of *K. paniculata*, those of this species are bipinnate, up to 18 inches long and 12 inches across at the base. They are not quite so gorgeous in the spring, although they still have the attractive bronze shades. The flowers are more freely produced than those of paniculata, but the panicles are not usually so large. However, *K. apiculata* then produces an additional attraction in its bladder-like seed vessels, which are a dark brick-red in colour. This not only starts to flower at an earlier age than *paniculata*, but also flowers with more freedom. If you have not room for both, it is difficult to decide which of the two to select. I am well acquainted with *K. paniculata* and have seen few plants of *K. apiculata*, but from what I have seen I would have thought that the better-known plant was somewhat superior in habit. Against this must be set the fact that *K. apiculata* appears to flower very much sooner than *paniculata*. *K. apiculata* is yet one more of the Wilson introductions to be chronicled. *K. paniculata* is also a Chinese native, but has been grown in this country since 1763 and the name of its introducer does not seem to be known.

LIGUSTRUM

The various privets have had to suffer for the popularity of *Ligustrum ovalifolium*, which is adequate as a hedging plant but not otherwise very exciting. There are, however, species with handsome leaves and copious flowers and these are followed by heads of dark-coloured berries, which, although less attractive than the red and orange berries of other shrubs, are by no means to be despised. Although one thinks of privets as being among the toughest of shrubs, able to grow in disgusting soil and polluted atmospheres, many of the choicer species are somewhat tender. Such is the case with *L. confusum*, which is noted for its dense panicles of grape-like fruit and which also will produce very fine panicles of clear white flowers in June and July. Most of the privets have somewhat yellowish-white flowers, but those of *L. confusum* are a good clear colour. However, it can only be enjoyed in the warmer counties.

An attractive hardy species is the evergreen *L. delavayanum*, which can reach up to 12 feet, but is usually not more than 6 feet high. It has small oval leaves, the largest being 1 inch long and ½ inch across of a dark shining green. On the other hand, the young shoots are covered with a grey down, which gives the plant something of the appearance of a cotoneaster. The flowers are produced in dense downy panicles in June, white, with violet-coloured anthers, and the egg-shaped berries are black. The seeds were sent to Vilmorin by the Abbé Delavay in 1890. The plant may be damaged in severe winters, but always appears to recover.

One always thinks of privets as evergreens, but there are some deciduous species, which are characterized by larger panicles of flowers than are usual among the evergreen species and which have purplish, rather than black, berries.

Ligustrum quihoui honours a superintendent of the Jardin d'Acclimation of Paris, whose name was Monsieur Quihou. It makes a rounded bush ranging from 6–10 feet in height, with oblong oval leaves up to 1½ inches long and barely ¾ inch across. Unusually for the genus, the flowers have an agreeable fragrance; most privets have a strong, but not very agreeable, scent. The plant is particularly valuable for its very late flowering, because the slender panicles of flowers, which may be 8 inches long, do not open before September and usually are still in flower in October. The disadvantage of this late flowering is that the purple berries are rarely formed in this country, so that its second attraction is somewhat notional, depending as it does on a warm October. However, the plant is so valuable for its late flowering, when a bush can transform itself into a mass of feathery white blossom.

Perhaps *L. sinense* is a more valuable shrub, although it does not have the advantage of the very late flowering season of *L. quihoui*. This is usually about 10 or 12 feet high, but can sometimes be obtained up to 20 feet high and trained as a small tree. The white flowers are produced in the greatest profusion in July, so that at that season it is difficult to see the leaves of a well-flowered plant. The flowers are followed by dark purple berries which can hang on the tree until February. The plant will do better in a sheltered position, although it is not usually affected by winter cold. It will, however, grow more vigorously in a situation that is not too exposed to the wind. There is a cultivar with white-variegated leaves, which may well be even more attractive than the type, but it is not very common. Although normally deciduous, the plant will retain most of its leaves in mild winters. The plant was introduced to cultivation by Robert Fortune and, since he introduced few wild Chinese plants, this would suggest that it is much cultivated in Chinese gardens or, at least, was so cultivated in the 1850s.

Although partially deciduous *L. yunnanense* has much of the aspect of *L. lucidum*, which makes an attractive small tree, but bears its fruits more reliably in Great Britain. It is less vigorous, growing from 10–15 feet high with oval-lanceolate leaves, tapered at each end, up to 6 inches long and 2 inches across. The creamy flowers are produced in large terminal panicles, 6 inches long and as much across, in July, and the black fruits are covered with a purple bloom, which does not, however, persist. Delavay sent seeds of this to the Paris Botanic Garden in 1888. None of the privets are very distinguished plants, but *L. quihoui* and *L. sinense* are extremely floribund and merit inclusion in most gardens.

LITHOCARPUS

I should not like to have to pass an examination to explain why the plant that used to be known as *Quercus densiflora* is now *Lithocarpus densiflorus* but, on consulting the authorities, I learn that the male catkins are pendulous in *Quercus* and erect in *Lithocarpus*, while the acorns are borne in some numbers on stout, stiff spikes. This last quality is not always apparent in our plant, which has the acorns either singly or in pairs. In any case, this plant is to all intents and purposes an evergreen oak, which can eventually reach 70 feet. It has only been in this country since 1874 and is not a rapid grower, so it is not easy to say if it will attain these dimensions easily here. The mature leaves are more or less elliptic in shape, up to 5 inches long and 2 inches across, and are a very dark green, markedly veined, with each vein ending in a sharp tooth. The main attraction of the plant lies in the new growth which is densely covered in white down—this provides a striking contrast to the nearly black mature leaves. The erect catkins, up to 4 inches long, appear in late June and early July and are pale yellow when the pollen is being distributed; they make a pleasing feature, though not, perhaps, wildly exciting. The young leaves soon lose their milky down on the upper surface, but it is retained on the underside for most of the first season. The leaves remain on the tree for two or three years.

In spite of coming from Oregon and northern California, the plant is perfectly hardy and is worth growing for the very striking picture it makes when the young growths are elongating. If you want to grow an evergreen oak, this is, undoubtedly, the best to obtain. No oaks grow very rapidly, but this will progress at a reasonable rate, making some 9 inches of new growth each year.

LONICERA

The differences between the climbing and shrubby species of this genus are so marked that it is not easy to appreciate that they do belong to the same genus. It is, indeed, divided into three sections: the long-trumpeted climbers with flowers in whorls belonging to the Periclymenum section; the climbing species with flowers in pairs and generally with evergreen foliage belonging to the section Nintova, and the shrubby species, with flowers in pairs, belonging to the section Xylosteum. This section has not very conspicuous flowers, but these are followed, often, by rather interesting fruits. Readers of Edward Lear may remember that at one stage of their voyage round the world, the Seven Children met with the Co-operative Cauliflower. Many of the Xylosteum honeysuckles must be related to this vegetable as often a pair of flowers combine to form only one berry. Although neither the floral nor the berry display of the shrubby honeysuckles is usually very brilliant, many of the plants have an elegance of habit which justifies their inclusion in any collection. Some of the species have additional attractions in their glaucous foliage. Among the two climbing sections, Nintova has many virtues, but the fruits are generally a rather dull black in colour and so none of them will be described here, whereas nearly all the Periclymenum species have handsome flowers and good red berries to follow and so should be included. It is probably best to discuss the two sections separately and we will start with the shrubs, in the section Xylosteum.

Lonicera albertii is a low growing, spreading, deciduous shrub. It has attractive glaucous blue, linear leaves up to 1 inch long and fragrant rosy-lilac flowers produced in pairs in May. Each flower is about ½ inch long and ¾ inch across, followed by distinct, purplish-red berries. All the best Xylosteums are liable to be damaged by late frosts and should not be planted where these are to be expected. The only other shrubby honeysuckle with these glaucous leaves is *L. korolkowii*, which should, therefore, perhaps be described now. This makes a largish spreading shrub from 6–10 feet high. The glaucous leaves are somewhat downy, oval in shape, up to 1¾ inches long and ¾ inch across. The shortly stalked, pale pink flowers are produced with some profusion in June and are followed by red berries. The plant is a native of Turkestan and requires hotter summers than we usually have here to give of its best, but even if it does not flower freely, it remains an attractive shrub. When it does flower and fruit well, it is really very valuable as a garden ornament, but the trouble with these shrubby honeysuckles is that, although they are delightful when they do perform well, so often they do not.

Lonicera deflexicalyx makes a very elegant shrub with pendulous branches and conspicuously purple young shoots. It can, eventually, reach a height of 10 feet. The oblong-oval leaves may be 3 inches long and 1¼ inches across and are produced quite thickly on the branches. From

93

every leaf axil springs a pair of yellow flowers that are quite large, as far as Xylosteums go, about ¾ inch long. As the branches tend to bend outwards and the flowers are produced on the upper side, this is somewhat more decorative than most of the species. The flowers come at the end of May and in early June, and are produced regularly enough. They are followed by conjoined orange-red berries.

Perhaps the best of all this section is *L. maackii podocarpa*. The variety is the Chinese form of this Manchurian shrub and has proved a much better garden plant. It makes a large, spreading shrub, up to 15 feet high and as much or more across. The dark green, oval-lanceolate leaves are 3 inches long and half as wide. The fragrant flowers are a very pure white when first open, but fade to yellow as they age and the berries are dark red. The flowers are small, individually, but both they and the ensuing fruits are produced with sufficient abandon to make the shrub look showy. Like the last species the flowers are produced on the upper side of the branches, and as these tend to grow horizontally, they are well displayed. The plant is a vigorous grower and so is not really suitable for small gardens, where it would take up more room than its charms warrant. Where sufficient space is available it should be borne in mind.

Lonicera ledebourii is a deciduous, rather gaunt shrub which can reach up to 9 feet in height, but is usually somewhat lower. The leaves are oblong-ovate, up to 4 inches long and 1½ inches across, of a shining green. The flowers open in pairs from June onwards and are tubular, about ¾ inch long, and orange-yellow in colour. Behind them are four bracts, two large and two small. After the flowers fade, these bracts enlarge and become bright crimson, and are much showier than the flowers. If seed has been set, black berries appear in the centre of the bracts, but they enlarge whether seed is set or no. The flowers appear in June and July, and the bracts are at their best from July onwards. The plant is thus very attractive for a long period, although its habit is somewhat graceless. It is a native of California and was introduced in 1838, which seems to suggest that Theodore Hartweg, the Royal Horticultural Society's collector, was responsible. A similar plant, but with yellow flowers and somewhat less attractive, is *L. involucrata*, which was introduced from North America in 1824.

Lonicera maximowiczii sachalinensis is notable for its dark purple flowers and fruits. Like many Korean plants it tends to start into leaf whenever there is a mild spell in the winter and may then be cut back by subsequent frosts. It makes an erect shrub, up to 10 feet high with leaves up to 4 inches long and half as wide, which are dark green and hairless above, greyish and downy underneath. The flowers are small, borne on stalks an inch long and produced fairly abundantly in late May and early June. The fruits are not always produced as profusely as one would wish, but when they are abundant they are attractive enough.

Lonicera quinquelocularis, a native of the Himalayas and China, makes a large shrub, up to 15 feet high and can apparently make a small tree in the wild. The downy leaves are oval, to 2½ inches long and 1½ inches wide. The flowers, which are large for the Xylosteums, are produced in June and are creamy-white, fading to yellow as they age. The point that distinguishes this plant from nearly all other shrubby honeysuckles is its translucent white fruits which, together with its flowers, it produces with great freedom, and it is thus to be preferred to some of the more showy but less reliable species.

In my opinion the above represent the best of the Xylosteums. The well-known *L. tartarica* grows with great vigour and flowers well, but is somewhat shy of producing fruit,[1] and the same can be said of the attractive *L. syringantha*, which is not always very free in producing its purple-pink flowers. Perhaps mention should be made of *L. thibetica*, a mound-forming plant up to 6 feet high, but 10 feet in diameter with attractive linear dark green leaves which are densely covered with white felt on the underside, while the flowers are lilac-perfumed and also the colour of a dark lilac. When young, this makes a spreading, prostrate shrub, but once it has reached its appropriate span it starts to rise and makes a very dense mass of intertwined branches. *L. rupicola* is similar in habit, but the leaves lack the felted underside and the flowers are not very freely produced. The two species appear to be unique in their curious mound-forming habit.

The climbing species of the Periclymenum group all bear red translucent berries which are probably at their best in our native honeysuckle, *L. periclymenum*. A really well-fruited specimen of this has a beauty that is all the more remarkable in that it goes so often unremarked. Another excellent fruit-bearing species is the North American *L. ciliosa*, a climber of moderate vigour with good yellow flowers and orange-red berries. Our other native species, *L. caprifolium*, has berries that are orange rather than red. The vigorous *L. tragophylla* does not seem to bear fruit very abundantly but that, too, has red berries. The free flowering hybrids *LL. americana*, *brownii*, *heckrottii* and *tellmanniana* are not at all prone to set seed, although they are not necessarily sterile. The berries do not hang for a very long time, but may give one from three to six weeks of pleasure.

As I said previously the Nintova section, which includes the popular *L. japonica*, has blackish berries which are not particularly attractive, nor are they borne with much freedom, so from the special point of view of this

---

[1] However, it is quite outstanding when it does, resembling a cotoneaster.

book they can be disregarded, though this is not to deny their valuable qualities.

MAGNOLIA

When I mentioned to a friend that I was including magnolia in this book, because of the ornamental fruits of some species, he raised his eyebrows and said: 'But surely no one grows magnolias for their fruits.' After this blinding glimpse of the obvious, his natural intelligence reasserted itself; obviously we grow magnolias principally for their flowers, but some do have very ornamental fruits and this fact might sway some of us to select one species rather than another.

Magnolia acuminata is, indeed, known for its fruit, as its popular name in its native North America is the cucumber tree. It is rather different from our general idea of a magnolia. It makes a large tree, up to 90 feet high, with oblong-oval, light green leaves up to 10 inches long and 5 inches across. The flowers are not large, and greenish-yellow in colour (but a good rich yellow in the dwarf variety *cordata*, sometimes given specific rank as *M. cordata*), the individual petals being about 3 inches long. The flowers appear at intervals from June onwards. The fruits are not much larger than the flowers, but a good dark red. The species is mainly grown as a rootstock for grafting other species or as a specimen tree. It was introduced to this country by Peter Collinson, a Quaker and an enthusiastic gardener of the eighteenth century. Together with various other enthusiasts he used to pay the well-known American botanist, John Bartram, to send them seeds and plants of his native wild flowers. Mill Hill School is built where his garden stood and some of his trees still persist. He received the seeds of *M. acuminata* in 1736, and it first flowered 26 years later, so it is obviously not a plant for quick returns. On the other hand, a mature tree is singularly handsome. The plant is completely hardy and a well-grown specimen looks very exotic.

Another North American species that makes a tree is *M. fraseri*, in this case one of more moderate size and greater floral beauty. This will eventually make a tree about 40 feet high, but it starts flowering when comparatively small. The leaves are large, up to 15 inches long and 8 inches across, obovate in shape and pointed at the end. The leaf is also characterized by two lobe-like auricles at the base, a feature that is only found in this and two other North American species, *M. pyramidata* and *M. macrophylla*. The parchment-coloured flowers, which turn to a milky-white as they age, appear in early June. The petals are each about 4 inches long; they are erect to start with, but spread out as the flower ages.

As a rough generalization it can be said that magnolias either have fruit like gherkins or like pine cones. The fruits of *M. fraseri* are cone-shaped, up to 5 inches long and about the same at the base; they are roughly pyramidal in shape and are coloured a delightful rose-pink. The seeds themselves, when they are displayed, are bright red. Although a native of the south-eastern United States—it was discovered by that great American naturalist William Bartram, in South Carolina in 1776—it appears to be perfectly hardy. Certainly it does well in southern England, and I have not heard of its failing farther north. In my far from exhaustive experience, this is the tree magnolia that comes soonest into flower. Magnolias have a reputation for slow growth which does not seem to be based on close observation. It is true that for the first three years from seed, the amount of aerial growth is not large, but once that period has been overcome, one can expect some 9 inches a year or even more in the larger species and some 6 inches in the smaller species such as *sinensis* and *wilsonii*. Magnolias are greedy plants and will respond enthusiastically to feeding. They do not like root disturbance and plants of any size may sulk for two years after being moved. *M. fraseri* will not thrive on alkaline soils.

Magnolia obovata (syn. *M. hypoleuca*) makes a large tree eventually, up to 80 feet high, and when sufficiently mature is handsome throughout the summer. It has large leaves, obovate as the specific name implies, up to 18 inches long, although such lengths are rare, and then about 8 or 9 inches across. They have a faint glaucous tint on the upper side and a pronounced blue-white underside. These leaves appear in clusters at the ends of the shoots, so that the flowers, when they appear, seem like some exotic sweet on a green plate. The flowers themselves are flattish, 8 inches across, creamy-white in colour, with the centre of the flower conspicuous because of its mass of purple stamens. They are also very fragrant. The cone-shaped fruits are eventually from 5–8 inches long and about 3 inches across and are a brilliant red in hue. The flowers open in June and the fruits have this red colour the whole time they are developing. Practically identical is *M. officinalis*, of which the variety *biloba* has the leaves divided at the apex. *M. obovata* itself is native to Japan, while *M. officinalis* is Chinese. Both these plants are completely hardy, although the young growths can be cruelly damaged by May frosts. As a young plant *M. obovata* is rather leggy and ungainly, but will eventually develop into a handsome tree.

Magnolia sieboldii (syn. *M. parviflora*) is more usually seen as a large shrub, up to 10 feet, than as a small tree. The oblong elliptic leaves are usually about 4 inches long, but occasionally attain 6 inches and are about half as wide. The flowers are borne at the ends of the shoots on stems that may be 2½ inches long; they are cup shaped, about 3 or 4 inches across and

D

a pure white, with a boss of crimson stamens in the centre. Most of the flowers appear in June, but the plant can behave like *M. virginiana* and flower spasmodically over three months. The fruits are rather slender, somewhat resembling gherkins, about 2 inches long and a brilliant carmine with scarlet seeds. The plant appears completely hardy. It is native to Japan and Korea but appears very close to two Chinese species, *M. sinensis* and *M. wilsonii* (and to the very rare *M. globosa*) and it is probably best to consider them all together.

The typical *M. sinensis* would be distinguished by the fact that the young growths are covered with brown silky hairs. It tends to make a larger plant than *sieboldii*, reaching up to 20 feet. The leaves are more or less rounded, up to 7 inches long and 5 inches across. The flowers are similar to those of *sieboldii* in colour, but tend to open more widely and to be slightly larger. The pendulous fruits resemble a ridge cucumber in shape, and are 3 inches long, half as wide and a rich pink. The seeds are a brilliant scarlet.

A typical *M. wilsonii* specimen has the young growths covered with pale brown down and in the second year the wood becomes purplish, while that of *M. sinensis* is greyish. The leaves tend to be more lanceolate in shape reaching a length of 6 inches but not more than 3 inches across. The flowers are pendulous, somewhat cup-shaped and about 4 inches across, white with nearly scarlet stamens. The fruits are also pendulous, about 3 inches long, 1 inch across and purplish-pink in colour. *M. wilsonii* will grow up to 25 feet. Unfortunately it is by no means easy to find plants that show the typical variations clearly and the plants appear to merge into each other in a baffling manner. To this list can be added the putative hybrid *M. × highdownensis*, which the late Sir Frederick Stern grew at his garden Highdown, near Worthing, Sussex. This is thought to be *sinensis × wilsonii*, but seedlings seem remarkably like the parent and there seems no good reason why it should not be an intermediate form. *M. wilsonii* tends to be somewhat less hardy than *M. sinensis* and does not grow so vigorously in colder districts. Damage is usually due to late spring frosts and it is to these that *M. wilsonii* seems more susceptible. A really typical *M. sieboldii* is quite distinct by its smaller leaves and the lack of brown hairs, or tomentum, on the young growth. I think it is probable that an amount of unconscious hybridization has taken place; whatever insects fertilize magnolias are unlikely to be trained botanists, and a hybrid swarm is now tending to supplant the three species. Since they are all very agreeable plants, the matter is not of great concern to the gardener, unless he feels strongly about having his labels correct.

Magnolia tripetala is grown mainly for its magnificent foliage and handsome fruits; its flowers are inconspicuous and have a most disagreeable scent. The plant can make a tree up to 30 or more feet high and bears huge leaves, up to 20 inches long, or occasionally longer, and half as wide. These leaves are oblanceolate in shape and tapered at both ends, but most noticeably at the lower extremity. The flowers are a rather dirty white and the petals are erect, so that although they may be 5 inches long, the flower is only about an inch across. In spite of its specific name, there may be 6 or 9 petals. The cone-shaped, freely produced fruits are about 4 inches long and a good dark pink in colour, eventually opening to reveal the scarlet seeds. The plant needs acid soil and some protection from wind, which can damage the huge leaves, but appears to be perfectly hardy as far as winter frosts are concerned. It is a native of the eastern United States and was first flowered by Peter Collinson in eight years from seed. Its leaves are only surpassed by *M. macrophylla* which can have leaves 3 feet in length, but is unfortunately by no means easy to grow. The plant used to be known as the umbrella tree, and one of its synonyms is *M. umbrella*. Once established, plants grow away very vigorously.

Magnolia virginiana (syn. *M. glauca*) is a more or less deciduous shrub, some forms retaining most of their leaves throughout the winter. It seldom exceeds 15 feet in this country, but can get larger in its native eastern United States. The leaves are oval, up to 5 inches long, but usually less and half as wide, a shining green on the upper surface and a glaucous blue-green underneath. This glaucous underside tends to fade as the leaves age. The flowers are produced in somewhat small numbers from June until September and have the best scent of any of the genus. They are globular, about 3 inches across, creamy-white when first emerged, but fading to a yellowish colour. They are notionally followed by bright red, cone-shaped fruits, but these are not produced with much freedom over here. The plant needs acid soil, but what else it requires I would find difficult to say. Some people grow it with ease, while with others it barely persists (and I can think of one gardener with whom it would not even do that). It really does appear to be a slow grower and possibly the magnolia's reputation for slow growth may be due to this plant, which was the first to be introduced to cultivation in this country. It was grown by Bishop Compton in the late 1600s in his famous garden at Fulham.

Most of the mahonias bear purple berries after their handsome flowers, but I would not consider that these are sufficiently ornamental to merit the mention of mahonia in this particular selection. The young leaves are also very handsome when they unfurl and I have a sneaking feeling that I am being too selective in omitting some of the species. However, bearing mahonia in mind we must move on.

MALUS

The crab apples are noteworthy for their flowers, their fruit and sometimes their gorgeous autumn foliage. There is also a group with rich
purple leaves during the spring and early summer. These all spring from
the variety 'Niedzwetzkyana' of our own wild crab, *Malus pumila*. The
genus is found throughout the north temperate zone, and some species
have been cultivated for so long in China that their wild forms are
unknown. Not all the species have all the qualities we require. *M. hupehensis*, for example, is one of the most gorgeous of the flowering species,
but the fruits are small and inconspicuous. However, a very large number
of species have beautiful flowers as well as fruits, and this section will have
to include also a large number of hybrids. Most of the species and hybrids
will grow in any soil, but some of the North American ones require
neutral or acid soil. Otherwise there appears to be no difficulty in cultivation. Owing to the size of the fruits, the birds tend to leave them more or
less untouched, at least as long as any other food is available. Some plants,
such as *M. baccata*, can carry their fruits through the winter until February,
and so give considerable decoration to the garden in winter. Very often it
is noted that the plants with the most attractive flowers lack ornamental
fruit and vice versa, so that a considerable amount of hybridization has
been done to attempt to combine the two main attractions, but the results
have not always been very convincing. The only real objection to the
principal fruiting species *MM. baccata*, *prunifolia* and *sargentii* is that the
flowers are white, not pink or red. But these white flowers are very
attractive on their own ground and the fruits of the pure species are better
than those of the hybrids, the only exception being *M. × robusta*, a hybrid
between *baccata* and *prunifolia*, which has extremely large and handsome
fruits, but still has the white flowers of the two parents.

The majority of the species and their hybrids make small trees and are
suitable for small gardens; a few make low bushes and even fewer will
make rather large trees. They are quite rapid growers and do not take
long to achieve a mature appearance.

Malus baccata generally makes a tree of 20 feet when fully grown, but it
has been recorded at twice this height. It makes a round, spreading head
with slightly pendulous branches and is of graceful habit. The white
flowers appear towards the end of April in clusters; each flower is $1\frac{1}{2}$ inches
across and is borne on the end of a longish stalk, which is erect, though it
becomes pendulous as the fruits form. These are bright red, about the size
of a cherry and can hang on the tree throughout the winter. The leaves
occasionally colour before falling, but this is not usual.

Of all the plants known as Siberian crab apples, this is the only one that is actually found wild in Siberia, whence it spreads southwards through Manchuria to northern China. It is the Manchurian form, variety *mandschurica*, that is most frequently grown, as this has the largest and best-coloured fruits.

Malus coronaria is a native of the eastern United States, where it makes a short trunked tree, which may reach 20 feet. The leaves are ovate and toothed, 4 inches long and 3 inches across. The flowers are produced in clusters and appear in late May and early June. They have a delicious fragrance of violets and are shell-pink in colour. The most usual form grown is 'Charlottae', with semi-double flowers that are 2 inches across. The fruits, which may be 1½ inches across, have little beauty, but the leaves will usually colour well in the autumn. Two related species, with the same violet-scented flowers, are *M. angustifolia* and *M. ioensis*. *M. angustifolia* is distinguished by its lanceolate leaves up to 3 inches long but not more than 1½ inches across, while the Iowa crab, *M. ioensis*, has downy young shoots, and the leaves are persistently downy on the underside. All these American plants do better in acid soil. There is a very good semi-double form of *M. ioensis* with pale pink flowers 2½ inches across, but neither this species nor *M. angustifolia* colour as well in the autumn as *M. coronaria*.

Malus × *floribunda* is thought to be a hybrid between *M. sieboldii*, a rather low, spreading shrub, and some other species, possibly *M. baccata*, although this is far from certain. The leaves are generally ovate, but occasionally on the stronger new growths are 3- or 5-lobed, a phenomenon that is also seen in *M. sieboldii*. However, the flowers are vastly superior to those of *M. sieboldii* and are also longer lived. These are a deep crimson in bud and a pale pink on expanding, so that the tree gives its most beautiful display when half the flowers are out and the other half have yet to expand. The berries are yellow, about ¾ inch in diameter. The hybrid character of the plant is deduced from the fact that it has only been found as a garden plant of Japan, but the cross must have been 'fixed', as seedlings breed true.

The plant with greener leaves and deeper flowers that used to be known as *M. floribunda atrosanguinea* is now correctly known as *M.* × *atrosanguinea* and is declared to be *M. halliana* × *M. sieboldii*. *M. halliana* is a Chinese species, long cultivated in Japan whence it was introduced to the United States. It is a small tree, up to 15 feet high with purple-tinted leaves and deep pink flowers, which does not thrive particularly well in this country and is usually replaced with *floribunda*. Crossed with *baccata*, *M. halliana* forms the hybrid × *hartwigii*, which has large flowers with a pink exterior and a white interior and rather showy red fruits. It is probably the best of the *baccata* crosses. All this group flower in May.

Malus glaucescens is an American species of moderate vigour, usually grown as a largish shrub, up to 10 feet high. It is one of those species with lobed leaves, and these are an attractive glaucous-blue on the underside in the early part of the season. In the autumn they turn yellow and dark purple. The large flowers are white and appear in May, and the yellow rounded fruits, which are about 1½ inches across, add a further interest in the autumn. The plant has not long been in cultivation and we do not know a great deal about it, but it seems to have charms of its own.

Malus kansuensis, a Chinese species, introduced by Wilson, makes a shrub or rather bushy small tree from 10–20 feet high. The leaves are basically ovate, 3½ inches long and 2½ inches across, but are usually somewhat deeply 3- or 5-lobed at their ends. The white flowers are not large, although produced abundantly, but the scarlet, rather small fruit is attractive, and the leaves usually colour well in the autumn. It would not be anyone's first choice for a crab apple, but its lobed leaves give it an unusual appearance.

Malus niedzwetzkyana should more properly be termed *Malus pumila* 'Niedzwetzkyana', but it is of so much importance both on its own account and as a parent that it merits separate treatment. The variety itself is not seen much nowadays, but it is still available. It makes a moderate-sized tree, about the same size as an apple tree which, since *M. pumila* is the ancestral species from which our apples have evolved, is not surprising. The whole plant, including even the young wood, is deeply suffused with anthocyanin, which gives a purple colour to the leaves, flowers, fruits and young wood. This variety is said to be not uncommon in Siberia and the Caucasus. As the season advances the leaves lose some of their purple colour and approximate to a dark green with purplish shades. Only a proportion of seedlings come true, but sufficient to perpetuate the plant without recourse to grafting. The main aim of the hybridists has been to maintain this overall suffusion of red-purple in rather more compact plants. There are quite a number of these, not differing greatly, except in the shape of the fruits. Crossed with *M.* × *atrosanguinea* is the popular plant known as *M.* × *purpurea*. *M.* × *aldenhamensis* and *M.* × *lemoinei* appear to be of unknown parentage, so far as the pollen parent is concerned; *M.* × *eleyi* is 'Niedzwetzkyana' × *spectabilis*. The 'Hopa Crab' is *baccata* × 'Niedzwetzkyana', and has green leaves with good dark purple flowers and fruits. All these hybrids are among the most popular plants for garden decoration and need no description.

Malus prattii makes a quite large tree, up to 30 feet or more, with ovate-lanceolate leaves up to 6 inches long and 3 inches across. The medium-sized white flowers appear in numerous clusters in May and are followed by red fruits covered with little white dots, which gives the plant an attraction although the individual fruits are only about $\frac{1}{2}$ inch across. In some forms the leaves have conspicuous red veins, and all forms usually colour well in the autumn.

Malus pumila, the wild crab apple, is the ancestor of our domestic apples and is found wild in this country as well as in most of Europe and north-west Asia. It makes a tree up to 30 feet high with white or rosy flowers in May and fruits of varying colours in the autumn. A number of cultivars have been selected for the beauty of their fruits, of which the best are 'Astrachanica' with bloom-covered crimson fruits, 'Elise Rathke' ('Pendula') with a weeping habit and bright yellow fruits and, perhaps the best of all, 'John Downie' with orange and scarlet fruits. None of these cultivars will breed true and must be propagated, either by grafts or cuttings.

Malus prunifolia makes a small tree, not exceeding 20 feet in height. It is one of the group of plants known as Siberian crabs, the others being *M. baccata*, and its hybrid with *prunifolia*, *M. × robusta*. *M. baccata* is found in Siberia, but *M. prunifolia* has not been found convincingly wild either in Siberia or in northern China, which has been suggested as an alternative locality. It may even be a hybrid between *baccata* and *pumila*. It is distinguished from *M. baccata* mainly by the fact that the calyx-lobes adhere to the top of the fruit in the case of *M. prunifolia* but do not in *M. baccata* or *M. × robusta*. The large flowers are produced in April and are a pure white, while the large fruits may be either red or yellow. The variety *rinkii* has pinkish flowers and very attractive bright yellow fruits, and is probably the best form to obtain, but they are all good fruiting plants.

Malus sargentii never makes a tree and is generally a rather low bush, although it can eventually reach a height of 8 feet. It bears quite large white flowers in May and has rather small, but very numerous bright red fruits in the autumn. This is useful, owing to its shrubby habit, but I have never been able to appreciate the somewhat excessive praise that is lavished on what seems to me a fairly undistinguished shrub. However, I am certainly in the minority, as the Royal Horticultural Society has awarded it both the Award of Merit and the more-to-be-prized Award of Garden Merit. The plant was discovered by Professor Sargent growing in a salt marsh in Japan in 1892, and it was subsequently named in his honour. If it will thrive in marshy situations over here, it will certainly have an added use.

Malus × soulardii 'Red Tip Crab' is a cross between *M. ioensis* and *M. pumila* 'Niedzwetzkyana'. This has bright crimson young leaves, which eventually fade to green, but colour up again in the autumn. The flowers are a good purple and the fruits a good red—the plant is one that might well be seen more frequently. *M. ioensis* seems to give extra size and substance to the flowers.

The most beautiful of the flowering crabs is *M. spectabilis*, a plant that has been cultivated for centuries in China, but which has yet to be found in the wild. Unfortunately its yellow fruits are so pale as to be inconspicuous, so that it cannot be included here.

On the other hand, *M. toringoides* merits inclusion, as much on account of its graceful habit as on account of the ornamental flowers and fruits. This makes a small tree, up to 25 feet high of a spreading, loosely branched appearance. The leaves tend to be deeply lobed into from 3 to 7 divisions. The flowers, which are creamy-white, open in May and are followed by yellow fruits, which are flushed scarlet where they get the sun. The fruits are only $\frac{1}{2}$ inch in diameter, but are so thick on the plant, that it is always one of the best features of the garden in September and October.

Malus trilobata, a plant of Lebanon and Syria, is something of a curiosity. The leaves are basically 3-lobed, but the lobes themselves are often divided, so that the leaf appears to be 7-lobed and takes on the appearance of a maple leaf. The individual leaves are about $3\frac{1}{2}$ inches long and 4 inches across. They turn various shades of crimson in the autumn and this autumn colour is one of the plant's main attractions. The large white flowers appear in May, but fruit, which can be either red or yellow, is not set with great freedom in this country.

Malus tschonoskii is one of the best of autumn colourers for those who live on alkaline soil. It is one of the largest crabs, capable of reaching 40 feet and makes a neat, pyramidal tree. The adult leaves may be 5 inches long and 3 inches across, and the emerging foliage in the spring is intensely silvery and is nearly as handsome as *Sorbus aria*. The white felt eventually falls from the upper side of the leaves, while remaining on the underside. The flowers are white, flushed with pink and are rather large for the genus. The fruit has little beauty, but the leaves turn in the autumn to shades of gold, orange and scarlet and are then among the most lovely of all trees. The plant is named in honour of a Japanese, Chonosuke Sugawa (1841–1925), who was an assistant of the great Russian botanist Maximowicz. When this gentleman wanted to honour his assistant he russified his first name to Tschonoski.

Very nearly as effective in its autumn colour and more effective in its fruits is *Malus yunnanensis*. This is very near *M. prattii* and has the same red fruits sprinkled with white dots. The form grown in gardens is the variety *veitchii*, which differs principally from the type in that the leaves are lobed in the variety, but more or less ovate in the type. These leaves are up to $4\frac{1}{2}$ inches long and 3 inches across, with a brown felt on the underside. The flowers, which appear in May, are somewhat small for the size of the plant, which can eventually be a tree from 20–40 feet high but, like all the genus, they are produced very copiously. They are generally white, but some plants have a pinkish tinge to the flowers. It was as a fruiting plant that the Royal Horticultural Society gave it an Award of Merit. The leaves tend to turn scarlet and orange in the autumn, so that the plant then becomes practically incandescent. It was discovered by Delavay, but was introduced by Wilson in 1900.

I think the above list includes all the best crabs for our purpose, but there is no species which does not have attractive flowers, and most have attractive fruits as well, so that it is really a question as to whether you wish to lay emphasis on the flowers or the fruit. You will have noticed that the best fruiting species have white or pale pink flowers, while the darker-coloured flowers generally have less ornamental fruits. Since the genus flowers at the time when most flowering shrubs are at their best, there are strong arguments in favour of growing the species with ornamental fruits. These are generally left by the birds and in some cases hang for a long time on the trees. In any case I cannot really see that pink flowers are necessarily more attractive than white ones. If you have a garden where the autumn colour is usually good, you can have two good displays with *M. coronaria*, which has the added advantage of a singularly delicious fragrance in the flowers.

MELIOSMA

With this genus we take a plunge into the obscure. It belongs to a family, the *Sabiaceae*, which must be only a name to most of us, and the plants themselves are rare in gardens. With the exception of the somewhat tender *Meliosma myriantha*, which Maries brought from Japan in 1879, the hardy species, most of which are Wilson introductions, have only been grown during this century. They do not appear to be very rapid growers, taking a considerable time for the arborescent species to come into flower, although the shrubby *M. cuneifolia* flowered within eight years of seed being sown. All the plants are deciduous, but they fall into two main groups, one with simple leaves and the other with pinnate leaves. The inflorescence is a very large, pyramidal panicle of white or cream flowers, which are individually very small. These are followed by small berries, which are black in most cases, but violet in the case of *M. veitchiorum*, the most desirable species. The plants to be described here have all proved themselves hardy, but the majority come from tropical south-east Asia and tropical America. The generic name means 'honey-scent' and the flowers are very fragrant. They are somewhat suggestive of the inflorescences of *Sorbaria* in appearance.

Meliosma beaniana is in many ways rather untypical of the genus. In the wild it makes a tree from 40–80 feet high; we do not yet know its ultimate height in gardens. The leaves are pinnate, up to 12 inches long, composed of a number of ovate leaflets of which the terminal one may be 5 inches long and half as wide, the lateral ones gradually becoming smaller, with the lowest pair only about 2 inches long. The flowers are creamy-white, borne in axillary, drooping panicles up to 8 inches long and 4 inches across, and emerge in May before the leaves are developed. The fruit is a small black berry. Once established, this must be a very imposing tree as, according to Wilson, it covers itself with blossom, and the huge panicles of black berries which follow must also be impressive. It seems probable that the interval between sowing seed and seeing the first flowers would be about twenty years.

Meliosma cuneifolia makes a shrub, up to 20 feet high in the wild, and has wedge-shaped leaves that may be 7 inches long and 3 inches across. The flowers are at first a pale yellow, but fade to a good white, and appear in July, which is a useful time to have flowering shrubs. They are in terminal pyramidal panicles up to 9 inches long and as much across at the base, and they have a delicious fragrance which is reminiscent of hawthorn. They are followed by black fruits. *M. myriantha* is similar, but has dark red berries and is, unfortunately, somewhat tender, particularly when a young plant.

Meliosma oldhamii, which makes a small tree in this country, is one of the pinnate-leaved species and a native of Korea. Like so many plants from that part of the world it is liable to start into growth too early and be damaged by early spring frosts. This is a pity, as it makes a handsome tree with leaves up to 15 inches long composed of numerous leaflets, increasing in size from the base upwards. The flowers, which appear in July, are in large, erect, terminal panicles of pure white flowers. These panicles may be a foot long and nearly as much across at the base. I presume the fruit is black, but I can find no reference to them in either English or American reference books that I have consulted. It suggests that they are not borne very freely in this country.

Meliosma veitchiorum seems to be the best of the pinnate-leaved species and flowers in 18 years from seed. It will probably grow to about 30 feet high and is characterized by its very stout, rigid, erect branches. The huge pinnate leaves may reach a length of 30 inches and are composed of about 11 leaflets each about 7 inches long and half as wide. The terminal flower panicles may be as much as 18 inches long and 12 inches across at the base. They are creamy-white in colour and appear in June or early July, to be followed later by the violet berries. The leaves turn a good, clear yellow in the autumn which, with the berries, give this species an attractive appearance.

As the fruits are very small, about the size of elder berries, they are not suffered to remain very long on the plants. It seems to be possible to move meliosmas when they are of a reasonable size, so that it should not be necessary to wait too long for the imposing flowers.

OSTEOMELES

Another somewhat way-out member of the rose family is *Osteomeles*. Either of the two semi-hardy species *O. schwerinae* and *O. subrotunda* can be recommended to those looking for rather small wall shrubs. The two species are rather similar in appearance, but *O. subrotunda* is considerably smaller in its leaves and in its ultimate height. The plants are evergreen with pinnate leaves composed of numerous minute leaflets, ¼ inch long in *O. schwerinae*, less in *O. subrotunda*. The leaves may reach a length of 4 inches in the larger species, but rarely exceed 1½ inches in the other. The leaflets are covered with grey down, which persists for a long time on the underside and the young growths are also covered with silky white hairs. The white, hawthorn-like flowers are produced in June in branching corymbs; each flower is about ½ inch across in both species. These are followed by haws which are at first dark red, but which turn blue-black when completely ripe. A plant that seems to link the two species is *O. schwerinae microphylla*, introduced by Wilson in 1908 and which appears to be somewhat hardier than either of the other two. Otherwise it is very close to *O. subrotunda*.

OXYDENDRUM

Oxydendrum arboreum is an ericaceous plant making either a large shrub or a small tree, related to *Arbutus*, but deciduous. It requires the acid conditions that most of the family need. All its display is concentrated into the second half of the year as it flowers in July and August, while the leaves turn a brilliant scarlet in October. The leaves are lanceolate with a tapering point, up to 8 inches long and 3½ inches across and dark green in colour. The lily-of-the-valley-like flowers are produced in panicles composed of terminal and axillary racemes, each some 6 inches long. This is a very valuable shrub for its late flowering and superb autumn colour, but is not a very rapid grower.

OZOTHAMNUS

Ozothamnus ledifolius is a rather stiffly erect evergreen shrub from 3–5 feet in height. The sticky young shoots are a brilliant yellow in colour and this yellow persists on the underside of the leaves, which become dark green above. The leaves are small and linear, rather like pine needles, but not more than ½ inch long. The white, daisy-like flowers are packed in numerous terminal clusters and, in the wild, they completely cover the plant. They open in June and July. The plant was introduced into cultivation from Tasmania by Harold Comber as recently as 1930 and is now considered to be a member of the genus *Helichrysum*. It appears to be hardy in the southern half of the country, but would probably need protection elsewhere.

PALIURUS

Paliurus spina-christi is an extremely thorny deciduous shrub or small tree. It will grow up to 20 feet high and is one of the plants from which the Crown of Thorns is reputed to have been made. The leaves are ovate, up to 1½ inches long, half as wide, arranged alternately on the stems. The flowers are minute, but produced in great quantities from every leaf axil of the current year's growth. They are greenish-yellow and, in July and August, when the plant flowers, it appears to be wreathed with myriads of tiny blooms. The fruits that follow are rounded, with a disc-like wing on the top, giving them the appearance of a broad-brimmed hat. They are about 1 inch across and greenish-yellow in colour, and are rather striking if examined closely. The plant is native to the eastern Mediterranean regions, but is perfectly hardy. It is not a showy plant by any means, but it has a quiet charm and interest, quite apart from its putative scriptural associations.

PARROTIA

Parrotia persica can be grown as a tree, when it can then reach a height of 30 or 40 feet, but is more often seen as a widely spreading shrub. Grown in this way it acquires an exceptionally graceful habit. It is a member of the *Hamamelis* family and bears clusters of flowers in March before the leaves emerge. These are remarkable for the conspicuous tufts of red stamens which give the plant distinction, although they are not remarkably showy. The ovate leaves, which are produced very thickly all over it, are some 5 inches long and half as wide. In the autumn they turn the most brilliant gold and crimson to make this one of the best of all autumn-colouring plants. Most of the *Hamamelidae* tend to grow rather slowly, but the parrotia, once established, grows very rapidly and ample room must be allowed. When grown with a trunk, it can be seen that the grey bark flakes off, much as that of a plane tree does. It does not seem at all fussy with regard to soil and, although usually seen growing on acid soil, there is no reason to suppose that it is essential. It is native to north Persia and the Caucasus, where the soil is often alkaline. The generic name commemorates a German, F. W. Parrot, who was the first man to climb Mount Ararat, which he did in 1829.

PERNETTYA

Pernettya mucronata is an ericaceous shrub from the extreme south of South America. It is an evergreen, which is said to be capable of reaching a height of 5 feet, but I have never seen plants of such a height and the most usual is 2 or 3 feet. It may spread more in diameter. It has a close affinity with *Gaultheria*, with which it has hybridized, as has already been noted.

Although the plants are not demonstrably unisexual, they appear to behave in such a manner, and it is necessary to ensure cross fertilization and also to have a male plant. This can most easily be obtained by the cultivar called 'Thymifolia' but if you have a group which sets fruit in the main, it is safe to assume that any failing to fruit is masculine. Most plants are clones, propagated from selections made by an Irish nurseryman, Tom Davis, in the 1880s, and have been selected for the colour of the berries.

The wiry branches are closely set with small, pointed ovate leaves, rarely more than ½ inch long and less than half as wide. Towards the end of May, the white bell-shaped flowers are produced singly in the upper leaf axils. Each flower is about ¼ inch long. The berries, which are the plant's main attraction, have usually coloured by August and will, in theory, remain on the bushes until the next flowering season. They are rather large for small birds, such as sparrows, to attack and so are generally fairly persistent in the neighbourhood of towns, but in the country they are liable to be gobbled down by pheasants and similar birds and, of course, wood pigeons, a menace wherever you garden.

There are named cultivars which have the berries in defined colours, including white, pink, lilac, crimson and dark red. These are propagated either by cuttings or by suckers. Although the usual peaty soil that suits most of the *Ericaceae* suits these plants very well, there is reason to suppose that they will thrive on limestone formations, although probably not on thin chalky soils. They do best in full sun.

There are a few other pernettyas that have been in cultivation rather spasmodically; these are principally creeping shrubs, suitable for the alpine garden. *P. leucocarpa* has white or pink berries, *P. pentlandii* has dark purple fruits and *P. pumila* white or pink ones. All these come from South America, but *P. tasmanica*, as its name suggests, comes from Tasmania, and has dark red fruits. One species is also found in New Zealand, but does not seem ever to have been introduced to cultivation.

Readers of Joseph Banks's Journal of his voyage with Captain Cook to observe the Transit of Venus, may recollect a disastrous expedition he made in Tierra del Fuego, before the Straits of Magellan were passed. He, with his botanical assistant Dr. Solander, went on a plant hunting expedition when they were cut off by heavy snow (this was in January 1770, when good weather might have been expected). Among the plants noticed were red and white cranberries, the first mention of *Pernettya mucronata*.

PHILADELPHUS

The Philadelphus do not have anything for us; their sole charm lies in their flowers, but mention should be made of the golden-leaved form of *Philadelphus coronarius*. The leaves are a good clear gold for the first part of the year, although they tend to fade to green in the latter half of the year. Unfortunately, in my opinion, the golden leaves make the white flowers appear to be of a rather dirty white, so that the attractive leaves make the generally attractive flowers lose their general air of purity. However, the combination of golden leaves and white fragrant flowers certainly constitute a double feature programme, so that the plant must be admitted here.

PHOTINIA

The so-called Chinese hawthorns comprise both evergreen and deciduous shrubs or small trees. Their main beauty is in the autumn when the haws are conspicuous and the leaves of the deciduous species usually colour well. The young growth of the evergreen species is a delightful coppery colour which makes the plants very handsome in the spring. Most species do best in neutral or slightly acid soil.

In general they have been introduced only during this century and there are conflicting reports about their hardiness, but it would seem fairly safe to say that the evergreen species are, on the whole, less reliable than the deciduous species and only do well from Sussex westwards. It is always a pleasure to grow new plants, but honesty would compel me to state that the true hawthorns are more ornamental.

Photinia amphidoxa makes a shrub or slender tree up to 10 feet high. It is most generally seen as a shrub and is deciduous, with willow-like leaves some 3 inches long which turn a good yellow before falling. The white flowers appear, like most of the genus, in late May and early June and are in rather few-flowered corymbs and not very conspicuous. It bears quite large scarlet fruits in the autumn.

Photinia beauverdiana is best replaced by the variety *notabilis*, which only differs from the type in its larger size and greater vigour. The lance-shaped leaves are up to 5 inches long and 2 inches across and the flower corymbs are about 4 inches across, produced with some freedom in established trees. These are up to 20 feet high in the type, 10 feet higher in the variety. The berries are a deep red and the leaves tend to turn scarlet in the autumn, so that at that season the plant is really splendid. It is less so in the spring, as the flowers are not very large individually, although they are quite showy in the variety *notabilis*. In the type the corymbs are only 2 inches across.

Photinia davidsoniae is the hardiest of the evergreen species and appears to be completely so in the southern half of the country. In China it makes a tree from 20–40 feet high and has proved fairly vigorous over here. The leaves are rather leathery, lance-shaped, up to 6 inches long and $1\frac{3}{4}$ inch across; a dark glossy green on the upper surface, pale green below. The young leaves and shoots are coppery in colour and are then striking. The small white flowers appear in quite large terminal corymbs and are followed by small, orange-red berries.

If the last species was the hardiest of the evergreen photinias, *P. priono-phylla* is the most tender and is probably only really satisfactory in situations with a Gulf Stream climate. It is rather valuable for its late flowering, as it is not until July that the flowers appear. It is a native of Yunnan, where it grows on limestone hills, so it may well be successful where other species would fail. Since it does not exceed 6 feet in height it is very suitable for treatment as a wall shrub. The leaves are obovate, 3 inches long and 2 inches across with an edging of spiny teeth. The flowers appear in corymbs some 3 inches across and are followed by rather small crimson haws.

The best of the evergreen species is *P. serrulata*, but it is somewhat tender. In severe winters it may be cut to the ground, although it appears to regenerate quite well. It is the species that has been longest in cultivation, having been introduced in 1804 and in favoured situations, as in Cornwall and Eire, it has made trees 35 feet high. It has large leaves, particularly on young plants when they may be 8 inches long and $3\frac{1}{2}$ inches across and are a really splendid colour when they first unfurl, a brownish-red like burnished copper. It does not appear to flower as a young plant, but when the flowers do appear it is in late April and early May, in corymbs that may be 6 inches across.

The fruit is much the same size as our wild May and of similar colour. Where this tree can be grown successfully it is one of the most handsome evergreens. The young growths maintain their coppery tinge for a long period, generally until the end of June, so that when it flowers and fruits the plant is in beauty for a longer period than most trees. If not checked it grows comparatively quickly, but spring frosts can retard it considerably and it will only do well in sheltered situations or in districts where the Gulf Stream brings mild winters.

Photinia villosa, a deciduous plant, is the most widely grown. It makes a shrub or small tree up to 16 feet high (up to 30 feet in the variety *sinica*) and has oval leaves which may be 3 inches long and 1½ inches across. In spite of its name the plant is not, generally, particularly villous; it is generally only the flower-stalk which is covered with grey felt, although the young growths are slightly hairy. The hawthorn-like flowers are produced in rather small corymbs in May and are followed by red haws. The leaves generally turn a very brilliant scarlet in the autumn, although there is a selected form 'Flava', in which the leaves turn a clear yellow. The plant is native to China, Korea and Japan and was introduced from the last-named country in 1865. The Chinese variety *sinica* was introduced by Wilson in 1901.

PHYSOCARPUS

Another plant with golden leaves, although these fade rather rapidly, is the plant now known as *Physocarpus opulifolius*, but which, in its day, has been a *Neillia* and a *Spiraea*. This makes a spreading shrub, which acquires some interest in winter when the peeling greyish bark can be observed. The flowers appear in June and are white with a rosy tinge that is less attractive than it sounds. The flowers are individually small, but produced in quite sizeable clusters. The plant is a fairly rampant grower and is tolerant of most soils and conditions. The golden-leaved form has the varietal name 'Luteus'. It is not one of the choicest shrubs, but it is reliable.

PICRASMA

Picrasma ailanthoides is not a well-known plant, but deserves to be so. It makes a slender tree from 20–40 feet high and has young bark of a reddish-brown colour which is picoteed with yellow spots. The pinnate leaves are up to 15 inches long, composed of from 9–13 ovate leaflets, each up to 4 inches long. The flowers are either perfect or unisexual, but both sexes are found on the same plant. They are inconspicuous, green in colour and disposed on a branched corymb, which may be 8 inches long. The female flowers set red, pea-shaped fruits which add a quiet charm. The plant achieves its real glory in the autumn when the leaves turn first orange and then a brilliant scarlet and are at that time among the most brilliant inhabitants of any garden.

PISTACIA

I mention *Pistacia chinensis* here for obvious reasons, although I have no idea whether it can now be obtained. It makes a large, deciduous tree, up to 80 feet high in its native China. It has pinnate leaves, which are peach-coloured when emerging. They may be 9 inches long and are composed of an even number of leaflets, usually 10 or 12, which are lanceolate in shape, with an elongated point, each some 3 inches long and ½ inch across. The flowers are unisexual, but the plant is monoecious, with both sexes produced together. The male flowers are on short spikes some 3 inches long, the female on a lax panicle some 9 inches long. The latter bear berries which are red when half-ripe and then turn to a blue colour. The leaves turn a brilliant crimson in the autumn, particularly after hot summers. The plant is perfectly hardy and it is not easy to appreciate why it is uncommon over here. It is apparently grown a great deal in the United States as a shade tree, so there should be no difficulty in obtaining seeds. Making so large a tree it is evidently a long-term investment in the garden, but with the beauty of the young leaves and their autumn colour it would start paying some dividends at once, and it sounds as though it should be reintroduced as soon as possible.

PRINSEPIA

A small genus of shrubs, all deciduous, belonging to the rose family and characterized by flowering early in the season and by their somewhat spiny stems. They are allied to *Prunus*, but fairly distinct in their habit.

Prinsepia sinensis grows to about 6 feet in height and has lanceolate leaves about 3 inches long and ½ inch across. The leaves emerge early in the season and at the same time the yellow flowers appear in the leaf axils of the year-old shoots. They are individually small, about ¾ inch across, but are produced fairly profusely. They are followed in August by small, cherry-like fruits, which are bright red in colour.

Prinsepia uniflora is similar but has white flowers and fruits that eventually turn a bluish-purple, but owing to the earliness with which the flowers open, the fruits are very rarely produced.

Very different is *P. utilis*, but this is only rarely a success in cultivation although it is easy enough to grow. It makes a more vigorous shrub than the other two species, reaching a height of 9 feet. The flowers are smaller, but produced in short racemes, generally in the autumn. If this occurs the fruit, which is purple and about the size of a barberry, should ripen in the following April and May. In point of fact the plant tends to flower in the early spring but is not very prodigal at that season and the plant is the least satisfactory of the genus as far as gardens in this country are concerned.

❧ Prunus - Rhododendron

PRUNUS

The peach, the plum, the cherry, the apricot, the almond; how many fruit trees with beautiful blossoms are contained in this genus. However, from the point of view of the gardener, the fruit is not of much importance, and the interest is concentrated mainly in the foliage. Many species have good autumn colour in the foliage, and there are also plants with leaves coloured purple all the year round. There are a couple of species in which the beautifully polished bark forms an attraction. A majority of the plants have only their flowers to recommend them and so will not be mentioned here. The genus has been divided into various sections, of which the evergreen *Laurocerasus* is of no interest to us, although it includes some useful garden plants.

Prunus avium, the wild cherry of our woods, is a plant of the greatest beauty in flower and in its autumn colour, while the shining bark, which peels horizontally, gives the plant distinction even in the winter. It is one of the largest species, (most of the genus are large shrubs or small trees), making a tree up to 60 feet high and fully deserving the amount of space that such a tree requires. It will grow very happily on chalky soils. The white flowers appear in April, before the leaves have unfurled, in such profusion as to hide the tree completely. The ovate leaves, up to 5 inches long and 2 inches across, turn gorgeous shades of crimson in the autumn.

There are two varieties, which can perhaps be considered as improvements on the type. The variety *decumana* is characterized by much larger flowers and really enormous leaves, sometimes up to 10 inches long and 4½ inches across. The variety *plena* has double flowers, so that it does not set any fruit, but makes a longer and more impressive, although slightly less graceful floral display. It cannot always be relied upon to colour so well in the autumn and I cannot agree with those who prefer it to the wild type. The fruits themselves are small, blackish-red and sweet, but are not particularly ornamental, even if they were not immediately taken by the birds. The plant is one of the ancestors of our sweet black cherries.

Prunus cerasifera (syn. *P. myrobalana*), the cherry plum, must have mention here for its purple-leaved form, *atropurpurea* (syn. *P. c. pissardii*). This makes a moderate-sized tree, up to 30 feet in height, which covers itself with rosy-white flowers in March. These flowers are followed by the leaves, which are a pleasant claret colour when they first unfurl, but afterwards turn to a rather dull dark purple. There seems to be little record of this setting fruit in this country, but when they are formed they are a purple colour. The plant appears to come fairly true from seed and was first noted growing wild in Persia by the gardener of the Shah, a M. Pissard, who sent the plant to France in 1880.

This purple-leaved plant has contributed its dark purple colouration to two hybrids. One is as large as the parent and known as *P. × blireiana*, having been bred by a M. Bliré. This has the same dark purple leaves of Pissard's plum, but has large double pink flowers, nearly as large as the double peach. It is thought that the other parent is *P. mume*, the Chinese apricot. This is an ornamental plant that has been cultivated in China and Japan for many centuries. Most of the cultivars in cultivation here have been brought from Japan and they include some double-flowered ones. It is presumably one of these that was the parent of × *blireiana*. The true *P. mume* is somewhat delicate in our climate and is seldom grown, but the hybrid has absorbed some of the vigour of *P. cerasifera* and is completely hardy.

The other hybrid is *P. × cistena*, which is *P. pumila* fertilized by pollen of *P. cerasifera atropurpurea*. This has the restricted growth of *P. pumila*, although the hybrid is somewhat larger than *pumila* itself, which rarely exceeds 4 feet in height, and it also has the myriads of very small flowers that characterize the seed parent. From Pissard's plum it has inherited the suffused leaves, although in *P. × cistena* they are less heavy and are deep red rather than purple. The flowers appear in late April.

Prunus canescens makes a rather spreading shrub, up to 8 feet high. It is notable, when sufficiently large, for its flaking bark, which falls away to expose the shining brown inner bark, much like that of *P. serrula*, although, owing to its bushy habit, the bark on *P. canescens* is less conspicuous. The lanceolate leaves, $2\frac{1}{2}$ inches long and 1 inch across, are covered with grey silky hairs, which persist for some time on the upper side and for the whole season underneath. The small rosy flowers are produced in May, but do not persist for very long, which is a disadvantage.

Prunus cerasus is a tree, to 10 feet and more, and the parent of the sour cherries, Morellos, Flemish Reds and the like. It gets a mention on account of an odd variant called 'Semperflorens' or the All Saints' Cherry. This flowers rather sparsely in April, before the leaves have emerged but then starts flowering again in June and continues doing so until September. These later flowers are not produced in any great profusion, but singly from the leaf axils and in small clusters from the ends of lateral shoots. In theory, by the time the later flowers have opened, the earlier ones should have ripened their scarlet fruits, but the birds usually put paid to this delightful idea. 'Semperflorens' is often grafted on to a standard form of *P. avium.*

Prunus dielsiana makes a small tree, up to 30 feet high and should be encouraged to form a tree as soon as possible, as one of its main attractions lies in the mahogany colour of the trunk and main branches. The pale pink flowers have markedly reflexed sepals and are similar to those of *P. cyclamina.* They open in April. The oblong leaves reach up to 7 inches long and are 3 inches across, and generally turn various attractive tints in the autumn.

In some districts it is a complete waste of time, trying to grow these early-flowering prunus. I had a garden once where every year the birds, mainly bullfinches, would strip nearly all the flower buds off as soon as they started to swell. At the moment there does not appear to be anything one can do to discourage them and if you live in a bird-infested area, the only way to avoid disappointment is not to grow these prunus at all.

Prunus maackii belongs to the Padus section, the bird cherries, which bear their flowers in tightly packed racemes and which generally flower with the leaves. *P. maackii* is not quite typical in that the flowers do not come on the current year's growth, but on the year-old wood. They open in late April. The plant's main attraction lies in its flaking brown-yellow bark, like that of a birch tree. It makes a respectably sized tree, up to 40 feet and is particularly striking in winter and early spring. The flowers are by no means to be despised and are packed into racemes some 3 inches long.

Prunus maximowiczii appears to be somewhat intermediate between the cherries and the bird cherries. It can make a largish tree, up to 50 feet high in the wild, although it has, so far, only reached about half that height in cultivation. The flowers do not appear until the middle of May and are borne on a raceme about 3½ inches long. Each flower is shortly stalked and the raceme is furnished with large, leaf-like bracts. The flowers are creamy-white, not very large, and there are from 6 to 10 on each raceme. The leaves are not particularly large either, 3 inches long and 1¼ inches across, but frequently turn a good crimson in the autumn. The plant is not one of the most attractive species, but is interesting with its bracted racemose inflorescence.

Prunus rufa requires only a brief mention. Apart from its pink flowers it also has the attraction of the young shoots being covered with umber down. However, this follows so soon after the rather exiguous floral display that it can scarcely be said to qualify for detailed consideration here.

On the other hand, the Japanese plum, *P. salicina*, has considerable charm and deserves to be seen more often. It makes a tree up to 25 feet high with oval leaves 4½ inches long and 2¼ inches across, so that the epithet 'willow-like' seems somewhat inappropriate. These generally turn bright red before falling. The flowers appear in early April, before the leaves, in great numbers. They are pure white and about ¾ inch across. In districts such as California, where they are grown as a commercial fruit crop, they bear reddish plums that are nearly 3 inches in diameter, but these are rarely formed in our climate and the plant must be grown for the sake of its flowers and autumn colour, with the occasional fruit ranking as an unforeseen bonus.

Of all the prunus species the one that has the most claim in this book, together with a few of its hybrids, is *P. sargentii*. This is a rapid-growing tree that can reach 80 feet and shows little delay in rapidly attaining half that height. The leaves are the usual cherry shape, up to 4 inches long and half as wide, and turn to various shades of red and orange in the autumn. They are one of the most reliable of autumn colourers. The blush-pink flowers are as much as 1½ inches across and are produced in the greatest profusion, completely smothering the tree. Why such a marvellous plant should have had to wait until 1893 before it was introduced is rather baffling. It is native to Japan and not uncommon there. Most of the Prunus species are rapid growers, but many have rather a short life of only 50 years or so; *P. sargentii*, however, seems to be longer lived. It is the parent of the following hybrids. *P. × hillieri* is from *incisa × sargentii* and has the smaller flowers of the seed parent, but the soft pink of the pollen parent, a more upright growth, and is not quite so reliable for autumn colour, although it usually colours well. *P. × juddii* is *sargentii × yedoensis*, which has the graceful flowers of *yedoensis*, but the colour of *sargentii*, and the most brilliant autumn colour of any cherry.

Prunus serotina is a North American bird cherry, growing up to 50 feet in this country, but occasionally up to 100 feet in its native state. The young bark is aromatic. The flowers are produced in early June and are in racemes up to 6 inches long. In this country the black fruit, which is used for flavouring rum in the States, is rarely borne. Unlike the crimson of most of the cherries, the leaves of this bird cherry turn a clear golden-yellow in the autumn. Cultivars with laciniate leaves and with a weeping habit have been in cultivation, but are now hard to obtain.

Prunus serrula, sometimes called *P. serrula tibetica*, is grown principally for its marvellous bark, which looks like the best polished mahogany. It peels yearly and is at its best during the summer months. It makes a moderately sized tree, up to 30 feet high, and is rather slower-growing than most species. The white flowers appear in April, but are not very distinguished, being neither very numerous nor of good texture.

Our native blackthorn, *P. spinosa*, has a purple-leaved cultivar, 'Purpurea', in which the young leaves are a good clear red, later fading to purple; the flowers are pale pink. This makes a good hedge plant.

Prunus subcordata is a North American shrub or small tree with reddish branchlets and broad oval leaves, which turn a brilliant red in their native haunts, but are less reliable over here. The small flowers appear in some quantity in April, opening white and fading to pink. The plant is perfectly hardy but is rare in cultivation.

Prunus ssiori makes a tree up to 75 feet in its native Japan and Manchuria, but there seems no record of its height over here, and it never seems to have been widely distributed. It was not brought into cultivation in Western gardens until 1915. It is one of the bird cherries and bears racemes of white flowers some 6 inches long in June. Apart from its flowers, it is remarkable on account of its white bark, which makes it very distinctive in winter, particularly if it can be planted in front of dark-leaved evergreens. How one pronounces the double 'ess' of its specific epithet and who Mr. Ssior was, may be stated somewhere but not in any book that I have been able to consult. The oblong leaves may be 6 inches long but are not more than 1½ inches wide. It sounds like a species that should be reintroduced, although the bird cherries are not very popular with gardeners. We have not many white-barked trees that also have ornamental flowers. I personally cannot think of any, apart from this plant.

PSEUDOLARIX

Pseudolarix amabilis, the only species, is a slow-growing tree that is not always easy to establish. Nor is there any agreement as to its requirements. Bean and Hillier agree that it dislikes lime in the soil, but William Dallimore, in the Royal Horticultural Society's Dictionary, says that it 'appears to need a slightly limey soil'. It is a native of Chekiang, in China, and was introduced in 1853 by Robert Fortune, who introduced comparatively few wild Chinese plants although he introduced the cream of all their cultivated ones. In favourable climes it can make a tree to 70 feet, but half that height appears to be the best that it can do over here. As its name implies it is very similar to the larch and, like that tree, is deciduous. The young growth is golden-green in colour. In June the male catkins produce their pollen and are then conspicuously yellow in their turn, while the leaves turn a brilliant gold in the autumn before falling. It is thus an extremely interesting tree and one that all agree is beautiful at almost all seasons. It should, therefore, be worth the trouble that it will apparently entail.

PTELEA

Ptelea trifoliata, the hop tree, is a rather low tree, not exceeding 25 feet, but with a greater spread. It is deciduous and, as its name implies, has trifoliate leaves. These are oblong, and the central lobe is the largest, sometimes reaching a length of 6 inches. They are aromatic, as is also the young wood. In late June the greenish-yellow flowers open. They are borne on pendulous corymbs some 3 inches across. The individual flowers are about ½ inch across and are unisexual, although both sexes are present in every inflorescence. Although not showy, they are extremely fragrant, somewhat resembling the honeysuckle in their perfume. The male flowers soon fall, but the female flowers develop the characteristic winged disc-like fruits, which persist well into the winter. Before falling the leaves turn a clear gold. There are selected forms with yellow leaves ('Aurea') and blue-green leaves ('Glauca') and also a fastigiate form, which might be useful in small gardens. Although there is little that is showy about this tree, it has these wonderfully fragrant flowers, conspicuous fruits and good autumn colour, and can thus claim to pay a good rental for the space it may take up.

PUNICA

The pomegranate, *Punica granatum*, is a Mediterranean shrub or small tree that requires to be trained on a warm wall in this country. Around the Mediterranean it is grown for the sake of its fruits, but in this country they are so rarely produced that they are not worth considering. The plant does, however, have delightful coppery young foliage and brilliant scarlet flowers from late June onwards. The leaves somewhat resemble those of a willow in shape, being up to 3 inches long and 1 inch across. They do not start to emerge until mid-May and are then a delightful shade of coppery-bronze. This slowly fades to a medium green. The flowers are tubular, up to 1½ inches across and 2 inches long and are scarlet in colour. The first ones generally appear before June is out and continue until early September, with the main display in mid-July. The plant is most successful when treated like an apple, pruning the leaders by about half in winter and spurring the laterals back to two or three buds. The plant takes a few years to reach flowering size. In this it differs from the so-called variety *nana*, which never exceeds 3 feet in height and comes into flower the second year from sowing, when it is a tiny shrub about 6 inches high. The type can reach a height of 25 feet.

The pomegranate is a plant of odd affinities. At one time put in the *Lythraceae*, it now has its own family, the *Punicaceae*, which contains only this genus. It is, however, reported that the Spaniards use it as a rootstock for oranges and roses. Grafting an orange on a pomegranate is said to give later ripening and red flecks in the pulp, the so-called blood oranges. The grafting of roses sounds suspect, but since oranges belong to the *Rutaceae* the whole story requires investigation. Generally, plants of different families are completely incompatible and it sounds in the highest degree unlikely the same plant could serve as a rootstock for two families that are not even supposed to have much affinity between them.

PYRACANTHA

A genus of evergreen shrubs, closely related to *Crataegus* and *Cotoneaster*. The leaves are entire, not lobed, which is the chief feature differentiating them from *Crataegus*. They are grown principally for their heavy crops of red or yellow berries and are often grown as wall-shrubs, presumably to discourage the birds from removing them too soon. When grown away from a wall, they tend to make rather sprawling shrubs and, although in theory the berries will hang for a long time on the plants, in practice they are rapidly stripped by the birds, unless protected in some way. The genus has a slightly peculiar distribution. The bulk of the species come from the Himalayas and their Chinese extensions, but one species is found in south-east Europe and Asia Minor. All the species have white flowers in corymbs in late May or early June and these flowers are about $\frac{1}{2}$ inch across.

Pyracantha angustifolia is somewhat distinct from the other species. It makes a spreading shrub, up to 12 feet high, with the young growths and the undersides of the leaves covered with thick grey down. The narrow, oblong leaves may be 2 inches long and $\frac{1}{2}$ inch across. The flowers are smaller than in the other cultivated species and appear much later, at the end of June or beginning of July. The immature fruits are covered with grey down, but they ripen to a brilliant orange and should remain on the tree until March. Like most of the genus, large plants do not move happily, and they are all best started when small plants.

Pyracantha atalantioides (syn. *P. gibbsii*) is, like the last species, of Chinese origin. It is the most vigorous of the species in cultivation. The leaves are more or less oval, up to 3 inches long and half as wide, and a dark, glossy green. The fruits are a rich crimson normally, but there is a yellow-fruited cultivar. The shrub will reach 20 feet and, if the lower branches are trimmed away it can be grown as a small tree. The fruit is said to hang until March, when the birds permit.

These two Chinese species are generally unarmed, but the European *P. coccinea* has spines up to ¾ inch long. This grows up to 15 feet high and has obovate leaves which can be 2½ inches long and ¾ inch across on the non-fruiting growths, smaller on the fertile shoots. The fruits are a very brilliant red, but do not persist into the New Year. The variety *lalandei* is larger in all its parts and has berries that are orange. At one time there was grown a form with white berries, but this seems to have dropped out of cultivation.

Pyracantha crenulata seems to be a very variable species which is found from the Himalayas to Yunnan. It is from this latter district that the best form, variety *rogersiana*, comes. This will grow up to 10 feet high and has a neat pyramidal habit when young, becoming more spreading as it ages. It has rather small leaves, which are set about ½ inch apart on the shoots and this gives them a rather distinct appearance in the genus. The leaves themselves are oblanceolate, up to 1½ inches long and ½ inch across, but generally considerably less. It is very profuse in its berries and these may be yellow or orange.

More or less half-way between *P. crenulata* and *P. atalantioides* is the plant known as *P. crenatoserrata* (syn. *P. yunnanensis*) which will grow up to 18 feet high. It is closest to *P. atalantioides*, from which it is distinguished by being more spiny, less downy and in having oblanceolate leaves with a broad rounded end. The fruit is smaller, lighter in colour, ripens later and persists for longer. One would not have thought that any of these differences were sufficient to give a specific entity.

A bigeneric hybrid between *Pyracantha atalantioides* and *Osteomeles subrotunda* was bred in France in the early 1920s. It had the pinnate leaves of the pollen parent, but the flowers and fruit of the seed parent and must have been a rather handsome plant. It grew about 6 feet high, but does not seem to be any longer in cultivation.

PYRUS

The various wild pears contain a number of attractive plants at the flowering stage, but few of them have any other attractions. They range in nature from the eastern Mediterranean through Asia to northern China and Japan.

Pyrus regelii (syn. *P. heterophylla*) is one of the most extraordinary of all plants. It is a small tree, eventually reaching from 20–30 feet. The young shoots are covered with grey down, and this persists until the second season, so that the plant is not unattractive in the winter. The white flowers are produced rather sparsely. It is the leaves that give the plant its great interest. The same plant may produce leaves that are ovate and entire, up to 3½ inches long and 1½ inches across, or pinnately lobed into from 3 to 7 linear lobes, each one of which may be 2 inches long but only ¼ inch across; shapes intermediate between these two extremes may also be found. The leaves are covered with a fairly persistent grey down.

This diversity of leaf-shape is, so far as I know, unique in broad-leaved trees. It can be paralleled in some of the aquatic *Ranunculus*, where the floating leaves are broad and the sunken leaves are divided into thread-like segments, but there is a sound explanation for this, whereas Regel's Pear appears to have no adequate reason for its differing forms. It is native to Turkestan, and the climate of this region may provide some explanation. The pinnatifid leaves may be better able to withstand the heat and windiness of the region, while the ovate leaves would represent the ancestral form of the pear, before it had adapted itself. Perhaps we have here a form that has not yet completed its evolution.

Pyrus salicifolia is well known for its graceful pendulous habit and its narrow leaves with a persistent silvery down on the underside. In April the abundant white flowers open and the young leaves are silvery on both sides. This silver persists on the upper side until June, and the underside gives silver flashes when it is disturbed by breezes. The plant is always given the varietal name *pendula*, but all forms are more or less pendulous in habit. The plant is native to Asia Minor and the Balkans.

Pyrus susuriensis is a largish tree from North China, growing up to 50 feet. In late April or early May it bears its rather large (up to 1½ inches across) flowers in dense corymbs. The leaves, which are rounded, are up to 4 inches long and 3 inches across. They turn a bronzy-red colour in the autumn, so that the plant is effective in flower as well as in its autumn foliage. *P. pyrifolia*, which is cultivated for its fruits in China and Japan, has leaves up to 5 inches long which also colour in the autumn, but not with the regularity of *P. ussuriensis*.

Some of the oaks, notably *Quercus coccinea* and *Q. palustris*, will produce wonderful autumn colour, but they are somewhat lacking in other attractions, apart from the attraction that all large trees present, and so they will be omitted here.

RHAMNUS

A genus of trees and shrubs of slight ornamental value, with small green flowers, which are followed by berries which generally turn first red and then black. They are found throughout the northern temperate zone. Of the two plants discussed here, one is worth growing on its own account, the other is more of a curiosity.

Rhamnus imeretina makes a spreading deciduous shrub, up to 10 feet high. It is noteworthy for its large, oblong leaves which are often 10 inches long and 4 inches across and occasionally even larger; Bean mentions leaves 14 inches long and 6 inches across. In the autumn these turn a deep bronzy-purple. Before they change colour, the fruits will have appeared; first red and later black-purple. This is a native of the Caucasus and will thrive anywhere. One shrub nurseryman suggests, rather oddly in my opinion, that it will make 'a splendid shrub for a damp, shaded site in a chalk meadow'. This is doubtless true, but it is not a problem that normally confronts gardeners. If they have a chalk meadow, it is unlikely to have a damp site in it.

Rhamnus purshiana makes a small tree, sometimes as high as 45 feet and is deciduous. The oval leaves may be 5 inches long and 3 inches across. The small green flowers are produced in small umbels in July and are followed by small, top-shaped, blue-black berries. It is not particularly attractive, but might serve to encourage a sense of one-upmanship. It is always agreeable to offer one's guests home-grown produce, and after the fruit and vegetables the aspiring gardener might be pleased to produce a home-grown *aperitif*. Although the plant is a native of the western United States its product, which is made from the bark, has always been known under a Spanish name, which when translated means the Holy Husk. The Spanish for holy is sagrada and for husk is cascara, and few things can be nicer than home-made cascara sagrada.

RHODODENDRON

This enormous genus has only been appreciated to its full extent in this century, and this is directly due to the exploration of the Chinese mountains by Wilson and even more by George Forrest. They have certainly introduced the largest number of new species, but the contributions of Kingdon-Ward from Tibet and Burma must not be underrated. During the late eighteenth century by far the largest number of species had come from North America, and rhododendron gardens were known at that time, and for long after, even when it was no longer appropriate, as American gardens. It is interesting to learn that the North American *Rhododendron maximum* was introduced to cultivation as early as 1736, 27 years before the European *R. ponticum* was brought into cultivation in Great Britain. The first of the Himalayan rhododendrons to be introduced was *R. arboreum*, in 1817 according to Sweet, in 1820 according to

Loudon. The two differ also as to the date of introduction of the next Himalayan species, *R. campanulatum*, for which Loudon gives 1817, Sweet 1824; subsequent writers seem to favour the later date. The first real influx of Asiatic rhododendrons dates from J. D. Hooker's expedition to Sikkim in 1848, which resulted in the introduction of such famous species as *RR. barbatum, cinnabarinum, campylocarpum, falconeri, grande, griffithianum, hodgsonii, niveum* and *thomsonii*, besides the tender *RR. dalhousiae, lindleyi* and *maddenii*. Other species were introduced subsequently by collectors such as J. T. Booth, and in the 1850s Fortune introduced *R. fortunei*, the first of the Chinese rhododendrons (apart from the 'Indicum' azaleas) to enter into Western cultivation. It was, however, first Wilson, and later Forrest and Kingdon-Ward, who opened the treasure chest of the mountains of Burma and western China, and it is only in this century that the majority of species have been introduced.

With the exception of the Falconeri and Grande series, which are grown principally as foliage plants, it is as flowering shrubs that the genus is chiefly grown. Some of the deciduous species, known generally as azaleas, have attractive autumn colour, and many of the evergreen species have very attractive young foliage; a few have attractive foliage all the year round. In a couple of species, *hookeri* and *auriculatum*, the young foliage is not outstanding in itself, but is accompanied by brilliant scarlet bracts, which are very striking for the rather short time that they are in evidence. A few species have very lovely, smooth, shining bark. There are a large number of species that have very attractive undersides to their leaves, but these attractions have to be sought for in the shrubby species, although they are apparent in the arborescent species, as, for example, *R. fictolacteum*.

Apart from the large-leaved tree rhododendrons and a couple of species with quite outstanding glaucous blue-green leaves, it is unlikely that anyone would elect to grow rhododendrons for features other than their flowers, but it can do no harm to list the ones that do have other attractive features in addition. It is not too easy to organize the list so that it makes a convenient tabulation, but it is probably best to consider first of all the deciduous plants of the Azalea series, then the two series of tree rhododendrons, and finally a rather heterogeneous list selected from the remaining series.

In the Azalea series, that old favourite, the fragrant *R. luteum*, a native of eastern Europe and western Asia, is the most reliable autumn colourer. This makes a bush up to 10 feet high and the fragrant, bright yellow flowers appear in May before the leaves start to unfurl. The latter eventually reach a length of 5 inches and a width of 1½ inches and turn various shades of crimson, purple and orange each autumn. The same phenomenon can be observed in many of the Ghent azaleas, in which *R. luteum* enters as a parent.

Rhododendron albrechtii is an attractive small shrub with rosy-purple flowers that appear slightly before the leaves, which are purplish in colour as they emerge, but soon lose this attractive tinge. They are obovate in shape and are usually arranged in clusters of 5 at the ends of the branches. They eventually can reach a length of 4 inches and half that width. The flowers generally appear at the end of April, but the shrub is often damaged by late frosts and should be put either in a very sheltered spot, where spring frosts are not a danger or else in a very exposed place, where it will not be hurried into unseasonable growth. All these deciduous azaleas seem to do best in full sun or in dappled shade. The plant is native to Japan and was discovered by Dr. Albrecht in 1860, but does not seem to have been much in cultivation prior to Wilson's collecting in 1914. According to Bean the leaves turn a good yellow in autumn, but I do not find that this happens consistently.

Rhododendron calendulaceum is not often seen nowadays, although it is the main parent in the glowing orange Ghent and other hybrid azaleas. It makes a leggy shrub, somewhat spreading, and up to 10 feet high, with elliptic leaves up to 4 inches long and 1½ inches across. The flowers are scarlet, orange or occasionally yellow, and appear before the leaves in May. In good seasons the leaves will turn orange and crimson, but after wet summers this display may be lacking. The shrub is so extraordinarily attractive in flower that it will always earn itself a place in the garden, but if it will also colour well in the autumn it is doubly welcome.

Rhododendron nipponicum, assuming that it still exists in cultivation, is one of the best species for autumn colour. It is also rather attractive in the winter as it has brilliant reddish-brown bark; this peels off during the summer. The obovate leaves are large for the series, reaching a length of 7 inches and a width of 4 inches. On the other hand, the flowers, although produced in quite large clusters of up to 15, are rather small and tend to be hidden among the expanding leaves. They are white and have no fragrance. The leaves turn orange and crimson in the autumn and could be relied upon to do this regularly, but owing to the rather inconspicuous flowers plants are now difficult to obtain.

Rhododendron occidentale is the main parent of many of the later breeds of deciduous azaleas: Knap Hill, Exbury and Occidentale. The plant was introduced from western North America by William Lobb in 1851, but it was some time before its virtues were appreciated. Like several other American species the flowers do not come out until the leaves are nearly fully developed, and it is from mid-June onwards that the plant is at its best. The elliptic leaves are up to 4 inches long and 1½ inches across and generally turn to yellow, scarlet and crimson in the autumn. The fragrant flowers appear in trusses of from 6 to 12 flowers, which are individually up to 2 inches across, white, flushed pink, with a yellow blotch. This has given its autumn colouring propensities to many of the Knap Hill and Exbury hybrids, but the species itself deserves to be seen much more often than it is.

Rhododendron pentaphyllum, from Japan, is a very graceful shrub, that can make a small tree up to 10 feet high. The leaves are produced in whorls of 5 at the ends of the shoots. It can be distinguished from the rather similar *R. quinquefolium*, to which we will come in a moment, by the fact that in *R. pentaphyllum* the flowers unfold before the leaves do so. The leaves are elliptic in shape, 2½ inches long and 1¼ inches across and turn to orange and crimson in the autumn, although this is dependent on the season and is not a yearly certainty. The flowers appear early in the year, in March if the season is mild, otherwise in April (another distinguishing characteristic) and are a very attractive rose-pink in colour. This again is a plant that is very susceptible to spring frosts, although the leaves emerge after the flowers and so the plant has a better chance of preserving its young growth. However, it should never be planted in known frost pockets and it cannot be regarded as amongst the easiest of species to grow.

Rhododendron quinquefolium, also from Japan and with leaves in whorls of 5, can be distinguished from the previous species by the fact that the flowers expand after the leaves have done so, and that they do this about a month later than those of *R. pentaphyllum*. The plant can be somewhat larger than *pentaphyllum*—plants up to 25 feet have been recorded in cultivation—although it is generally a rather low, bushy shrub. The flowers are generally white with a green blotch, but occasionally they are pale pink, but never so rosy a pink as in *R. pentaphyllum*. The young leaves have an attractive purple margin, which fades out as the season advances and they generally colour well in the autumn. This is one of the most graceful of the deciduous species, but young plants are somewhat shy in flowering and patience is required.

Rhododendron reticulatum, yet one more Japanese species, makes a rather gaunt shrub that can reach 15 feet in height, but is generally seen around 5 feet. The leaves are a distinctive diamond shape, up to 2½ inches long and nearly as much across. They are a purplish colour when young, but then become a rather dull green. The underside is covered with finely netted veins, which give the plant its specific epithet. The leaves turn a rather dark purple before falling. The flowers, which appear before the leaves in late April or early May, are produced singly or in pairs, and are a brilliant rosy-purple, and the plant then makes a very graceful effect.

Rhododendron schlippenbachii is surely one of the loveliest of deciduous, or indeed of all, rhododendrons. It is not a particularly rapid grower, but can eventually make a plant up to 15 feet high. The leaves are in whorls of 5 at the ends of the branchlets, obovate in shape, up to 4½ inches long and 3 inches across, sometimes purple-tinged when young. The flowers open before the leaves in late April and early May, in trusses of about 6 flowers, each flower rather flat and about 3½ inches across in colours ranging from a rather pale pink to a deep rosy colour. The plant is native to Japan, Korea and Manchuria, and plants from the more northerly stations have the usual unfortunate habit of starting into growth at the first mild spell and then being at risk with subsequent frosts. They should, therefore, be grown either in elevated positions or in very cold situations, where they are not liable to be excited into premature growth. The Royal Horticultural Society's *Rhododendron Handbook* states that the leaves turn yellow, orange and crimson in the autumn, but my own experience does not bear this out. It would seem that this is a matter of situation.

Rhododendron tschonoskii may, on occasion, be semi-evergreen. It is a rather curious species with tufts of nearly linear leaves, about 1½ inches long and ¼ inch across, which turn orange-red and crimson in the autumn and really give the plant its only attraction. The very small, white flowers are produced in May in trusses of from 3–6 blooms, which are nearly hidden in the leaves. It would seem that this plant must at some time have entered into the parentage of the evergreen 'Kaempferi' azalea 'John Cairns', which has dark orange-red flowers in late May and whose second-year leaves turn a good orange-scarlet in the autumn. Autumn colour is not usual among the evergreen azaleas and its appearance in 'John Cairns' is exceptional.

Rhododendron vaseyi, one of the most beautiful North American species, was not discovered until 1878, when it was found by Mr. G. Vasey on mountains in North Carolina. It makes a sizeable shrub, up to 15 feet high, and seems to grow best in full sunshine. The flowers open in late April and early May, before the leaves, in clusters of 4–8. They are about 2 inches across and are in various shades of pale pink (a white form also exists) with red dots. The elliptic leaves can be 5 inches long and 2 inches across, and sometimes have a slightly reddish tinge; they can usually be relied upon to turn bright red before they fall. However, like too many of the Azalea section, this display is very fleeting and the leaves generally fall very soon after colouring up. The plant is one of the most charming of a charming series and merits inclusion in any connection.

All the azaleas require acid soil, preferably with a rich humus content. This is indeed regarded as essential for all rhododendrons, but it is worth noting that Forrest and Kingdon-Ward drew attention to the fact that many of the Chinese rhododendrons were growing on magnesian and dolomitic limestone. I have never, alas, been to these districts, but I have seen the European *R. hirsutum* growing on limestone in the Alps. The plants actually grow in humus-rich soil lying on the rocks and one would imagine that the amount of alkalinity that seeps into this soil is not very great. It would be interesting if gardeners in the Yorkshire Dales, for example, would experiment with rhododendrons in similar situations. One would expect the chalk districts of southern England to be quite unsuitable, but there is some reason for doubt even here. At Birling Gap in Sussex there is an extensive tract of chalk down, which appears to have amassed sufficient humus on the surface to allow ling, *Calluna vulgaris*, to grow successfully, and few botanical phenomena are more extraordinary than to see this native of acid soils growing among the typical chalk-down flora. Rhododendrons are not deep-rooting plants and they might well thrive where sufficient depth of soil exists, regardless of the alkalinity or otherwise of the subsoil. Evidently not all species would thrive under these conditions, but it would be worth trying.

The various tree rhododendrons of the Falconeri and Grande series are all plants with handsome leaves and respectable flowers. Very few of the Grande series are reliably hardy and their growth is confined to such districts as Hampshire, Dorset, Devon, Cornwall and the West coast regions that are affected by the Gulf Stream. Apart from a mild, moist climate they also require protection from wind, so that their huge leaves are not damaged. The leaves of the Falconeri series are less magnificent in size, but equally attractive in colouration and the plants are considerably hardier, although again protection from strong winds is desirable. Both series require shady conditions when young, although they should later be able to emerge into conditions that are less obscured. They are not extremely rapid growers, but can usually be relied upon to make about 9 inches of growth each year. They take some time to come into flower, and if young plants flower it would rather suggest that they are not thriving. Although they usually end up as trees, they tend to make large spreading shrubs in their youth, although, of course, it is always possible to remove the lower branches so as to emphasize their tree-like qualities.

Of the Grande series, the species that appear to be the hardiest are *RR. coryphaeum, macabeanum, mollyanum, praestans, puderosum, sinogrande* and *watsonii*. None of these would thrive in very cold districts, but should be happy in most of southern England and in sheltered spots elsewhere, although they never appear to do so well as in districts such as Cornwall and western Scotland. Of the species listed neither *R. puderosum* nor *R. watsonii* are particularly outstanding, as many of the hardier Falconeri series have equally attractive leaves, so our discussion will be confined to the remaining five species.

Rhododendron coryphaeum is closely related to *R. praestans* and is sometimes considered to be a form of this species. It makes a spreading shrub up to 20 feet high with oblong leaves that may be 18 inches long and 5 inches across. The colour of the indumentum which covers the young growths and persists on the underside of the leaves may be white, grey or beige. This plant seems to flower earlier than most of the series and produces in April a large truss of campanulate flowers which are creamy-white or very pale yellow in colour, with a purple or red blotch in the throat. The young growths, which are arguably the most attractive feature of the plant, appear in May, usually late enough to avoid frost damage. *R. praestans* will reach up to 30 feet and has broader obovate leaves, sometimes reaching a length of 24 inches and about 10 inches across. It is likely to become tree-like with age. The flowers, which come slightly later than those of *R. coryphaeum*, are either pink or a pale magenta with a crimson blotch. Both these species are Forrest introductions from Yunnan.

Rhododendron macabeanum is, in my opinion, the gem of the whole series. It was introduced by Kingdon-Ward as recently as 1928 and since it received an Award of Merit in 1937, it evidently does not take too long to reach flowering size. It makes a tree up to 45 feet in height. The bud scales are red and, since the buds are as large as small pine cones, they are quite an attraction in themselves. The new growths and young leaves are densely covered with silver felt and glisten in a highly attractive manner. The mature leaves reach a length of 12 inches and a width of 6 or 7 inches and carry a silvery tomentum on the underside. The flowers emerge early in the season, frequently at the end of March, and range in colour from pale yellow to a real rich buttery yellow blotched with purple at the base. Owing to its relatively small leaves, it is less liable to wind damage than some of the larger-leaved species.

Rhododendron mollyanum was collected originally in 1925 in Tibet by Kingdon-Ward and subsequently by Ludlow, Sherriff and Elliot in 1947. Originally it was thought to be a form of *R. sinogrande* and was not until it flowered that it was discovered to be a new species. It makes a small tree, up to 30 feet, but generally less, in height and has leaves that are 12 inches long and 4 inches across. The young growths are covered with a silvery tomentum which persists on the undersides of the leaves, which are dark green above. The campanulate flowers appear towards the end of April in a large truss. They are sometimes frilled at the edges and are in various shades of pink, from nearly white to a deep rosy colour. There is always a crimson blotch at the base.

The most magnificent leaves of any rhododendron belong to *R. sinogrande*. This was discovered by Forrest in 1912 and introduced in the following year. It first flowered in Cornwall in 1919, a remarkably short time after the seeds had been received. It makes a tree about 30 feet high and has silvery young growths. The emerging leaves are also glistening and silvery. The dark green leaves with well-marked veins retain a silver underside. They can reach a length of 3 feet and would then be 12 inches across, but these dimensions are unusual and a more general description would give a length of 2 feet and a width of 10 inches; impressive enough in all conscience. When mature the leaves are tough and leathery, but even so they need protection from violent winds, even more so in their juvenile stages. Very severe frosts will cause partial or complete defoliation, but do not seem to do any further damage. The flower truss, although it is very large, up to a foot in height, still seems rather small in proportion to the enormous leaves. The flowers open in April and are generally a rather dull cream colour, although the plants from northern regions, variety *boreale*, have flowers of a soft yellow, which is more attractive. All forms have a crimson blotch. Some of Forrest's later gatherings came from very high elevations and they are certainly hardier than his original sendings. *R. grande* itself, of which this is claimed to be the Chinese form, never has leaves more than 12 inches long and is considerably less hardy.

The Falconeri series have less magnificent leaves than the Grande specimens, but they are far hardier and thrive in less protected situations. They tend to make rather taller trees and seem to be rather slower in coming to flowering size. Most of the species are available commercially; those that do not appear to be are omitted in these descriptions.

Rhododendron arizelum makes a small tree, up to 20 feet in height. The young growths, the petioles and the underside of the mature leaves are all covered with a dense cinnamon-coloured tomentum, which makes the plant especially striking in late May when the new growths are emerging. The flowers, which appear in April in trusses of from 15–25 flowers, are generally in various shades of cream, ivory or pale yellow, but occasionally deep yellow and from Tibet have come forms with crimson and purple flowers. The plant is not easily distinguished from *R. falconeri* itself and is slightly less hardy. Even more akin to *R. arizelum* is *R. basilicum*, which can reach 30 feet in height and in which the cinnamon felt of the underside of the leaves tends to fade to grey as the season advances. The diagnostic distinction lies in the winged petioles of *basilicum*, those of *arizelum* being rounded. In both species the leaves themselves are about 10 inches long and half as wide. Both these species are Forrest introductions.

Rhododendron eximium was originally regarded as a variety of *falconeri*, from which it is distinguished by the rusty tomentum adhering to the upper surface of the leaves and by its pink flowers. It makes a tree up to 30 feet with the young shoots, the buds and for the first year, both surfaces of the leaves covered with a rust-coloured tomentum. In the second year the upper side of the leaves becomes dark green. The flowers, which appear in early May, are in various shades of pink.

Rhododendron falconeri itself is a Hooker introduction of 1850. It can make a sizeable tree, up to 50 feet, and then its flaking reddish bark makes an additional attraction. The young growths are covered with a greyish down, but the underside of the leaves is covered thickly with rust-coloured felt. The upper surface is dark green and the veins are somewhat sunken to give a wrinkled effect. In wet districts they can reach a length of 12 inches and a width of 6 inches, in dry parts they are considerably smaller. The flowers, that appear in early May, are in various shades of pale yellow, from ivory to lemon, and have a purple blotch inside the tube.

Rhododendron fictolacteum makes a tree up to 40 feet in height. The young shoots are covered with a cinnamon-coloured tomentum and the leaves have a dark brown felt on the underside. The leaves are variable in size, but the most frequent dimensions seem to be up to 10 inches long and 4½ inches wide; on the other hand larger measurements are known and smaller ones are frequent. The flowers appear in a large truss of campanulate flowers, which are white or creamy-white with a crimson blotch, and sometimes show a pink suffusion. They open in late April or early May according to the district. The plant appears to have been first introduced by Delavay and the plants from his seeds had rather small leaves and flowers. The subsequent sendings by Forrest and Rock have introduced vastly superior forms.

A plant that is by no means easy to distinguish from *R. fictolacteum* is *R. rex*, introduced from Szechwan by Kingdon-Ward in 1921 and originally diagnosed as *R. fictolacteum*. It is, to all appearances, a superior form of *fictolacteum*, and the only apparent distinction lies in the fact that the young shoots are covered with a grey-white tomentum, rather than a cinnamon-coloured one, and similarly the indumentum on the underside of the leaves is grey or fawn, not dark brown. Whether this is sufficient distinction to permit the creation of two species seems rather dubious. Its other distinction lies in the old botanical cliché 'larger in all its parts', a distinction which might be apparent if you had two plants growing side by side which were both typical of their respective species. Since nearly all rhododendron species are extremely variable, this distinction really means very little.

In the garden *R. rex* seems to grow more rapidly and come into flower sooner than the other plants in the series. Most of the ones of which we have some record appear to take nearly twenty years between the seed germinating and flowers appearing, considerably longer than most of the

Grande series, but *R. rex* was awarded an F.C.C. in 1935 (as *R. fictolacteum*, Ward's form) 14 years after sowing the seed. Of course the gardener who can purchase large plants does not have to wait so long for his flowers, but the Falconeri series do seem to need to make a sizeable plant before they start to flower.

Of all the plants in the series *R. fictolacteum* and *R. rex* appear to be easily the hardiest and are, indeed, as hardy as any rhododendron, getting the rating H4 in the *Rhododendron Handbook*.

For the rest of the rhododendrons which seem to me to warrant inclusion here, and this has been the hardest portion of the book to select, I propose to follow alphabetical order to a certain extent. On some occasions it may be convenient to discuss other species in the same series together with whatever species comes first and at other times it may well be that the desirable feature of a species is also to be found in some of its hybrids, so that they will be discussed along with the species.

Rhododendron araiophyllum, of the Irroratum series, makes a slender shrub up to 16 feet high with narrow, lanceolate leaves which are up to 5 inches long and an attractive red colour when young. They retain this colouration for four weeks. The cup-shaped flowers appear in April in rather few-flowered clusters; each flower is about 1½ inches long and is white, sometimes flushed pink, with a crimson blotch and crimson spots in the interior. The plant is probably reliable enough in southern England from Sussex westwards and along the West coast, but would require a sheltered situation elsewhere.

Rhododendron argyrophyllum is the type species of its subseries of the Arboreum series and one of the most attractive species in this very attractive genus. Capable of making a shrub up to 20 feet high, it starts flowering when quite small. The young growths are covered with a silvery-white down, which persists on the underside of the leaves. These leaves eventually reach a length of 6 inches and are 1½ inches across. The funnel-shaped flowers emerge in May and are white or pink in colour. The plant is extremely variable and several varieties have been named; of these the variety *nankingense*, with larger leaves, which are shining on the surface, and deep pink flowers, is the most attractive if it can be obtained.

Rhododendron auriculatum is one of the very last of rhododendrons to flower, coming into blossom in late July and early August. It makes a large shrub or a small tree, up to 20 feet in height, and has large leaves up to 12 inches long and 5 inches across. It frequently appears to happen with this genus that young plants carry their largest leaves before they start to bear flowers and that once flowers are produced the leaves are somewhat smaller. The flowers of *R. auriculatum* are not produced until the plant is fairly sizeable, and are large, up to 4 inches long, and either white or, somewhat rarely, pale pink. They are extremely fragrant. The lower parts of the young growths are furnished with bright crimson scales, which are extremely colourful. This feature is transmitted to some of its hybrids, notably 'Isabella' (*auriculatum* × *griffithianum*). *R. auriculatum* was one of Wilson's first introductions. He found it growing in semi-wooded country, but in this country it appears to do better with very little shade and seems quite happy in full sunshine.

Rhododendron bureavii is a member of the Taliense series, which for long had a reputation for being very slow growing and for their reluctance to flower. There seems to be some justification for this in the Roxieanum subseries, which are characterized by very narrow leaves, but most people find that the others are no shyer than other rhododendrons to flower and do not take an excessive time to do so. The species we are discussing belongs to the Adenogynum subseries and makes a shrub up to 8 feet high. The young shoots and first-year leaves are covered with a reddish-brown indumentum, which soon disappears from the upper surface but adheres to the underside. The leaves are thick and leathery, ovate in shape, up to 5 inches long and 2 inches across. The young growths with their bright indumentum are almost more attractive than the white or pink flowers, which appear towards the end of April and the beginning of May. The plant is perfectly hardy. Herbarium specimens from Delavay date from 1886, but the plant was not introduced to cultivation until 1908, when Forrest sent it from Yunnan.

The variety *aeruginosum* (sometimes regarded as meriting specific rank) of the very variable *R. campanulatum* is grown for its surpassing foliage, which is silver-green when young and a glaucous blue when mature. It is thus a focus of interest for the whole year and this wonderful display compensates for the rather wishy-washy mauve of the flowers. The leaves are elliptic in shape, up to 6 inches long and half as wide.

Rhododendron cinnabarinum, with which for the purposes of this discussion may be ranked *R. concatenans* and *R. xanthocodon*, is characterized by its long, pendant, tubular flowers and its glaucous foliage. This is an attractive shade of metallic blue when young and it retains a tinge of blue even when mature. *Cinnabarinum* and *xanthocodon* will make shrubs up to 15 feet in height, when fully grown, but *concatenans* has not been recorded higher than 8 feet. In all the species the leaves are obovate-elliptic, up to 3 inches long and 1¾ inches across. In *R. concatenans* the underside is sometimes purplish. The colour of the flowers is very variable. *R. xanthocodon* is always some shade of yellow; *R. concatenans* is generally a rather apricot shade of yellow-orange, but is sometimes purplish on the exterior; *R. cinnabarinum* ranges from cinnabar-red to purplish-mauve and there are many forms (*blandfordiaeflorum*, *aestivale*) with a red exterior and a yellow interior. Occasionally bad forms occur and these should be destroyed, but generally the flowers are among the most attractive of all rhododendrons, quite apart from being markedly dissimilar to the majority in the shape and port of the flowers. *R. cinnabarinum* has been used a great deal in hybridizing and many of the hybrids have the same attractive foliage as the parent. Among these may be mentioned 'Lady Roseberry', 'Lady Chamberlain', 'Lady Berry', 'Yunncinn' and 'Oreocinn', to name but a few. Most of the species flower in May, but *R. cinnabarinum aestivale* does not flower until July. Although the plants are normally completely hardy, the flower buds may be damaged by late spring frosts before they have opened. The young growths start to emerge towards the end of May and are occasionally damaged by very late frosts, but this is not usual. It is necessary to emphasize the plants' hardiness, as they look so extremely exotic that one would expect that they required greenhouse cultivation.

Rhododendron clementinae is named in honour of Mrs. George Forrest, whose husband discovered and introduced the plant in 1913. It is not easy to obtain. It makes a small shrub, occasionally reaching 10 feet in height, but usually somewhat less, with rather stout branches. The brilliant blue young growths are dusted with a beige-coloured felt, which persists on the underside of the leaves. These are oval in shape, up to 6 inches long and half as wide. The funnel-shaped flowers are produced in trusses of up to 15 flowers, which open in early May. The colour range extends from white, through cream to quite a deep pink and the interior of the flowers is generally dotted with crimson. This is a member of the Taliense series and subseries, but flowers when still quite small. The fruits are said to be purple-black, but it is bad policy to let rhododendrons set seed (unless of course seed is required) and growers tend to remove the trusses as soon as the flowers are faded. This is one of the most striking species for beauty of foliage.

If this was not the best treatment for rhododendrons, one would be interested to learn whether *R. cyanocarpum* really does have blue fruits. The plant is allied to *R. thomsonii* and has the same rounded leaves—these are blue-green when young. They are rather larger than those of *R. thomsonii*; they can reach a length of 5 inches and a width of 3 inches. The flowers appear in late March and early April in loose trusses and are usually creamy-white, sometimes tinged with pink. They are fragrant. Owing to its early flowering it thrives best in the south-west, although it does well at Leonardslee in Sussex. The leaves emerge in May, so that the plant is quite suitable for growing in other regions, although there is then the risk of damage to the flowers with spring frosts. Bean states that the seed-vessels are bluish-purple. The plant can make a tree up to 20 feet high, but is more usually a bush of half that height or even less. The plant is not easy to obtain and is inferior to *R. thomsonii*.

Rhododendron exasperatum belongs to the Glischrum subseries of the Barbatum series. The petioles of all this subseries are covered with bristles of varying colours, all of which tend to make the foliage rather striking at all times. In most of the species the leaves, too, are bristly and make a striking contrast with the smooth leaves of most other species. *R. exasperatum* can eventually make a small tree up to 15 feet high. The young shoots and leaves are a warm bronzy colour. The fully developed leaf is ovate in shape, up to 7 inches long and 4 inches across, with a bristly midrib. The top side is dark green, the underside somewhat paler. Most of the Glischrum subseries resemble *R. barbatum* itself with their plum-coloured smooth bark, which is very attractive in the autumn and winter. It tends to peel off in the early summer. The flowers of the Glischrum subseries are generally in a rather loose truss and are tubular-campanulate. Those of *R. exasperatum* appear in late April and are a brick-red in colour but rather small.

Among the other plants in this series, *R. erosum* makes a striking-looking shrub, with its leaves arranged in fours at the ends of the branches, and the young growths covered with glandular bristles. It can make a tree up to 20 feet. It has crimson flowers in early April and attractive peeling bark. *R. habrotrichum*, which can reach 10 feet, has young growth that is purple and the petioles are always covered with purple bristles, which give it an interesting appearance at all seasons. It has elliptic leaves up to 7 inches long and 3 inches across. It flowers in April with a truss of up to 20 funnel-shaped flowers which vary in colour from white to rosy-pink and is, in my opinion, the most charming member of the subseries with which I am acquainted. All the species seem to be well worth growing both for their flowers and their bristly foliage. Some forms of *R. exasperatum* and *R. glischroides* are slightly tender, where others, presumably from higher elevations, appear to be quite hardy.

Rhododendron fulgens, which is related to *R. campanulatum*, makes a shrub up to 12 feet high, with peeling bark, which is usually obscured by the shoot. The young growths, which appear in late April, about a month after the flowers, are accompanied by extremely brilliant crimson bracts which, like those of *R. auriculatum* and *R. hookeri*, are a feature in themselves. The young growths are also colourful on account of the brown indumentum which persists on the undersides of the leaves. The flowers will open in March in most years, but very mild winters may see flowers in February, while during hard winters flowering may be delayed until April. The flowers are a bright red, nearly scarlet and are extremely welcome so early in the year. There is always a risk of frost damage with all these early flowering rhododendrons and if space is limited one should perhaps play safe and go for the later flowering species and hybrids. However, in favourable districts and where space permits in less favourable ones, there is so much more pleasure to be got out of red rhododendrons in March than there is in May that the risk is worth taking. The plant is shy to flower until well established.

Rhododendron fulvum is so variable a plant that it is worth visiting the nursery to select your plant or plants personally. The best forms have brownish-yellow young growths and leaves with a bright cinnamon indumentum on the underside. Less attractive forms have greyish young growths and a pale yellow indumentum. In the same way the flowers range from a rather dirty white to good pinks and deep rose colours. The plant can eventually make a small tree up to 20 feet high, but most specimens in cultivation are only about half this height. The broad oblong leaves can reach a length of 10 inches and a width of 3 inches and are a dark shining green on the upper surface. The flowers, which even in the best forms are not among the most striking in the genus, open in late March or early April. The new growths elongate a month later.

The only objection that can be levelled at *R. haematodes* is that it takes rather a long time to establish itself and to reach flowering size. Since there is no difficulty in moving large plants of most rhododendrons, including this one, this is an objection that can easily be overcome, if finances permit. This generally makes a dwarf-spreading shrub in the garden, but Forrest reported it as sometimes from 6–10 feet in height. The young growth is clothed with dense, rust-coloured wool, and the undersides of the leaves retain this. The flowers are a brilliant crimson, bordering on scarlet, and are tubular in shape. They are arranged in trusses of from 6–12 flowers; each flower is about 2 inches long. The flowers open in late May and early June and the young growths follow shortly afterwards. This is a very hardy and satisfactory plant.

Closely allied to *R. haematodes* is *R. beanianum*, which tends to make a rather more upright shrub, but does not exceed 8 feet in height. The elliptic leaves are 4 inches long and 1½ inches across, covered on both sides with a good reddish-brown indumentum when young and retaining it on the upper side until quite late in the season; similarly the young wood is covered with this indumentum. The plant is variable in flower and the best forms with scarlet or crimson flowers should be sought out. The flowers generally open in early May; they are about 1½ inches long in trusses of 6–10 flowers.

Superficially similar in appearance, but belonging to a different series, is *R. tsariense*. This is a rather dwarf plant with the leaves in whorls at the end of the branches. The leaves are elliptic, 2½ inches long and 1¼ inches across.

When young the shoots and leaves are densely covered with a yellowish tomentum, which gradually wears off, but remains, even on the upper side, till late in the season. The few-flowered trusses of campanulate flowers open in early May and are pale pink or white, often with red spots. *R. lanatum* is larger, but not dissimilar. It has a reputation for not being an easy plant to grow, but has attractive pale yellow, purple-spotted flowers in quite large trusses. The leaves can reach a length of 5 inches and the tomentum is white on the young growths, but tawny on the underside of the leaves.

Rhododendron hookeri makes a shrub up to 14 feet high and has very beautiful reddish-brown bark, which is smooth and polished. It produces deep blood-red flowers in March and the new growths, which do not emerge until May, are richly ornamented with scarlet bracts. It is distinct from other rhododendrons by having tufts of down on the underside of the main veins of the leaf. It is somewhat tender, although T. J. Booth who first collected it in Bhutan in 1852 found it in a region where frost and snow were severe and prolonged. For most gardeners, therefore, its hybrid with *R. barbatum*, 'Alix', is a better plant. It has equally attractive bark and is perfectly hardy so far as winter frosts are concerned. It makes a larger plant than *hookeri* itself and, in a mild season, will flower as early as February, when it is the most brilliant inhabitant of the garden. It seems rather odd that none of the collectors who have visited Assam and Bhutan in recent years seem to have sent back any further material of *R. hookeri*, as there may well be hardier strains in the wild. Kingdon-Ward's 8238 was described as a purple-flowered form of *hookeri*, but otherwise no one who has visited Bhutan and Assam seems to have seen it.

Rhododendron lutescens is a charming shrub, which may reach up to 12 feet. It has lanceolate leaves up to 3 inches long, which are a delicious coppery-red when young and which retain this colour for six weeks. The rather few-flowered trusses of yellow flowers, which are widely funnel-shaped, appear very early in the year, sometimes in late February. The young growth does not start until May, so that it generally escapes frost damage. Some forms are slightly tender and a more satisfactory plant is its hybrid with *R. moupinense*, known as 'Bo-Peep'. This has the same yellow flowers and attractive foliage, but the flowers are in larger trusses and the plant is very hardy. The leaves are rounder in shape than in the species. The plant flowers in March in most years, but later, in April, if the winter is severe. It does not seem to exceed 8 feet in height and is generally less. The long gap between the flowers and the young growths means that its two displays are well separated.

Rhododendron makinoi is a Japanese plant belonging to the Caucasicum subseries of the Ponticum series, and makes a rounded shrub up to 8 feet in height. It has very distinctive leaves, which are dark green above, leathery in texture, and with an orange indumentum below. These leaves, which are somewhat arched, can be 7 inches long, but are only 1 inch across and, since the edges are recurved, they appear to be practically linear. The rose-pink flowers appear in June in few-flowered trusses and fade to white before they fall. The new growth, which is covered with a white indumentum and is striking in appearance, does not start to emerge until August. As by this time most of the leaves in the garden are starting to look somewhat tired, this new growth, which would be effective at any time, is strikingly so at so unexpected a season.

There are other members of the subseries which are attractive in leaf, although rather less so than *R. makinoi*. *R. smirnowii*, a native of the Caucasus, can make a tree up to 15 feet in the wild but, in cultivation, is usually only about 6 feet high, although generally wider. The oblong leaves are up to 6 inches long, but only 2 inches across and when young are covered with a dense white felt, which remains permanently on the underside of the leaves, but tends to darken in colour. The flowers appear in loose trusses of from 10–12 flowers at the end of May and are some shade of rose-purple.

From the same district comes *R. ungernii*. This makes a shrub up to 20 feet in the wild with leaves that can be 8 inches long and 3 inches across. When young they and the shoots are densely covered with white tomentum, but as the leaves mature the surface becomes dark green and glabrous, while the underside is covered with grey or fawn wool. The flowers are borne in large trusses of from 20–30 flowers, which are each about 1½ inches long and are pale pink in colour. They do not open until July. Unfortunately by this time the young growths have started to elongate and they sometimes hide the flowers. Both these Caucasian species are extremely hardy and it is surprising that they have not been used more in hybridization to obtain very hardy hybrids. The excessive use of *ponticum* and *catawbiense* has given rise to hybrids that may be attractive enough in flower, but which have no interest in their foliage (the plant of unknown parentage, 'Moser's Maroon', which has bright red young growth, is the only exception I can think of). If *ungernii* or *smirnowii* were employed one might have interesting foliage as well. It is interesting to know that one does not have to travel to China to find new species of rhododendron. Both *R. smirnowii* and *R. ungernii* were only discovered in 1885, by Baron Ungern-Sternberg. Plants were distributed by the St. Petersburg Botanic Garden the following year.

Rhododendron yakusimanum was introduced from the island of Yakusima in Japan even more recently; probably in 1939, although there seems no certainty about this. In the wild it is apparently a very variable species, but the form that is most usually seen and which received an F.C.C. from the Royal Horticultural Society, is a small, dome-shaped shrub that does not exceed 4 feet in height. The young growths are covered with a brown tomentum and this is maintained on the underside of the mature leaves, when the upper surface has become dark green and glossy. The leaves have recurved edges and are some $3\frac{1}{2}$ inches long and $1\frac{1}{2}$ inches broad. The flowers are large for the size of the plant, deep pink in bud, pale pink on first opening fading to white. The plant makes a very pretty little dome in the winter, although it may be regarded as inferior at this time to another Japanese plant of the same series, *R. degronianum*, which has longer leaves, but less attractive young growth. Both these species flower in May.

Rhododendron niveum, of the Arboreum series, can make a small tree up to 15 feet high and occasionally even higher. It is more generally seen as a shrub up to about 8 feet. Its most striking feature is the brilliant white young growth, which is due to all parts being densely clothed with thick white wool. This eventually disappears from the upper surface of the leaves and fades to a greyish-brown on the undersides. The upper surface is then dark green. The leaves may reach a length of 6 or 7 inches and a width of $2\frac{1}{2}$ inches. The mauve-purple flowers appear in late April or early May and are usually a rather unpleasing shade, but some forms are more agreeable. The colour is unusual among rhododendrons, which is, perhaps, just as well. I should, however, mention that many people appear to find the colour quite agreeable and it is as well to see what your own reaction is, before committing yourself either for or against. The plant is one of Hooker's 1849 Sikkim introductions.

Rhododendron lepidostylum is a member of the Trichocladum series, of which most have attractive leaves and comparatively inconspicuous flowers. From the foliage point of view, this is the best of the series. The ovate leaves are small, some $1\frac{1}{2}$ inches long and $\frac{3}{4}$ inch across, and are for most of the year a very attractive blue-green; much like the colour of *R. campanulatum aeruginosum*. It makes only a small plant, up to 3 feet high, and though normally evergreen it is deciduous in cold districts. The pale yellow flowers appear singly or in pairs in late May and early June and are sometimes concealed by the foliage, a vice that others of the series exhibit.

Rhododendron pseudochrysanthum should, so far as this book is concerned, be obtained from the A.M. clone, which has young growths of an extraordinarily attractive metallic blue-green. The plant makes a compact shrub up to 9 feet high with ovate leaves 3 inches long and half as wide which are produced in great abundance. In April the flowers, which are deep pink in bud and pale pink with crimson spots when expanded, appear. This belongs to the Maculiferum subseries of the Barbatum series, most of which have very attractive flowers, and two more of which have attractive foliage as well. *R. pseudochrysanthum* is a Formosan endemic. The other two attractive species in this subseries are both Wilson introductions. They are *R. pachytrichum* and *R. strigillosum*.

Rhododendron pachytrichum makes a large shrub or small tree up to 18 feet high. The young growths are covered with brown shaggy hairs. The leaves are arranged in whorls of five. Each leaf is up to 5 inches long and 2 inches across. The colour of the flowers varies from white through pale pink to a deep pink and even a rather unpleasing magenta; all forms have a conspicuous purple blotch. The white and pink forms are very charming. The plant normally flowers in April, but may be in flower in March in mild springs. The same season sees the flowering of *R. strigillosum*. This makes a shrub or tree up to 20 feet and has all parts of the young growths covered with bristles, which persist until the following spring and which give the plant a very unusual appearance. The long, narrow leaves are also attractive; they can reach a length of 7 inches and, although they may be 2 inches across, the edges are recurved so that they appear narrowly lanceolate. The flowers which are quite large and in sizeable trusses are a brilliant glowing crimson.

Rhododendron thomsonii is, like most rhododendrons, a very variable plant, but it could easily be argued that the best forms show it to be the best shrub that has ever been introduced to gardens. There is not one feature that is unattractive, from the bark to the young growth and the mature growth, and an incomparable display of flowers. It will not thrive in dry districts and does not start to flower until it is fairly sizeable, about 4½ feet high, but otherwise it is fairly trouble-free. It can make a shrub up to 20 feet high, but is worth pruning to make it a small tree, so that the smooth, peeling, purplish-red bark can be appreciated. In the best forms the young growths are glaucous blue-green, a colour that persists for some time, and permanently on the underside of the leaves. These are orbicular in shape, up to 3 inches long and 2 inches across. The flowers are blood-red in the best forms, produced in loose trusses in April and backed with red calices which are large and look attractive after the flowers have fallen. Each flower can be 2½ inches long and is wide in proportion. Once the plant does start to flower it is liable to do it with such enthusiasm that it must be dead-headed as soon as the flowering is over, otherwise it could flower itself to death.

The plant was one of Hooker's 1849 introductions from Sikkim and he named it in honour of his friend, Thomas Thomson, then on the medical staff of the East India Company. The plant has been used as a parent in a large number of hybrids, but no hybrid has managed to produce all the charms of the original species; the best is *R.* 'Shilsoni' (*R. thomsonii* × *R.*

barbatum), which lacks the blue bloom of the emerging foliage of the best types, but is otherwise a satisfactory alternative.

On the other hand, R. *williamsianum* has managed to transmit its attractive young leaf colour to many of its hybrid offspring. The plant makes a spreading, dome-shaped shrub, sometimes reaching as high as 5, but generally little more than 3 feet. The leaves are rounded, coppery-bronze when young and with a red petiole. Mature leaves measure up to 2 inches long and nearly as much across. The nodding pale pink flowers open in April in trusses of from 2–3 flowers, which are extremely large in proportion to the size of the plant, being 2 inches long and somewhat wider at the mouth. The plant was introduced by Wilson in 1908, who found it growing in isolated thickets on cliffs at Wa-Shan in Szechwan. It was not widely distributed. In this country it seems to do best in very light shade or in full sun. Some people complain that it is a very shy flowerer, while others have no difficulty at all. Whether the shyness in flowering is a clonal affair, or whether it is due to chemical deficiency in some soils, is not clear. It is certainly shy-flowering when grown in dense shade, but this is almost certainly due to the shade and to no other cause.

Among its hybrids with equally attractive foliage, but which tend to make larger and more upright shrubs, may be mentioned 'Bow Bells' (*williamsianum* × 'Corona', which is an early hybrid of unknown parentage), 'Humming Bird' (*williamsianum* × *haematodes*), 'Arthur J. Ivens', to which Part 2 of the *Rhododendron Handbook* seems unnecessarily severe (*williamsianum* × *houlstonii*), 'Cowslip' (*williamsianum* × *wardii*), and 'Brocade', which is *williamsianum* crossed with one of the Indian azaleas that are so popular at Christmas. 'Humming Bird' was used as a parent with R. *griersonianum* and the resultant hybrid 'Winsome' still retains the coppery young growth, although the leaves are far removed in shape from the rounded leaves of *williamsianum*, being oblong and pointed. All these hybrids, like their parent, have delightful flowers and attractive young growth. 'Arthur J. Ivens' is lilac-pink and 'Cowslip' is ivory, otherwise they are all various shades of pink and red.

The hybrid 'Yellow Hammer' (*flavidum* × *sulfureum*) is a small shrub with numerous, rather small yellow flowers in early April, which usually has a second flowering in September. The plant is perfectly hardy and, although the second display is not so showy as the main display in the spring, it is sufficiently extensive to make the plant remarkable in the autumn.

❧ Rhus – Viburnum

RHUS

It is surprising how often sex seems to be coming into this list. Some of the sumachs are unisexual, and it is the female plants that are the more attractive. All the plants to be discussed are deciduous shrubs with large pinnate leaves that generally colour very brilliantly in the autumn.

Rhus glabra is a medium-sized shrub, rarely exceeding 6 feet in height, but occasionally reaching 10 feet and liable to sucker to an embarrassing extent. The pinnate leaves are up to 18 inches long composed of a large number of lanceolate leaflets that may individually measure 4 inches long and ¾ inch across; they colour a rich red in the autumn. The flowers are unisexual, but both sexes are borne on the same plant and the fruits form a rich red pyramidal panicle up to 10 inches long, which is more striking than some writers suggest. The plant flowers in July and the fruits are coloured by September, so that the plant is then of interest until the leaves fall in October. It is also a handsome foliage plant in the earlier parts of the year. It is a native of the eastern United States and as tough as old boots.

Rhus potaninii makes a small, round-headed tree and should be grown more frequently than it is. The pinnate leaves can reach a length of 16 inches, and are composed of a number of rather large oblong leaflets, each one being up to 5 inches long and 2 inches across. They turn a rich red in the autumn. The flowers appear in June in terminal panicles up to 7 inches long; these panicles are covered with brown down, to such an extent that the minute greenish-white flowers are barely visible. The flowers are hermaphrodite and are followed by deep red fruits, which are also downy to the touch. As the fruits ripen the panicles tend to droop. The individual fruits are the size of peppercorns. The plant is native to Szechwan and Henry sent back seed in 1888.

Rhus typhina is the species seen most frequently as, not only will it grow anywhere, but is also tolerant of any amount of pollution in the atmosphere. The plants are dioecious and the female is the one to obtain. This can make a tree up to 25 feet high, but is more usually seen as a rather gaunt shrub, which has an unfortunate tendency to sucker and will form thickets if allowed. Although it makes a larger tree, it is similar in appearance to *R. glabra*, but can easily be distinguished by the reddish hairs which cover the young bark, whereas *R. glabra*, as its name suggests, is hairless. The pinnate leaves may reach a length of 2 feet and are composed of numerous oblong-lanceolate leaflets up to 4½ inches long and 1 inch across. They turn red, orange and purple in the autumn. The female inflorescence is a deep crimson, pyramidal panicle, up to 10 inches long, and is conspicuous from late July onwards. The male plant has the same good autumn colour, but a pyramid of rather inconspicuous greenish flowers and is only grown if ripe seed is required. Since the plant is so easily propagated by suckers, there is no need to burden your ground with an inferior form. The plant is native to the eastern United States and has been cultivated since the early seventeenth century.

ROBINIA

In a wide sense it could be argued that all these North American trees and shrubs merit inclusion in our list, as they all have attractive flowers and handsome pinnate foliage. The best-known species is the false acacia, *Robinia pseudacacia*, of which many cultivars exist. That known as 'Frisia' with golden foliage makes an extremely handsome tree. If, however, we are going to be more selective, our choice will be restricted to *R. kelseyi*. This makes a largish shrub or small tree, up to 10 feet high, and has the unfortunate extreme brittleness, which is the genus's only disadvantage. The pinnate leaves are up to 6 inches long, composed of 9 or 11 leaflets, which are ovate in shape, up to 2 inches long and ¾ inch across. In June the rose-pink pea-shaped flowers, each about 1 inch long, are produced in racemes that may contain 8 flowers, but generally somewhat less. These flowers are followed by pods which are covered with reddish bristles so thickly that they appear to be bright red and form an attractive later decoration for the tree.

It is worth while pausing a moment over *R. viscosa*, a pleasant small tree, which has been given the extremely unconvincing vernacular name of Clammy Locust. 'You should see our Clammy Locust; it's a mass' sounds like a non-remark to me.

ROSA

Although the barrier is becoming increasingly tenuous we can still divide the roses into species and the remontant hybrids. These latter, whether they be Hybrid Teas or Floribundas, are perhaps the most popular of garden plants and merit inclusion here for their long flowering season. However, it seems to be generally agreed by all gardeners that they are plants that will not integrate with other genera and they are usually put into ghettoes called rose gardens and treated as bedding plants. Under these circumstances they need not be further discussed here.

The various species are a different matter and can be grown with other shrubs with no feeling of incongruity. Many have extremely attractive foliage, but, except in the case of *Rosa rubrifolia*, I am not considering this to be a distinctive feature in the following notes. Indeed, the list that follows has been rather rigorously pruned, in keeping with its subject. With the exception of *R. pimpinellifolia*, *R. spinosissima* and all the yellow-flowered species, most roses have red heps of some brilliance and for plants to be recommended for their fruits you will only find included here those that are outstanding either for size or for quantity. Some species, all from the United States so far as I know, also tend to have good autumn colour, which can sometimes be exceptionally brilliant. There is one species, or rather a variety of a species, *R. sericea pteracantha*, which is grown as much for its very large, transparent red thorns as for any other feature.

It is not particularly easy to organize these plants in a more satisfactory manner than that provided by alphabetic order, but it seems simplest to deal first with the few climbing species and then to deal with the shrubs.

There are a number of climbing roses belonging to the Synstylae section, all characterized by great vigour, large heads of fragrant white flowers, and in four species with brilliant heps. Of these the most desirable, in my opinion, is *R. helenae*, named in honour of Mrs. Wilson. This is one of the later flowerers and has the most brilliant scarlet heps which persist until Christmas. *R. multiflora* is also very brilliant in the autumn, but is not often seen in gardens, although it is a parent of many of the ramblers. *R. filipes* and *R. rubus* are both among the later flowerers of the section and have heps that are somewhat less brilliant than the other two species. All of them are far too vigorous for training on to walls and should be trained into trees. *R. multiflora* can be grown as a large arching shrub and is used in the United States as a crash barrier on motorways, as it forms so compact a thicket that crashing cars cannot penetrate it. It has been in cultivation since 1862, whereas the other three species are Wilson introductions.

To turn to the shrub roses we appear to start with *R. foliolosa*. This is native to the south-western United States. It is not a tall grower, rarely getting higher than 3 feet, and spreads by underground suckers. The plant is generally unarmed, but some forms have a few prickles. The leaves are usually composed of 7 leaflets. The flowers are characterized by their very long sepals, their extreme fragrance and by a rather unfortunate mauvy-pink colour. The red heps are not very conspicuous, but the leaves generally colour red and yellow in the autumn. The plant is also valuable for its very late flowering; it does not start until mid-July and may continue into September. Unlike many roses it does not make one brilliant display, but staggers its flowers over six weeks or so.

Rosa forrestiana is a splendid rose, making a large shrub up to 7 feet high and as much across. The large flowers, up to 2 inches across, are borne in clusters in June; they are carmine with a suggestion of purple and very fragrant. They are followed by large flask-shaped heps which are a bright red and covered with bristles.

Rosa macrophylla is sometimes excessively vigorous and needs ample space to give of its best. It is generally about 8 feet high, but there was a famous plant in the Cambridge Botanic Garden which reached a height of 18 feet and a spread of 25 feet. Some forms are spineless and there is a variant called, sometimes, *korolkowii* and sometimes *rubricaulis* (Forrest's 15309), in which the young growths are purplish-red. The leaves are, as the name implies, large, reaching a length of 8 inches. The leaflets are from 7–11 in number and are each some 2½ inches long in the largest forms. The deep red flowers may be 3 inches across and are produced in clusters of varying numbers. They are followed by pear-shaped heps about 1½ inches long. The Forrest form with purple stems is the most desirable, but has proved somewhat tender.

Rosa moyesii is, I suppose, the most frequently grown of the rose species. In favourable conditions it can reach 12 feet, but is usually between 6 and 10 feet in height. The leaves can reach a length of 6 inches and these are made up of numerous small leaflets, sometimes as many as 13 in number. The flowers are a deep crimson and unique in their colour among roses. It is not the most usual colour of the plant in the wild, where the colour ranges from deep pink to deep red. These flowers are followed by very large, scarlet, flask-shaped heps which may be 2 inches or more long. They colour in August and persist until October. *R. moyesii* has been used in several hybrids, of which 'Geranium', 'Highdownensis', *hillieri* and *wintoniensis* are all excellent plants.

Rosa roxburghii (syn. *R. microphylla*) is a rather distinct plant, known for a long time in its double form; the wild plant was not introduced before 1908. It makes a rather spreading shrub, up to 8 feet high, but sometimes somewhat wider. It has, unusually for the genus, flaking, buff-coloured bark which gives it some interest in the winter. The plant is heavily armed and has leaves up to 4 inches long which are composed of as many as 15 very small leaflets; a feature which gave it its synonym of *R. microphylla*. The individual leaflets may be ¾ inch long. The flowers vary from very

145

pale pink to deep rose in colour and, in the single form, are rather hidden under the foliage. In the double form the outer petals are pale pink, while the centre is much deeper in colour. The flower stalks, calyx tube and calyx are covered with prickles and so later is the hep, which resembles somewhat the fruit of the sweet chestnut, and gives it its common name of the Burr rose. It is rather large, 1½ inches across, and yellowish in colour and is also fragrant, although this feature must usually be taken on trust as the hep is rather painful to handle. The fragrance of the flowers, on the other hand, is easily appreciated, and Bean notes that they attract bees more readily than any other species.

Rosa rubrifolia is native to Central Europe. It makes quite a tall shrub, up to 7 or 8 feet in height and is conspicuous in winter by reason of the purplish young shoots. It is grown mainly for the sake of its very ornamental foliage, which is coppery-mauve when grown in full sunshine and grey-mauve when grown in partially shaded situations. The flowers are borne in quite large clusters, but are small and not particularly conspicuous, although they are quite a deep pink in colour. On the other hand the heps are a good bright red with a tinge of brown and they are produced very freely, so that the plant gives a good account of itself in the late summer and early autumn. The plant is somewhat straggly and inelegant in shape and looks best in the least formal parts of the parterre.

Rosa sericea may be taken to include all the plants with only four petals to the flower, although some forms have been separated on somewhat minor grounds, into *R. omeiensis*. *R. sericea* proper is found in Northern India throughout the Himalayas to north Burma, while *R. omeiensis* is exclusively Chinese. The main difference between the two putative species lies in the number of leaflets which are numerous in *R. omeiensis* (from 11–19) and comparatively few in *R. sericea* (from 7–11). In what Wilson and Rehder regarded as the typical form of *R. omeiensis* the scarlet hep is borne on a short, bright yellow stalk. All the forms tend to make rather spreading shrubs, up to 9 feet high and as much across, and the *omeiensis* forms have a delightful ferny appearance with their numerous small leaflets. Most roses have 5 petals, but *R. sericea* has, normally, only 4 which are arranged like a Maltese cross and are white in colour. They are among the earliest of roses to open and are often seen by early May. The heps are pear-shaped and about 1 inch long and decorate the plants in late summer. They are generally scarlet, but in the variety *chrysocarpa* they are a rich butter-yellow and very striking. The variety *R. o. pteracantha* is grown mainly for the sake of the enormous deep red prickles, which are sometimes an inch across at the base and which are very attractive when the sun shines through them. This translucent red colour is only present for the first season, so that the plant should be pruned in winter to encourage fresh new growths. The flowers are said to be rather smaller than those of the other garden forms, but are still sizeable. The cultivar known as 'Heather Muir' has unusually large flowers, up to 2½ inches across, which are produced freely and which are followed by orange-red heps on red stalks; this is probably the best red-hepped form to acquire. There are some forms with no prickles at all, but most are armed to some extent, although not with the fearsome armature of *pteracantha*.

Rosa soulieana requires a great deal of room and so is not a suitable plant for the small garden. It makes a spreading shrub throwing up great arching stems, which will eventually make a plant 10 feet high and as much across. The young shoots are grey and are densely covered with yellow prickles, which look charming but are painful to negotiate. The leaves are up to 4 inches long, usually composed of 7 leaflets, and are a distinctive grey-green in colour. The plant flowers in July and has large corymbs of white flowers which emerge from yellow buds; each individual flower is 1 inch across, but the general effect is of an enormous mass. They are followed by small heps of a distinctive orange colour. Graham Thomas has noted that young, very vigorous plants are sometimes damaged by early autumn frosts, but says that the plants become hardier as they age.

Rosa setipoda is another rather large plant, capable of reaching a height and width of 9 feet. It has large leaves, sometimes 7 inches long, composed of 7 or 9 leaflets. This is one of those unusual plants where the flower buds are almost as attractive as the flowers, as the flower stems, the calices and the sepals are purple in colour. The flowers themselves are up to 2½ inches across and are deep pink with a paler centre. The heps are large, up to 1½ inches long and are bottle-shaped, scarlet in colour but studded with black hairs. The leaves have something of a sweet-briar fragrance and the plant is very desirable.

Rosa villosa (syn. *R. pomifera*) is a not very common British native, but is found over a large part of Europe and extends to Asia Minor. It is related to our dog roses and makes a spreading shrub, up to 7 feet high, but generally somewhat wider and not so tall. The leaves are up to 7 inches long, composed of from 5–7 rather large leaflets, and have a greyish tinge. The flowers, which open in late June, are deep pink and up to 2½ inches across. They are followed by large heps, about 1½ inches long and 1 inch across, which are orange-red to start with, but later turn to a more crimson shade. The cultivar known as 'Duplex', or Wolley-Dod's rose, is a hybrid between *R. villosa* and some garden rose and was nurtured by the Reverend A. H. Wolley-Dod, who split the dog rose into far too many species. He might be considered the Arch-splitter. His rose is not very different from the parent, but has semi-double flowers which may make it more attractive when in flower. It has the same numerous and attractive heps, but they are not borne so freely.

Rosa virginiana (syn. *R. lucida*) may be said to have a longer season of attraction than any other rose species. It forms a rather low suckering shrub, which can reach a height of 5 feet, but is generally little more than 3 feet. The new growths are reddish-brown in colour and preserve this colour through the following winter. The leaves are about 4 inches long, composed of 7 or 9 leaflets and are a very shining green. In the autumn they turn first dark red and then orange and yellow. The flowers, which are cerise in colour, open in July and August and are followed by red, rounded heps which persist on the plant for most of the winter. The plant does not thrive in very heavy soils, but on light soils it gallops away with what may sometimes be excessive vigour. However, it is not difficult to control if it spreads farther than is required.

Rosa webbiana makes a dense shrub up to 6 feet high and as much or slightly more across. The young growths are a handsome plum colour, but lose this as the season progresses. The small leaves are very dainty in appearance and are up to 3 inches long and composed of 7 or 9 tiny leaflets. The lilac-pink flowers are up to 2 inches across and are usually borne early in the season, although some forms seem not to flower until July. The heps are not very large but of a brilliant shining scarlet and, according to Graham Thomas, it is one of the showiest of roses in fruit. There is no arguing with his authority, but my own experience does not bear this out. Presumably I had a bad form.

Rosa woodsii fendleri is native to western North America from British Columbia to Mexico. *R. woodsii* itself is of little attraction, but the variety *fendleri* is a charming shrub of moderate dimensions with greyish leaves, up to 5 inches long, composed of 5 or 7 leaflets. The soft lilac-pink flowers are about 2 inches across, borne in clusters rather early in the season. They are followed by round heps about $\frac{3}{4}$ inch across, which pull the slender branches down with their weight so as to give a rather strange appearance, which Mr. Thomas compares to strings of red currants. These persist on the shrub until November which is longer than most heps do, and help to decorate the garden in early winter.

RUBUS

The brambles and raspberries do not contain a great deal from our point of view. If they have showy flowers, they do not have any other features of much interest and where these do exist the floral display tends to be disappointing. The plants are also generally tremendous spreaders and must be given plenty of room; even so one must be prepared to take steps to limit their spread. On the other hand, the white-stemmed species are attractive throughout the winter and have considerable foliar distinction in the summer.

Rubus amabilis, one of many Chinese species introduced by Wilson, is one of the pleasantest species. It is deciduous with dark reddish-purple stems, which are attractive in the winter. The pinnate leaves are up to 8 inches long and made up of from 7–11 leaflets. These leaflets are deeply toothed, up to 2 inches long and 1 inch across and give a very laciniate effect. The solitary flowers are white and up to 2 inches across. They are followed by red conical fruits, about the size of a loganberry and quite as palatable.

Rubus cockburnianus (syn. *R. giraldianus*) is the first, alphabetically, of a number of *Rubus* with biennial stems which are covered with a white or blue-white waxy covering. This particular species may reach a height of 8 feet, and the stems are branched at their summits and bend over. The stems are covered with a pure white waxy covering, which gleams in the winter in a most impressive way. The large leaves are up to 8 inches long, composed of from 5–7 leaflets, ovate in shape, the terminal one being twice the size of the lateral leaflets. It is not so very different from the Himalayan *R. biflorus*. In both cases the white flowers are of little distinction and the fruits, although edible, are also not very conspicuous. It is probably best to deal with the other white-stemmed brambles here.

Rubus coreanus grows up to 10 feet high and has blue-white stems. The pinnate leaves are from 6–10 inches long, composed of 7 leaflets. The flowers and fruits are of little interest.

Rubus lasiostylus is a better plant with stems up to 6 feet high, which rarely branch, and are covered with blue-white bloom. The leaves are usually about 8 inches long, but have been found as much as 14 inches long. The leaflets are laciniate and give the plant a graceful appearance. The small flowers are reddish-purple in colour, but very short-lived. On the other hand, the fruits are quite large, up to 1 inch across, red with an agreeable flavour, and quite freely produced.

Rubus leucodermis from the western United States is now a rare plant, having been supplanted by the better species from China. The blue-white stems are from 4–6 feet in height and the leaves are composed of only 3 or 5 large ovate leaflets. The white flowers appear in June and are followed by purple, rather succulent fruits.

Rubus thibetanus is one of the best of this group, with branching stems up to 6 feet in height covered with a rather more purplish bloom. The leaves, which may be 9 inches long, are composed of a large number of leaflets, sometimes as many as 13, which gives a very agreeable laciniate appearance to them. They are dark green above, but white-felted on the

149

underside. The flowers are only ½ inch across and are dark purple. They are either solitary from the upper leaf axils or in a terminal cluster. The fruit looks like a blackberry. This is a less rampant grower than most of the other white-stemmed species.

All these species with biennial stems should have the stems cut out as soon as fruiting is completed. Probably the best of them is the vivid white *R. cockburnianus* and the elegant *R. thibetanus*.

Rubus flagelliflorus is a climbing, evergreen species. The young shoots, which can be as long as 6 feet in a single season, are covered with whitish down and look rather remarkable. The leaves are entire, more or less heart-shaped, up to 7 inches long and 4½ inches across with a yellowish felt on the underside. They are borne on quite long stalks. The white flowers are borne in clusters springing from the leaf axils and are followed by rather small black fruits, which are edible. There are quite a number of evergreen, scandent species that Wilson introduced from various parts of China and they are all ornamental, chiefly on account of their foliage. Of these *R. flagelliflorus* is the best for our purposes, as the white, young growths give the plant a distinction that the other evergreen species lack. In partly shaded conditions the leaves sometimes assume a variegated appearance. These climbing rubus need to be trained to their supports, otherwise the growths may fall to the ground, where they root at the tips like our own native brambles and you find yourself with an unwanted jungle. On the other hand, this makes propagation very simple.

The ornamental rubus poise a problem for the gardener. Although they have many attractive features they also have a somewhat weedy appearance and are at their best in the wild garden or whatever its modern equivalent may be. Owing to their vigour they are probably not the best of plants for the small garden, although the appearance of the white and blue-stemmed species are so effective in the winter, that many will feel tempted to admit them and prevent their spreading too far by rigorous excisions. The evergreen scandent species are more easily accommodated and, in spite of their hardiness, give an exotic appearance, which is often welcome.

SALIX

We had to strain our terms of reference somewhat to include *Rubus*, but we have to bend them even further to admit the willows. The plants to be mentioned here are chiefly grown for their colourful winter bark, and for this reason they are generally pollarded in the spring. This means that they produce plenty of young wood during the summer, but this is not really very ornamental. If they are not pollarded, they will make small trees which will bear catkins in the spring. The plants are dioecious and it is generally the male trees that have the most conspicuous catkins, as they are the ones that produce the pollen. We all know the golden male catkins of the Palm or Sallow. However, flowering trees do not produce so much young wood and so are not so ornamental in the winter. The foliage is generally attractive, but in no way striking.

Salix alba is a well-known tree with grey-green foliage which can attain a height of 70 feet and is often grown for ornament. It is, however, with some of its varieties that we are concerned here. *S. aurea* has golden young wood and pale yellow leaves, and makes a rather upright, slow-growing tree. The catkins appear in early May, rather later than those of most species, and are not particularly conspicuous. This is an attractive plant with its coloured young bark and coloured leaves, and is best left to grow unpruned. On the other hand, *S. a. vitellina*, sometimes known as *S. vitellina*, is usually pollarded yearly so as to encourage the very brilliant yellow shoots to develop. There is a variety of *alba* called 'Britzensis' or 'Chermesina' in which the young wood is orange-scarlet. The leafless branches look most impressive during the winter.

On the other hand, *S. daphnoides* has a perfect right to be present. This makes a small tree, up to 40 feet high, which is most conspicuous in the winter when the violet-purple young wood shows itself to full advantage. The plant can be pollarded to give more of this purple wood, but if the tree is allowed to grow naturally it will produce very effective catkins early in the season. The male ones resemble those of the sallow and cover themselves with yellow stamens when developed. They reach to as long as 2 inches. The female catkins are as long, but slenderer and lack the stamens. Young plants will always produce plenty of new growth to give winter beauty, so that there is no real need to restrict the growth and the catkins will then provide additional attractions. The leaves are somewhat leathery, elliptic in shape and up to 4 inches long and 1 inch across.

Salix fargesii is very different. It is not a tree but a shrub up to 8 feet high with stout shoots that become a shining red-brown and retain this colour for more than one season. The overwintering buds are large and bright red in colour, so that the plant is really very striking in its leafless state. The leaves are large for the genus, elliptic in shape, up to 7 inches long and 3 inches across. They are somewhat wrinkled on the upper surface and a dark glossy green in colour. In spring the large, erect catkins appear. Apparently only the female plant is in cultivation and this produces catkins up to 6 inches in length, although only $\frac{1}{4}$ inch in diameter. They are produced before the leaves have developed, so that a well-flowered plant is quite a sight.

Salix irrorata, a native of the south-western United States, makes a

151

shrub up to 10 feet high. Its main attraction lies in the young bark and this seems to vary somewhat. In the form with which I am acquainted it is a glistening silver which gives the appearance of the plant being covered with hoar frost. Other forms, apparently, are 'purple covered with white bloom' and 'smooth, purple or yellow, waxy'. The plant that I know is one of the most effective of shrubs for decorating the garden in winter. The catkins are small, but produced abundantly in April. The leaves resemble those of *S. alba* being long and narrow, reaching up to 4 inches long and ¾ inch across.

SAMBUCUS

The elderberries are somewhat weedy-looking trees and shrubs which can be very effective both in flower and in fruit. We probably do not appreciate them as much as we should. The forms with black fruit are not really very ornamental at that stage, but the plants with red or blue fruits are more striking.

Sambucus caerulea, a native of California, is a vigorous shrub up to 10 feet high over here, but can apparently make a large tree in its native land. Like all the species it has pinnate leaves. In this case they may reach a length of 10 inches and are usually composed of 7 oval leaflets, which may be 6 inches long and 2 inches across. The flat umbels of flowers, up to 7 inches across, open in June and are creamy-yellow in colour. The berries are basically black, but are densely covered with a blue bloom, which gives them a very attractive appearance. I am not sure if this attractive shrub is still in cultivation, but if it is not it might well be possible to obtain seed from the United States.

From the same districts of California and Oregon comes *S. callicarpa*, a rather small shrub, not exceeding 6 feet in height. The leaves are composed of 5 or 7 leaflets, which are not more than 4 inches long. The very characteristic inflorescence is hemispherical in shape and only some 3 inches in diameter. The flowers are white and they open in late June or early July, to be followed by scarlet berries in the autumn. Unfortunately, all these scarlet-fruited elderberries are extremely attractive to birds and one day you have a shrub that is a pleasure to look at and the next day you find it has been stripped.

Sambucus canadensis is a vigorous shrub much like our own *S. nigra*, but its outsize variety, *maxima*, deserves notice. This requires plenty of room as it makes a vigorous shrub up to 10 feet in height. The huge leaves have been known to reach a length of 18 inches and may be composed of 11 leaflets. The large, slightly convex flower clusters appear in July. They have been measured 18 inches across and a width of 12 inches is by no means unusual. They are white in colour. The plant does not generally set fruit, but when the flowers fall they leave the rosy-purple flower stems still standing and giving a very charming, rather smoky effect. This is really a valuable shrub for its late flowering with its enormous flower-heads.

Sambucus racemosa is one of the most brilliant of red-berried shrubs, but its flowers, which appear in April, are greenish and inconspicuous. On the other hand, the cultivar known as 'Plumosa Aurea' is well worth growing. This is not particularly vigorous, but has the leaflets very deeply laciniated and golden-yellow in colour. This cultivar is less liable to flower than the type, but when it does the berries are scarlet by July. *S. racemosa* grows far better in the north of the country and has naturalized itself in Scotland. The other species seem perfectly happy in any part of the country.

SCHINUS

Schinus dependens comes happily into our requirements, but I have no idea how it could be obtained. It has also been called *Duvaua dependens*. It is a Chilean plant and makes an evergreen shrub up to 15 feet high. The twigs are tipped with spines. In May it produces inflorescences like small catkins about ½ inch long and greenish-yellow in colour. They spring from every axil of the previous year's growth. After flowering the inflorescence elongates and the plant becomes covered with deep purple berries by the autumn. Each berry is the size of a peppercorn and since there is no pulp the birds tend to ignore them. The plant appeared to be quite hardy at Kew; the form with smaller, more ovate leaves, variety *ovatus*, being slightly hardier than the type. Although the catkin-like inflorescence is small, it is borne very profusely and the plant is attractive both in May and in the autumn.

SCHIZANDRA

A genus of climbing plants, whose inclusion is somewhat open to question. The plants are dioecious, although there is little to choose between the flowers from the point of attraction. On the other hand, the female plants will also bear berries, which in some cases are very brilliant. However, in order to have these berries you also have to have a male plant, which will have no later season of attraction. This may well be tolerated in *Schizandra rubriflora*, which covers itself in late May and early June with ruby-red flowers about an inch across and which is one of the most delightful of all climbers. If there is room for two climbers, this is the species to obtain and there is no reason why they should not both be trained up the same support. *S. propinqua sinensis* does not produce its rather small yellowish flowers until the end of June, but these are followed by bright scarlet berries in clusters.

SKIMMIA

A genus of low-growing evergreen shrubs with fragrant flowers and persistent red berries. They have no objection to being in a somewhat shady position and prefer a slightly acid soil. *Skimmia reevesiana* (syn. *S. fortunei*) has hermaphrodite flowers; *S. japonica* is dioecious, so that one male plant must be provided for every half-dozen females, but it is, however, lime tolerant.

The plants are not dissimilar in appearance, having elliptic leaves about 4 inches long and 1 inch across, and heads of flowers in early spring. In *S. japonica* the male flowers are always more fragrant than the females. The plants can be distinguished by the fruits, which are globular in *S. japonica*, and oval in *S. reevesiana*. Although *S. reevesiana* has bisexual flowers, fruiting is best when cross-pollination can take place.

There appear to be several hybrids between the two species, of which × *rogersii* has the bisexual flowers of the Chinese plant. *S. reevesiana* was introduced by Fortune in 1849 and to him also is due the popularity of the Japanese plant. This had been known in England since 1838, but its dioecious character was not appreciated and it was not until Fortune introduced plants of both sexes from Japan in 1861 that the real merits of the plant became apparent.

Both the species are very useful with their by no means unattractive flower panicles and their red berries, which the birds generally ignore. They will grow very happily in shaded conditions, so long as the shade is not too dark. The berries are borne underneath the current crop of leaves, but are large enough to be conspicuous.

SORBARIA

Sorbaria is a genus allied to *Spiraea*, from which it may be distinguished by its pinnate leaves and by the very large flower panicles. They are all elegant shrubs, but the only one to interest us here is *S. aitchisonii*.

This makes a spreading shrub up to 9 or 10 feet high and has attractive reddish young wood, which looks conspicuous in the winter. The leaves, which are composed of from 11–23 leaflets, may reach a length of 15 inches and a width of 8 inches. The leaflets are long and narrow, up to 4 inches long but only ¾ inch across. The white flowers open in late July and early

August and are borne in immense panicles, up to 18 inches long and 15 inches across at the base. These are followed by red seed pods which are by no means unattractive. The specific epithet *aitchisonii* is an indication that the plant is native to Afghanistan and was collected by Dr. Aitchison, who, until the recent expeditions by Admiral Furse, was the last plant collector to visit that country. This sorbaria, which can easily be kept to manageable dimensions, is a useful shrub for its late flowering and is admirably suitable for small gardens.

SORBUS

A genus of trees that are generally not very large, deciduous, and distributed throughout the north temperate zone. They have been divided into two sections; Aucuparia, the section that contains our own native rowan, is characterized by pinnate leaves, while Aria, the section that contains our wild whitebeam, has simple leaves. The Aria section has been subdivided into Aria proper and Micromeles, but the main distinction appears to lie in the fact that the calices adhere to the top of the fruits in Aria and fall off in Micromeles, so that the distinction is not very considerable. In the garden the Micromeles section can usually be distinguished by the smaller leaves and by the fact that they are generally coloured, sometimes very strikingly, as they unfurl in the spring. Since they appear to be perfectly hardy it is regrettable that they are so rarely seen.

The whole genus is usually remarkable for the beauty of its foliage and of its fruits. The flowers are pleasant enough, but rarely outstanding, but in many species the leaves colour well in the autumn. The fruits are very popular with birds and, if the latter are pestilential, one will lose one of the plant's greatest attractions. Our native *Sorbus aucuparia* seems to thrive as a street tree and when it is well fruited, can compare with any Flamboyant for brilliance of effect. Birds appear to be less destructive in towns and so the various sorbus are particularly suitable for town gardens.

The genus is not too easy to describe and it will certainly be easier to consider the two main sections separately. Let us start then with the section Aria.

Sorbus alnifolia, a Micromeles, can eventually make a tree up to 40 feet high, but is in no hurry to do so. It makes a somewhat columnar tree. The leaves are a soft bronze as they unfurl. When mature they are green on both surfaces and are rather like those of an alder in shape, as their name suggests. They are up to 4 inches long and 1½ inches across. In May the white flowers open in smallish corymbs, up to 3 inches across. The individual flowers are ½ inch across. The largish fruits are a very bright red. The Chinese form of the plant, known as variety *submollis* (but also as *S. zahlbruckneri*) is a smaller tree with somewhat darker fruits. In the autumn the leaves are liable to turn orange and scarlet.

Sorbus aria is our native whitebeam, which is so often a prominent feature on the chalk downs and which must be ranked as among the most beautiful of all trees. This can vary in dimensions from a large shrub to a tree up to 50 feet, and occasionally greater dimensions have been recorded. The oval leaves are covered with silver down as they emerge, and retain this on the underside throughout the season, so that any gust of wind will suddenly turn half the tree silver. The white flowers, which appear in late May or early June, are nearly the same colour as the leaves at that period and so are not very conspicuous. The fruits, on the other hand, which are large for the genus, are a good red speckled with brownish dots. The leaves turn beige or ash-grey before falling and, although not brilliant, have a certain charm. There are a certain number of cultivars that deserve consideration. That known as 'Lutescens' has both surfaces of the leaves covered with silvery tomentum, and has also the bark of the trunk and branches coloured pale orange-buff.

The oval leaves of the type are generally up to 4 inches long and 2 inches across, but in the cultivar 'Decaisneana' ('Majestica') they can reach a length of 7 inches and a width of 4 inches. The fruits are also somewhat larger than in the type. As a young plant the leaves are almost too large, but once the tree has become sizeable it is one of the most effective of all trees. In his fascinating article on various arias in the Royal Horticultural Society's *Journal* for June 1965, David Wright has very happily likened the unfurling leaves to small silver magnolia flowers. In *S. aria* 'Decaisneana', they look like full-size magnolias.

Sorbus chamaemespilus is a smallish shrub, native to the Alps. It has been found as tall as 6 feet, but is usually not more than half that height and is very slow-growing. The young shoots are covered with white down, but the leaves are green on both sides and not particularly attractive. On the other hand, the flowers, which have markedly upright petals, are rosy-pink in colour and are outstanding. The scarlet fruit is as large as that of the rowan and is therefore very attractive.

Sorbus cuspidata, a native of the Himalayas, is the most impressive tree in this section but, alas, is somewhat tender and apparently is liable to die suddenly without any warning. However, in a sheltered situation it is certainly worth an attempt.

This does not seem to have ever exceeded 35 feet in this country, although in the Himalayas it makes a tree of the largest dimensions. The young shoots are covered with white down, which disappears before the leaves fall, to leave purplish-brown young wood. The leaves are somewhat less rounded than most of the Aria section and can reach a length of 9 inches and a width of 5 inches. The upper surface is covered at first with white down, but this soon falls away. The underside is covered with a thick white tomentum that turns grey as the season advances. The large white flowers appear in early June and are followed by quite large but not very brilliant reddish fruits which are speckled with brown.

The plant has been hybridized with *S. aria* and the resultant hybrid, called 'Wilfred Fox', is an excellent substitute for *S. cuspidata* in colder districts. Its leaves are longer and narrower than those of *S. cuspidata*. The fruits are bronzy-yellow and not outstandingly conspicuous. The leaves of both *S. cuspidata* and 'Wilfrid Fox' turn either ash-grey or dark brown in the autumn.

Sorbus folgneri, a Wilson introduction, sounds one of the most attractive of all this section and one wonders why it is seen so rarely. It makes a small tree, up to 30 feet high so far as is known, with rather pendulous branches. The young growths are covered with white down which, in some forms, persists throughout most of the winter, so that the young wood then resembles that of the white-stemmed rubus. When it does fall off the wood underneath is seen to be a dark purple-brown. The leaves are lanceolate in shape, up to 3½ inches long and 1 inch across, dark green on the upper surface, but a very vivid silver-white on the underside. Indeed, there are very few leaves of any genus which are quite so dazzling. In the autumn the upper side of the leaves turns orange and scarlet, while the underside still retains its silver tomentum. The flowers are in rather large corymbs and are followed by large red fruits, which are, apparently, pendulous. This is evidently a rather variable species and the difference between good and bad forms seems considerable, so it is obviously best to select your plant from the nursery if that is practicable. The brilliance of the underside of the leaf is sometimes lacking or inferior to the best forms and this is a feature which is of importance. Some plants are also more pendulous in habit than others, but this is not a feature that can be detected in young plants.

Sorbus intermedia, the Swedish whitebeam, is useful for its tolerance of extreme cold and polluted atmospheres, but since the leaves are a dull grey on the underside, it is inferior to our own *S. aria*. It is interesting for the fact that its leaves are lobed at the base; hence its name which suggests that the plant is intermediate between the Aria and Aucuparia sections. The plant has been hybridized with the rowan, *S. aucuparia*, to give the plant known as *S. × hybrida*, which has leaves that are grey felted beneath and partially pinnate, and extremely brilliant large crimson fruits. A plant allied to *S. intermedia*, but with a whiter underside to the leaf, is *S. mougeottii*. This has hybridized in the wild with *S. chamaemespilus* to give the very attractive *S.* × *hostii*. This is a small tree, not more than 15 feet high, with oval leaves, 4 inches long and 2¼ inches across which are light grey on the underside. The plant has the pink flowers of *S. chamaemespilus*, although they are somewhat paler, and bright red fruits. This is a delightful plant for the small garden.

Sorbus lanata is similar to *S. cuspidata* and may be easier to grow, but there seems to be very little known of it. Plants are offered in a leading shrub nurseryman's catalogue as are also plants of *S. vagensis*, a plant about which all my reference books are silent. The catalogue description is that the leaves are broad, regularly and shallowly lobed and toothed, dark glossy green above, felted beneath. It does not mention the colour of the felt, nor the colour of the fruits.

Sorbus megalocarpa must be mentioned, although it is only suitable for a sheltered position, on account of its early flowering. It makes a rather low spreading tree, not more than 20 feet high and probably as much across. The cream-coloured flowers appear in late March or early April, before the leaves have started to unfurl, which makes this unique in the genus. The leaves are dark green and wrinkled, elliptic in shape and up to 9 inches long and half as wide. In favourable seasons they turn crimson before falling, but this is not to be relied upon. The very large fruits, up to 1 inch long, are russet in colour and are not, therefore, very conspicuous. The plant can tolerate as much winter frost as is offered, but is liable to damage in the spring.

Sorbus meliosmifolia can make a tree up to 35 feet high, but its natural habit is shrubby and it will make a large bush, unless pruned to encourage a tree-like habit. The leaves start to unfurl in early March and are sometimes a delightful salmon-pink and sometimes a bronze colour. These leaves will tolerate at least ten degrees of frost (Fahrenheit) without any damage, so that, in spite of their early emergence, they maintain their charm. The elliptic leaves can reach a length of 7 inches and may well turn crimson before falling. The rather handsome white flowers open in April, earlier than any other sorbus, except for *S. megalocarpa*. The fruits are rather a dull red, but the plant has such charm that it deserves to be far better known than it is.

A plant that does not appear to be in cultivation in this country, but which is highly praised by Alfred Rehder in his *Manual of Cultivated Trees and Shrubs*, is *S. japonica*. This makes a tree, up to 60 feet, and the young branches are covered with a greyish-white tomentum. The ovate leaves are up to 4 inches long and half as wide, slightly lobed and toothed, dark green above and with either a white or grey tomentum below. The variety *calocarpa* is the one to obtain apparently, as the leaves have a better white tomentum and turn a good yellow before falling, while the fruits are orange rather than scarlet in colour. The flowers are produced in May and the fruits are ripe in October. The variety was introduced to North America in 1915, but has not, so far as one can find out, reached this country.

The Aucuparia section contains our own mountain ash or rowan and is easily distinguished by the elegant pinnate leaves, which make the plant attractive during the summer. There are a very large number of species and it is not always easy to choose between them. As a general rule they are good-tempered plants that will grow in most soils. They vary considerably in their final dimensions and also in the size of the leaves, but, perhaps from our point of view, they are best distinguished by the colour of the fruits. Although the largest number have these scarlet or dark red, there are a few with yellow fruits and rather more with white fruits and so I propose to classify them according to their fruit colours.

(a) Species and cultivars with yellow fruits

The most outstanding plant in this series is so far unnamed. It was sent from China by Joseph Rock under the number 23657 and is at the moment in commerce under the name *Sorbus* 'Joseph Rock'. This has pinnate leaves from 5–7 inches long and composed of 13 or 15 oval, toothed leaflets with a reddish main stem. The ultimate height of the tree will be around 30 feet and it is a vigorous grower when young. The white flowers appear in late May and are followed by pale yellow fruits which persist for some time if the feathered songsters of the grove will permit it. Since the plant apparently comes true from seed it would seem to be a distinct species, but at the moment it lacks official confirmation of this fact. Let us hope that it is not too disturbed.

This is the only species to have yellow fruits that is in cultivation, but two yellow-fruited cultivars of normally scarlet-fruited species are available. These are *S. aucuparia xanthocarpa* (*S.* × *fructu-luteo*) and *S. esserteauiana flava*. The so-called yellow-fruited form of *S. aucuparia* is more accurately described as having orange-yellow fruits, but the cultivar of *S. esserteauiana* does have very brilliant yellow fruits.

(b) Species with white or pale pink fruits

Sorbus cashmeriana makes a small tree with very elegant, fern-like leaves, up to 5 inches long, but narrow in proportion, composed of numerous leaflets that are only about ½ inch long. The white flowers (sometimes pink) open in early June and are followed by extremely large, shining white fruits that will persist on the tree until December if permitted. The fruits are 1 inch in diameter and sometimes more, as large as cherries. The plant is native to the Himalayas, notably Kashmir, and has, I would imagine, the largest fruits of the genus.

By contrast the enormous *S. harrowiana* has nearly the smallest. The plant itself makes a tree from 25–40 feet high, and is characterized by its very large leaves. They may be 10 inches long, but are composed of not more than 9 leaflets, which may be 8 inches long and 2 inches across. The small white flowers are in corymbs up to 6 inches across, and the tiny fruits are white or pale pink.

The plant was introduced by Forrest from Yunnan in 1912, but nearly all his introductions died in the 1962–3 winter, whereas plants from a later introduction by Kingdon-Ward survived. However, the plant must be regarded as tender and only suitable for mild localities. The related *S. insignis*, with equally large leaves, but browny-red fruits, appears to be considerably hardier.

Sorbus hupehensis is one of the most delightful of all the species and a first choice out of a bewildering medley. It will eventually make a moderately sized tree up to 40 feet in height. The leaves are as long as 8 inches consisting of up to 17 oval leaflets, which are about 2 inches long and 1 inch across. These are glaucous blue-green on the surface and very pale green on the underside. The white flowers (blush-pink in the variety *rosea*) are produced on long-stalked corymbs in June and droop as the small white, pink-tinted, fruits develop. The foliage is liable to colour well in the autumn, but is less reliable in this respect than the related *S. discolor* (syn. *S. pekinensis*). This makes a somewhat smaller tree, with somewhat longer leaves, which may reach 10 inches. The individual leaflets are quite large, up to 3 inches long and $\frac{1}{2}$ inch across. The flowers appear in late May in a flat inflorescence which may be 6 inches across, and are followed by milk-white fruits with a slight yellowish tinge. At the same time the leaves generally turn a good crimson and the plant is then extremely impressive with its red leaves and white fruits.

Sorbus koehneana is a small tree or shrub of not more than 12 feet in height. The leaves, which differ markedly in length between those on flowering shoots and those on growth shoots, are composed of a large number of very narrow leaflets, although they can be as long as 1 inch. The leaves on the flowering shoots are about 3 inches long, those on the growth shoots may be twice as long. They are dark green on the surface and grey-green below. The white flowers appear in panicles about 3 inches across in May and subsequently white berries on red stalks are produced. The plant is very close to *S. vilmorinii*, which is much more frequently seen, but can perhaps be most conveniently discussed here. This Chinese plant was raised by Maurice de Vilmorin from seed sent by Delavay. It makes a small tree, sometimes attaining 20 feet, but usually less, and rather slow-growing. The leaves are among the most elegant of the genus, up to 5 inches long composed of very many small leaflets, each not more than ½ inch long and ¼ inch across. The young shoots are covered with a brownish tomentum. The leaves are a dark green and somewhat glossy. The white flowers are produced in slender corymbs in some quantity to form an inflorescence some 4 inches across. They open in June. The fruits are pale pink when first ripe and then fade to nearly white. This is the best known of the group, which includes *S. koehneana* and a species that appears to be only a variety of the last named, but which has been named as *S. glomerulata*, and which may no longer be in cultivation. These white-fruited sorbus are just as attractive to the birds as the red-fruited species.

Sorbus prattii is near these species, but is slightly more vigorous. The leaves reach up to 5 inches in length and in the variety *subarachnoidea* have the underside covered with a rusty, cobwebby, tomentum. The flowers are in rather small clusters, not more than 2 inches across and open in May, followed by pearl-like fruits. Somewhere between this and *S. vilmorinii* comes *S. poteriifolia*, with leaves composed of a great number of leaflets and fruits that are white with a pink flush. With the exception of *S. cashmeriana*, which is readily recognized by its very large fruits, none of these white-berried species are easily distinguished. They are all small, elegant trees with fern-like leaves and they are all desirable garden plants. *S. vilmorinii* is distinct with its pale pink fruits, but the others are very easily confused.

(c) Species with red fruits

We may as well begin with *Sorbus sargentiana*, which is so very distinct from all the others in this section, although it is close to *S. harrowiana* and *S. insignis*. This makes a rather spreading tree up to 25 feet high and has large sticky buds like those of the horse chestnut. The leaves may attain a length of 12 inches and are rather like those of an ash. They are composed of 9 or 11 leaflets, which are oblong-lanceolate, up to 5 inches long and 1½ inches across. They usually turn various shades of red before falling. The white flowers which open in June are in a hemispherical corymb that may be 6 inches across. The red fruits are very small, but are generally numerous, so that the plant may be nearly as brilliant as the species with larger fruits.

The other species to be discussed are not too easily recognized, as they all have pinnate leaves composed of numerous, rather small pinnae, white, flattish inflorescences and heads of medium-sized red pomes. They are typified best by our own mountain ash, *S. aucuparia*, a plant that is not bettered by any exotic introductions. This makes a tree that is usually not more than 30 feet high, but which on occasions attains twice this height. The leaves are downy as they emerge and unfurl to be up to 9 inches long and composed of 13 or 15 leaflets. The panicles of creamy flowers open in late May and early June, and may be 5 inches across. The bright red fruits colour in late August. This is now regarded as an aggregate species and numerous small differences have been observed between various sub-species. From the gardener's point of view ssp. *edulis* (*moravica*) with extra large fruits is to be recommended, and there is a cultivar from this, 'Beissneri' ('Dulcis laciniata') in which the leaflets are themselves lobed, which is perhaps the most desirable form of all. There are also fastigiate and pendulous forms in cultivation and a cultivar with laciniate leaflets which give a fern-like effect, called 'Asplenifolia'. Unfortunately the colourful fruits are seldom left long for our enjoyment, but town-dwellers will probably be able to get considerable pleasure from them. *Sorbus americana*, which will make a tree to 30 feet, but is generally smaller, is not of any greater interest than *S. aucuparia*, but is a slower grower and may be more suitable for small gardens.

Sorbus commixta is the Japanese representative of this group. It makes a rather upright tree with a pyramidal top and usually reaches only 25 feet. The leaves are from 5–7 inches long and are composed of 11 or 13 leaflets. They are dark green above and glaucous below. The somewhat similar *S. rufo-ferruginea* has the leaf-stalks and the underneath of the midribs and principal veins covered with red-brown down. The white flowers are produced in May and the red fruits follow in the autumn. Both the Japanese and American plants have glutinous winter buds, while those of *S. aucuparia* are downy. The Japanese species very often have brilliant red foliage in the autumn and this is certainly an added attraction. If a choice is necessary I suppose the reddish down of *S. rufo-ferruginea* gives an additional interest to the plant.

Sorbus esserteauiana, a Chinese plant, is very close to *S. aucuparia*, from which it is most easily distinguished by the grey-white down which clothes the undersides of the leaves. The flowers are in corymbs that may be 5 inches across and open in June, rather later than the majority of sorbus. The fruits are smaller than those of *S. aucuparia*, but very numerous and, if allowed, will persist on the tree until December. The leaves can reach a length of 10 inches and the tree will attain 45 feet.

On the other hand, *S. gracilis* is usually no more than a large shrub and will not exceed 12 feet in height. It is the most charming of the small species, as the leaves are a delightful bronzy-purple when they emerge and they can usually be relied upon to turn a brilliant crimson in the autumn. This autumn colouring seems to be a feature of all the Japanese sorbus. The leaves are from 3–6 inches long, composed of from 7–11 leaflets, which are quite large: up to 2½ inches long and about two-thirds as wide. The flowers are in rather small inflorescences, not more than 2 inches across and the red fruits are small.

Sorbus matsumurana is yet another Japanese plant that will give good autumn colour. This makes a moderately sized tree up to 30 feet with leaves composed of quite large, acuminate leaflets. The leaves themselves may reach a length of 7 inches and the leaflets are about 1½ inches long. The flowers are not particularly conspicuous, although they are in flat inflorescences some 6 inches across, but the orange-red fruits, although not very large, are of the greatest brilliance and in the autumn this may be one of the most striking of all trees.

Sorbus pohuashanensis gets its curious specific epithet from the Po-hua mountains. It is very close to *S. aucuparia* but tends to be 'larger in all its parts' and has inflorescences and fruiting heads up to 7 inches across and is thus one of the most showy plants in this section.

Sorbus scalaris makes a tree up to 25 feet and has leaves somewhat reminiscent of those of *S. vilmorinii*. They may reach a length of 8 inches and are composed of up to 37 small leaflets, which may be 1½ inches long and ¼ inch across and are not set very closely together. They are a very dark green on the upper surface and have a cobwebby down on the underside. The flowers are in large heads, up to 5 inches wide, and the berries are smallish but numerous and a very bright red. They are usually the last to be attacked by the birds. The fern-like leaves make this an unusually graceful small tree. Closely allied, but less desirable, is *S. pluripinnata*. This makes a large shrub or small tree and the young growths are clothed with grey down. The leaves do not exceed 5 inches in length, but may be composed of 25 leaflets, which are 1 inch long and perhaps ¼ inch across. They are dark green above, grey and woolly below. The inflorescence is not more than 3 inches across and the fruits are bright red and on the small side.

Sorbus scopulina (syn. *S. americana nana*) is a slow-growing American shrub that will eventually reach 12 feet. It is characterized by unusually thick, erect branches. The leaves are similar to those of *S. americana*, up to 10 inches long, composed of from 7–15 leaflets, which may be 5 inches long and 1 inch across. The inflorescence may be 6 inches across and the flowers are followed by fruits which are large for the genus and a very brilliant red. The height of 12 feet is the maximum and it is more usually around 4 or 5 feet high. It is thus a particularly good plant for the small garden.

So is our last species, *S. tianshanica*. This makes a shrub from 6–14 feet high, which can be pruned to be a small tree. The leaves are about 6 inches long and composed of from 9–15 leaflets, up to 2 inches long and ½ inch across. The flowers are produced in rather loose corymbs in late May and are the largest of the genus, being ¾ inch across. They are followed by bright red, round pomes which are ½ inch across. The plant comes from Central Asia, notably Turkestan and Afghanistan, but appears to thrive in our very different climate. This is again a very pleasant species.

Since there are very few sorbus that are not desirable plants, the choice is by no means easy, but as a short list for this section I would put *S. hupehensis* and *S. aucuparia* 'Beissneri' among the larger species, *SS. cashmeriana*, *gracilis* and *tianshanica* among the smaller ones.

STACHYURUS

Stachyurus praecox is a Japanese shrub which produces catkin-like flowers very early in the season, before the leaves unfurl. The plant makes a spreading shrub, that may reach 10 feet in height, but is usually from 6–7 feet. The young wood is reddish in colour and quite ornamental in the winter. The ovate leaves, which taper to a thin point, are up to 7 inches long and 2½ inches across, and on established plants they turn crimson in the autumn. The flower spikes appear from the axils of second-year wood in the autumn, before the leaves fall. They are frost-tender as they emerge, but once they have attained their full length they will tolerate very low temperatures. The small pale yellow flowers resemble those of the corylopsis, and open in February in mild seasons, otherwise in March. At this stage they are again frost-tender and late frosts will often destroy the flowers just as they are opening.

The other species in cultivation, *S. chinensis*, which is similar in appearance, is more vigorous, flowers later, has greeny-brown young growth and no autumn colour, so far as my own observation goes.

STAPHYLEA

The bladder nuts have attractive flowers in the spring, followed by inflated seed capsules, which have an attraction of their own and which give the genus its vernacular name. They also have attractive foliage, and most species are of moderate dimensions and suitable for the small garden. They are all deciduous and are found throughout the northern temperate zone.

Staphylea bumalda makes a small shrub, not more than 6 feet high and generally around 4 feet. The leaves are composed of 3 leaflets, each up to 3 inches long and 1 inch across, and ovate-lanceolate in shape. In June it produces panicles of greenish-white flowers which are followed by inflated seed-capsules about an inch in length. The leaves turn a good golden yellow in the autumn.

Staphylea colchica is a more vigorous shrub, which will eventually reach 10 feet. The leaves are composed of 3 or 5 leaflets, the central one of which is stalked. These leaflets are ovate, up to 3½ inches long and a bright green. The flowers, that appear towards the end of May, are in erect panicles that may be 5 inches long and as much across, and which are pure white. They are followed by large, inflated capsules, up to 4 inches long and 2 inches across, which are quite striking. This plant is superior to the 5-leaved *S. pinnata*, although this latter is more usually seen. This has drooping, not erect, panicles of flowers and the 'bladders' are not more than 1½ inches long and about as wide.

Staphylea holocarpa, a Chinese species, is the most vigorous in cultivation, reaching up to 30 feet in height. It is not very rapid growing and seems to be rather a touchy subject, doing very well in some situations and being far from satisfactory in others. Where it does do well, as in the late Sir Frederick Stern's garden at Highdown, in Sussex, it is one of the loveliest of spring shrubs. The leaves are trifoliate, and a delicate bronze-green as they unfurl and the leaves have red petioles, so that there is always a touch of colour about the shrub. The leaflets are ovate, the central one stalked, the two laterals sessile and they may reach a length of 4 inches. The flowers appear in early May in axillary racemes of 2 inches or more. The flowers are pink in bud, opening white in the type, but pink in the variety *rosea* and are followed by inflated pear-shaped capsules, which are 2 inches long and 1 inch across at the widest. Where this will thrive it is certainly the best of the genus. Highdown is on a very chalky soil, so that alkaline conditions would appear to suit the plant.

STEPHANANDRA

This genus is related to *Spiraea* and is characterized by graceful leaves which colour yellow and orange in the autumn, and brown young wood, which is attractive in the winter. Two species are in cultivation. *Stephanandra incisa* has basically triangular leaves, which are deeply lobed; they reach a length of 3 inches and a width of about 2 inches. The dirty white flowers appear in June in panicles some 3 inches long. *S. tanakae* is somewhat more desirable as the stems are a brighter brown and the leaves are larger, as is the lax branching inflorescence, which is also a better colour. The plants are grown mainly for their attractive autumn tints and winter stems, as well as for their foliage, which is much in demand for floral arrangements. The flowers are somewhat inconspicuous.

STEWARTIA

This genus, sometimes spelled *Stuartia*, is related to the camellias, but its species are very distinct in their deciduous character and their late flowering. They are plants that have a large number of attractions and they deserve to be far better known, and to be planted more extensively. They require acid soil and like a well-lit situation, but otherwise they appear to have no special requirements, and to be perfectly hardy. The species to be described all have attractive flowers in July and August, which is a period when any flowering tree is particularly welcome. Three of the four species have very brilliant autumn colours in all but very wet seasons and three will eventually develop very attractive creamy-pink bark which makes these plants a joy during the winter months.

Stewartia koreana is, as its name implies, native to Korea, where it makes a tree up to 50 feet high. It has only been in cultivation since 1917, so we do not know its ultimate dimensions over here. The ovate leaves are 4 inches long and 3 inches across and the white flowers, which are produced in July and August, are 3 inches across. This is generally one of the most reliable species for autumn colour, which is characterized by varying shades of red. Mature plants produce peeling bark which discloses a silvery-grey trunk.

Stewartia pseudo-camellia is the Asian species that has been longest in cultivation (two North American species have been in cultivation for over 100 years, but have never proved very long-lived). It was introduced in 1874. In its native habitat in Japan it makes a tree up to 50 feet high with a trunk 6 feet across, but is, so far, considerably less in cultivation. Although the petals are as long as those of *S. koreana*, the flowers are cupped and so appear smaller. After about 15 years the tree starts to develop a delightful beige-pink bark which peels yearly during the summer and makes the plant quite outstanding in the winter. The obovate leaves are about 3 inches long and can generally be relied on to turn golden and crimson in the autumn.

Stewartia sinensis is, perhaps, even more desirable. The plant was introduced by Wilson in 1901 and makes a smallish tree, up to 30 feet high. The oval leaves, 4 inches long and half as wide, turn a vivid crimson in the autumn; the flowers, though rather smaller than those of the two previous species, have the added advantage of being fragrant, while the plant starts to produce its attractive bark at an earlier age.

Stewartia monadelpha, another Japanese species, makes a fairly large tree eventually, and has handsome ivory flowers and very attractive pale brown smooth bark. It is not, however, so reliable for autumn colouration and so, for our purposes, less desirable than the other species. Even so it is a very ornamental plant with a particularly graceful habit.

STRANVAESIA

A genus of evergreen shrubs related to *Photinia*, with large corymbs of whitish flowers which are followed by red haws. The plants are very vigorous growers and should be allowed ample room.

The generic name is a curious example of what happens when one latinizes some English names. The genus is named in honour of Hugo Fox-Strangways. The number of species is difficult to determine, so similar are *Stranvaesia davidiana*, *S. salicifolia* and *S. undulata*. The first two are now telescoped into *S. davidiana*; some authorities accept *S. undulata* as specifically distinct, but most consider it simply as a variety of *S. davidiana*.

Stranvaesia davidiana was discovered by Père David in 1869, but not introduced until Forrest sent back plants in 1917. It makes a vigorous, spreading plant up to 30 feet high and nearly as much across. The leaves are bronze colour as they unfurl and become narrowly elliptic, up to 4 inches long and 1¾ inches across, finally dark green and rather leathery. The flower heads are about 3 inches across and consist of numerous pearly-white flowers. These are followed by crimson berries, but these are not freely produced without cross fertilization. Although the plant is ever-green the older leaves will turn crimson or scarlet before they fall. This is in their second year and they detach themselves singly, usually from October to May, so that there are some coloured leaves on the plant over a long period, although never very many at any one time. The plant is attractive enough, but not so much as the description would suggest, owing, I suspect, to its rather ungainly habit.

Although David's type plant was not introduced until 1917, Wilson had 10 years earlier introduced the plant that was called *S. salicifolia*. This has narrower leaves, not more than 1 inch across, but does not seem to be otherwise distinct.

Stranvaesia davidiana undulata is somewhat more distinct. It was the first of the three to be introduced, Wilson having sent seeds to Messrs. Veitch in 1901. It is lower and more spreading than the type and has orange-red, not crimson fruits. There exists also a yellow-fruited variety. The leaves are oval-lanceolate, 3½ inches long and 1¼ inches across, and they frequently have an undulate margin, although this is not invariable. The flower heads are somewhat smaller and the fruits slightly larger than those of the typical *S. davidiana*. In all the forms the flowers are very fugacious and persist for a very short time.

SYMPLOCOS

Symplocos paniculata had better be included for the sake of the record, but it does not seem very satisfactory in this country, although it does splendidly in North America. It makes a shrub or small tree, usually not more than 10 feet high. The ovate leaves are up to 3½ inches long and 1¾ inches across, and taper at each end. In May it produces terminal and axillary panicles of small, white fragrant flowers. These are followed by berries, about the size of haws, that are a really brilliant blue. Well, you may say, what could be better than that? Unfortunately, there are three objections to this otherwise admirable plant. Cross fertilization appears to be essential to get a good set of fruit and so at least two plants must be grown. The flowers are perfect, not unisexual, but even so two or more plants are necessary. Even with this, the set of fruits tends to be unsatisfactory in all but hot summers: and it is the fruits that are the main attraction of the plant. Finally, even if there is a good crop of fruits, the birds will at once make a set for them, so that they have to be protected either by netting or something similar, otherwise the display is very fugitive.

TAMARIX

Tamarix parviflora is the only one of the tamarisks to deserve inclusion here, although they are all interesting when not in flower, owing to their feathery appearance, caused by the tiny, closely imbricated leaves that cover the branches. In *T. parviflora* the young wood is reddish-purple in colour and this gives the plant distinction in winter when the leaves are fallen. Together with *T. tetrandra*, it differs from the other species by flowering off the old wood in May. The remainder flower on the current year's growth in late summer and autumn. The flowers are a good deep pink and though individually minute, cover the branchlets to dazzling effect. The tamarisks are somewhat undervalued in gardens, perhaps owing to the fact that *T. gallica* is often used as a hedge near the coast and tends to look rather tattered and ragged. Species such as *T. pentandra*, flowering in August and September, are among the best of late flowering shrubs and should be seen more often.

TILIA

The limes make rather large trees with fragrant yellowish flowers in July and August. The species which merit inclusion here are all characterized by the silver underside to their leaves, which makes them very attractive when there is any wind about. All the species are deciduous and have rather broad leaves.

Tilia oliveri is the most restrained of the species under consideration, since it does not exceed 40 feet in height when fully grown. It has a somewhat pendulous habit and is like a more compact *T. tomentosa* from which species it is easily distinguished by the glabrous young shoots. The young shoots of *T. tomentosa* are woolly. The roundish leaves are 4 inches long and about 3½ inches across, with a sharp point at the apex and a heart-shaped base. They are dark green and smooth on the upper surface, but the under surface is covered with a thick white felt. The flowers appear in late July and are strongly perfumed. The plant is a native of China and was introduced by Wilson in 1900, although Henry had sent back herbarium specimens in 1888.

Tilia petiolaris makes a large tree, up to 80 feet in height eventually, and has a very graceful appearance with its pendulous habit. It is sometimes referred to as the weeping silver lime. The rounded leaves are up to 4½ inches long and about 3 inches across, the same shape as the previous species and dark green above, silvery on the underside. They are borne on exceptionally long petioles, up to 2½ inches long. This compares with a length of 1½ inches in *T. oliveri* and 1 inch in *T. tomentosa*. The dull white flowers open in August or in late July and are possibly the most fragrant of all, scenting the air around for a great distance. The fragrance appears to act as an anaesthetic to bees, which may be often see in large quantities lying underneath the tree incapable of movement. The origin of this tree has never been satisfactorily established, but south-east Europe appears to be most likely.

Tilia tomentosa can reach a height of 100 feet and is rather graceless in its youthful stages, although very handsome when mature. The leaves are up to 5 inches long and as much across, with a straightish base and a slender point at the apex, dark green above and silvery on the underside. The flowers appear in early August and are similar to those of *T. petiolaris*, but the fruits differ in appearance. This plant is certainly a native of south-east Europe and has been in cultivation since 1767.

Tilia tuan is a moderately sized species, reaching perhaps to 50 feet. It has rather large, thin leaves which may be nearly 6 inches long and 4 inches across, green on the surface and grey on the underside. The yellowish flowers are produced more abundantly than those of most other species, from 15 to 20 in each cyme and subtended by a bract up to 5 inches long. They make this a plant worth having, but it is difficult to obtain. 'Tuan' is apparently a transliteration of the Chinese name for a lime tree. Like *T. oliveri*, the plant was discovered by Henry and introduced by Wilson.

VACCINIUM

The blueberries are a large genus of plants requiring acid soil, ranging in height from prostrate creepers to small trees and containing both deciduous and evergreen shrubs. They all appear to need acid soil and many are found in damp, marshy situations in the wild. The fruits are frequently very ornamental and are usually palatable, but the birds will make rapid inroads on them. Our own native whortleberry, *Vaccinium myrtillus*, is fairly typical of the smaller species, but those of larger size often have quite large racemes of white or pink urn-shaped flowers. Most species show fairly brilliant leaf colour in the autumn. The genus is generally confined to the northern hemisphere, but there is at least one species, *V. floribundum* (syn. *V. mortinia*), which is found in Ecuador, practically on the Equator. Curiously enough this is quite hardy in southern England, as it is found high in the mountains in its wild stations. A large number of species are offered in catalogues, but I am only including a few here of the larger species.

Vaccinium arctostaphylos is a native of the Caucasus range. It is not a rapid grower, but will eventually attain a height of 10 feet. The elliptic leaves may be 4 inches long and 1½ inches across and turn a purple-red in the autumn. The flower racemes open in June and spring from the second-year wood, so that one has the new growth and below that bare wood from which the flower racemes spring. The racemes are some 2 inches long and carry about 6 greenish-white flowers, reminiscent of lilies-of-the-valley. These are followed by purple fruits in September. Sometimes, at the same time, it produces a second crop of flowers from the current year's growth, but this autumn flowering is not invariable.

Vaccinium corymbosum is the commercial blueberry and many named cultivars have been selected for the best fruiting. It seems, however, that best results are obtained when cross-fertilization is possible and if the plants are to be grown for their fruits, two cultivars should be planted. The fruits require some protection against birds. The plant is in any case very attractive in itself and will ornament the shrubbery.

Vaccinium corymbosum is either very variable or else should be regarded as an aggregate species with a number of subspecies. Its height is variously given as 6 or 12 feet, but the lower number is that most frequently met with. The plant forms a thicket of rather thin, erect, branched stems. The leaves are elliptic, about 3 inches long and half as wide and usually turn a brilliant red before falling. The pale pink flowers are produced in terminal and axillary clusters in May before the leaves are fully expanded. The berries, which may be ¾ inch across in the named cultivars, are black covered with a blue bloom and very attractive to see, although the birds find them as palatable as we do. The plant is native to the eastern United States.

The above are the two best deciduous species for most gardens. Two evergreen species deserve a brief mention. *V. glauco-album* is a Himalayan plant and is only hardy in mild counties in southern England and along the west coast elsewhere. The leaves tend to be held rather upright, enabling one to see the very vivid blue-white undersides of the leaves, which are very striking. These leaves are up to 2 inches long and 1 inch across, oval in shape. The racemes of pink flowers are up to 3 inches long, produced from the leaf axils and they, too, are ornamented by blue-white persistent bracts. The blackish fruits are also covered with this blue-white bloom. The plant may reach 4 feet in height, but tends to grow outwards rather than upwards.

Vaccinium ovatum will begin life as a spreading, prostrate shrub, but will then start to ascend and may reach up to 10 feet, although 6 feet seems more usual. The young wood is purple and the young leaves are an attractive coppery colour. As the name suggests they are ovate and measure up to 1½ inches long and ¾ inch across. In May and June the white flowers are produced in axillary racemes, according to the Royal Horticultural Society's Dictionary (but one authority says they are not produced until September), followed by berries which soon turn red and ripen to black, but it is not often that they do ripen in this climate.

VIBURNUM

A fairly large genus of deciduous and evergreen shrubs from the north temperate zone, which generally have attractive flowers and fruits and which sometimes colour well in the autumn. The species with blackish fruit are not usually very attractive at this stage, but a few species have these black fruits covered with a blue bloom and these are attractive. Most species have rather small, perfect flowers usually white in colour, but a few resemble hydrangeas in having the outside of the cyme edged with sterile flowers which are much larger than the fertile ones. Our own native guelder rose illustrates this feature very well. By selection, forms have been propagated which consist only of sterile flowers and these are the various 'snowball trees'. Cross fertilization is generally necessary to produce fruits and one species, *Viburnum davidii* with blue berries, is dioecious, so that plants of both sexes must be obtained to secure the fruits. Most of the species require well-lit situations, but one or two, notably *V. alnifolium*, do better in semi-shaded conditions. The plants often have a rather ragged appearance, but contain also some of our best garden shrubs.

Viburnum alnifolium has not proved among the easiest species to cultivate, which is a pity, as it is one of the most attractive. As already mentioned it seems to do best in rather shady conditions, and needs an acid soil.
It makes a rather straggling, deciduous shrub up to 6 feet or more in
height. The rounded leaves are large, up to 8 inches long and as much
across and turn wine-red in the autumn. The inflorescence, which opens in
late May, is up to 5 inches across with a ring of sterile flowers, each 1 inch
across, on the outside. They are followed by fruits which quickly turn a
bright red and then darken to nearly black. The plant is native of the
eastern United States, but is scarcely to be distinguished from the Japanese
V. furcatum, which is equally difficult to cultivate successfully, but which
has leaves that often turn a brilliant scarlet before falling, so that it might
marginally be considered a better species.

Viburnum betulifolium makes a rather tall shrub, up to 12 feet in height,
and is deciduous. The dark green leaves are up to 4 inches long and
3 inches wide, broadly ovate, but tending to end in an elongated point.
The white flowers, in cymes up to 4 inches across, open in early June. They
are followed by the most brilliant red fruits, which persist long into the
winter. This is one of the very best of berrying shrubs, but does not fruit
well until the plant is fairly mature. Young plants flower with some
freedom, but seem loth to produce fruits. Eventually the plants will fruit
so well as to cause the branches to bend under the weight of the berries, but
patience is necessary to reach this state. It is also best to have more than one
specimen, so as to ensure cross fertilization, although this is not essential.

Viburnum davidii is a very low growing, spreading shrub, not more than
3 feet high and generally less. It is evergreen and has attractive elliptic dark
green leaves, which are somewhat wrinkled. They reach up to 6 inches
long and are 2 inches across. The whitish flowers are produced in cymes up
to 3 inches across and are followed by turquoise-blue berries. As already
mentioned the plants are dioecious and one male plant should be provided
for every five females. The flowers are of little interest and the plant is
grown for the sake of its handsome leaves and attractive berries.

Viburnum dilatatum is a Japanese species reaching to about 8 feet in
height, with rather large obovate leaves, up to 5 inches long and sometimes nearly as much across. The white flowers are produced in great
profusion in June in cymes up to 5 inches across. They are followed by
scarlet fruits, for the production of which cross-fertilization seems to be
essential and, like most of the Japanese species, the leaves will also colour in
the autumn. The plants are sometimes rather shy to set fruit and seem to
do better in the drier eastern counties.

Fairly close to *V. dilatatum* is the Chinese *V. hupehense*. This makes a
shrub up to 7 feet high with downy young wood and leaves. These are

rounded with a slender point, up to 3 inches long and wide, and they colour well early in the autumn. The floral cymes are about 2 inches across and open in late May or early June and are followed by berries which are first orange and later a brilliant red; it is one of the best of all shrubs for autumn display.

Our native wayfaring tree, *V. lantana*, would probably be grown with enthusiasm if it came from exotic parts. It can reach up to 15 feet in height, but fits happily into 6-foot hedges in most chalky districts. The velvety leaves are 5 inches long and 4 inches across. The white flowers open in June in cymes up to 4 inches across, and are followed by berries which are at first bright red, but later turn black. Sometimes the foliage will turn crimson before falling, but this is not invariable.

On the other hand, our other native viburnum, *V. opulus*, the guelder rose, will generally have crimson leaves in the autumn and is, in any case, one of the most agreeable species. It forms a rather tall shrub, up to 15 feet high with lobed, maple-like leaves up to 4 inches long and sometimes wider at the base. In early June the white flowers open. The cymes are 3 inches across with an outer ring of sterile flowers, ¾ inch across. The small fertile flowers produce translucent red berries with great regularity. There is also a yellow-fruited form, 'Xanthocarpum', on which the fruits hang until well into the winter. The snowball tree, *V. o. sterile*, has a large rounded inflorescence composed entirely of sterile flowers and so fails to set any fruit, but will still give good autumn colour. The cultivar known as 'Notcutt's Variety' has larger flower heads and fruits than the wild plant. The plant is represented in China by *V. sargentii* and in North America by *V. trilobum*, but neither are to be preferred to our own guelder rose.

Viburnum setigerum (syn. *V. theiferum*) is an attractive species, reaching to about 10 feet in height. The leaves are ovate-lanceolate, up to 5 inches long and half as wide and are bluish when they first unfurl, turning later to a dark green, and orange-yellow before they fall. The flowers are borne in corymbs some 2 inches across, which are produced with great freedom in early June. They are followed by berries which are at first orange-yellow and finally bright red. This is one of the best of the genus for its interest in foliage, flower and fruit.

Viburnum tomentosum, although one of the best of all flowering shrubs, only gets into this list on other people's recommendations. It makes a deciduous shrub rarely more than 6 feet high, as it tends to grow horizontally rather than elongate vertically and produces a series of horizontal branches, ranged above each other in diminishing lengths—a form of growth known as tabular. The flowers open in June and wreathe the branches. Each inflorescence is an umbel some 4 inches across with a ring of large sterile flowers, up to 1½ inches across in the type, but larger in the clones known as 'Mariesii' and 'Lanarth'. I have never seen the fruit, for which presumably cross fertilization is necessary, but it is said to resemble that of *V. lantana*, being first coral-red and then blue-black. The leaves, which are oval in shape, up to 4 inches long and 2½ inches across, are said to turn ruby-crimson in the autumn. I am bound to state that I have not experienced this. The sterile form, the Japanese snowball, used to turn a rather dull purple with me, but *V. tomentosum* itself never obliged.

Tabulated List

TREE OR SHRUB (E = evergreen SE = semi-evergreen)	Flowers	Orna. fruit	Autumn leaf colour	Orna. adult leaves	Bark	Orna. young wood	Orna. young leaves
Acer argutum	x		x	x		x	x
A. capillipes			x		x		
A. circinatum	x	x	x				
A. davidii			x		x	x	
A. fargesii	x	x					x
A. ginnala	x		x				
A. griseum			x		x	x	
A. grosseri hersii			x		x		
A. henryi		x	x	x			
A. japonicum	x		x				
A. j. aureum	x			x			
A. palmatum 'Osakazuki'		x	x				x
A. p. 'Senkaki'			x			x	x
A. pennsylvanicum			x		x		x
A. p. erythrocladum			x		x	x	x
A. platanoides	x		x				
A. rubrum	x	x					
A. r. 'Sanguineum'	x	x	x				
A. rufinerve			x	x	x	x	
A. saccharinum	x		x	x			
A. tartaricum	x	x	x				
Aesculus californica	x			x			
Alnus incana ramulis coccineis	x					x	
A. i. aurea	x					x	
Amelanchier asiatica	x		x				
A. canadensis	x		x				x
A. × grandiflora	x		x				x

TREE OR SHRUB (E = evergreen SE = semi-evergreen)	Flowers	Orna. fruit	Autumn leaf colour	Orna. adult leaves	Bark	Orna. young wood	Orna. young leaves
A. laevis	x		x				x
A. ovalis	x		x				
Amorpha canescens	x			x			
Arbutus andrachne (E)	x	x			x		
A. menziesii (E)	x	x		x	x		
A. unedo (E)	x	x			x		
Arctostaphylos manzanita (E)	x				x	x	x
A. patula (E)	x				x		
Berberis aemulans	x	x	x			x	
B. angulosa	x	x					
B. aristata	x	x					
B. beaniana	x	x					
B. chitria	x	x				x	
B. dasystachya	x	x					
B. dictyophylla	x	x	x			x	
B. francisci-ferdinandii	x	x				x	
B. jamesiana	x	x	x			x	x
B. kansuensis	x	x				x	
B. koreana	x	x	x			x	
B. ludlowii	x	x		x			
B. morrisonensis	x	x	x			x	
B. poiretii	x	x					
B. prattii	x	x					
B. replicata (E)	x	x				x	
B. × rubrostilla	x	x					
B. telomaica	x	x		x			
B. thunbergii	x	x	x				
B. t. atropurpurea	x	x		x			
B. vernae	x	x				x	
B. virescens	x	x	x			x	
B. vulgaris	x	x					
B. v. purpurifolia	x	x		x			
B. wilsonae (SE)	x	x	x				
B. yunnanensis	x	x	x				
Betula albo-sinensis					x		
B. ermanii					x		
B. jacquemontii					x		
B. lutea				x	x		

TREE OR SHRUB (E = evergreen, SE = semi-evergreen)	Flowers	Orna. fruit	Autumn leaf colour	Orna. adult leaves	Bark	Orna. young wood	Orna. young leaves
B. pendula					x		
B. p. dalecarlica			x	x			
B. p. 'Tristis'					x		
B. p. 'Youngii'					x		
Callicarpa bodinieri giraldii	x	x					
C. dichotoma	x	x					
C. japonica	x	x					
Camellia cuspidata (E)	x						x
C. 'Cornish Snow' (E)	x						x
Carya cordiformis			x	x	x		
C. myristicaeformis				x		x	
C. ovata			x	x	x		
C. tomentosa			x	x			
Castanopsis chrysophylla				x			
Catalpa bignonioides 'Aurea'	x			x			
C. × *hybrida* 'Purpurea'	x			x		x	x
Cladrastis lutea	x		x				
C. sinensis	x			x			
Clematis orientalis	x	x					
C. serratifolia	x	x					
C. tangutica	x	x					
Clerodendron fargesii	x	x					x
C. trichotomum	x	x					x
Cornus alba		x				x	
C. a. 'Gouchaltii'				x		x	
C. a. 'Spaethii'				x		x	
C. a. sibirica 'Variegata'				x		x	
C. capitata (E)	x	x					
C. florida	x		x				
C. f. rubra	x		x				
C. kousa	x	x	x				
C. k. chinensis	x	x		x			
C. mas	x	x	x				
C. m. 'Aurea'	x	x		x			
C. m. 'Elegantissima'	x	x		x			
C. m. 'Variegata'	x	x		x			
C. officinalis	x	x					
C. stolonifera						x	

177

TREE OR SHRUB (E = evergreen SE = semi-evergreen)	Flowers	Orna. fruit	Autumn leaf colour	Orna. adult leaves	Bark	Orna. young wood	Orna. young leaves
C. s. flaviramea						x	
Cotinus americanus	x		x				x
C. coggygria	x		x				
C. c. atropurpureus	x	x	x				
C. c. 'Foliis Purpureis'	x	x	x			x	
C. c. 'Rubrifolius'	x	x		x			
Cotoneaster bullatus		x	x				
C. b. floribundus		x	x				
C. conspicuus (E)	x	x					
C. 'Cornubia'	x	x					
C. frigidus	x	x					
C. harrovianus (E)	x	x					x
C. hupehensis	x	x					
C. × hybridus pendulus (E)	x	x					
C. lacteus (E)	x	x		x			
C. multiflorus	x	x					
C. m. calocarpus	x	x					
C. rotundifolius (SE)	x	x					
C. salicifolius (E)	x	x					
C. s. floccosus	x	x		x			
C. s. rugosus	x	x					
C. s. 'Fructu-luteo'	x	x					
C. serotinus (E)	x	x					
C. turbinatus (E)	x	x					
C. wardii (E)	x	x	x	x			
C. × watereri (E)		x					
Crataegus altaica	x	x	x				
C. aprica	x	x	x				
C. arkansana	x	x	x				
C. arnoldiana	x	x					
C. azarolus	x	x					
C. brachyacantha	x	x					
C. calpodendron	x	x	x		x		
C. × carrierei	x	x		x			
C. chlorosarca	x	x					
C. coccinea	x	x					
C. coccinioides	x	x	x				
C. crus-galli	x	x	x				
C. × dippeliana	x	x					

TREE OR SHRUB (E = evergreen SE = semi-evergreen)	Flowers	Orna. fruit	Autumn leaf colour	Orna. adult leaves	Bark	Orna. young wood	Orna. young leaves
C. dsungarica	x	x					
C. durobrivensis	x	x					
C. flava	x	x					
C. × grignonensis	x	x					
C. heterophylla	x	x		x			
C. macracantha	x	x					
C. missouriensis	x	x				x	x
C. mollis	x	x	x		x		
C. monogyna 'Aurea'	x	x					
C. orientalis	x	x					x
C. oxyacantha	x	x					
C. phaenopyrum	x	x	x				
C. pinnatifida	x	x	x	x		x	
C. prunifolia	x	x	x				
C. punctata	x	x	x				
C. p. 'Xanthocarpa'	x	x	x				
C. saligna	x	x					
C. stipulacea	x	x		x			
C. submollis	x	x					
C. tanacetifolia	x	x		x		x	x
Daphne alpina	x	x					
D. giraldii	x	x					
D. mezereum	x	x					
Davidia involucrata	x	x					
Diervilla sessilifolia	x			x			x
Dipteronia sinensis	x	x		x			
Elaeagnus angustifolia		x		x	x	x	
E. argentea		x		x		x	
E. macrophylla (E)	x			x			x
E. multiflora	x	x		x			
E. umbellata	x	x		x			
Enkianthus campanulatus	x		x				
E. cernuus	x	x	x				
E. c. rubens	x	x	x				
E. perulatus	x		x				
E. sinohimalaicus	x		x				x
Eucryphia glutinosa	x		x				

TABULATED LIST

TREE OR SHRUB (E = evergreen, SE = semi-evergreen)	Flowers	Orna. fruit	Autumn leaf colour	Orna. adult leaves	Bark	Orna. young wood	Orna. young leaves
Fothergilla gardenii	x		x				
F. major	x		x				
F. monticola	x		x				
Fraxinus bungeana	x		x				
F. chinensis	x		x	x			
F. c. rhynchophylla	x		x	x			
F. dipetala	x			x			
F. excelsior aurea			x	x		x	
F. longicuspis	x		x				
F. mariesii	x	x	x	x			
F. ornus	x		x	x			
F. spaethiana	x		x	x			
Gaultheria cuneata (E)	x	x					
G. fragrantissima (E)	x	x					
G. hookeri (E)	x	x					
G. miqueliana (E)	x	x					
G. semi-infera (E)	x	x					
G. veitchiana (E)	x	x					
G. wardii (E)	x	x					
× *Gaulthettya wisleyensis* (E)	x	x					
Ginkgo biloba			x	x			
Gleditschia caspica		x	x	x			
G. japonica			x	x		x	
G. triacanthos		x	x	x			
G. t. 'Sunburst'			x	x			x
Gymnocladus dioica			x	x			x
Halimodendron argenteum	x			x		x	
Hamamelis japonica	x		x				
H. j. zuccariniana	x		x				
H. mollis	x		x				
H. m. pallida	x		x				
Hippophaë rhamnoides		x		x		x	
Hydrangea quercifolia	x		x	x			
H. radiata	x			x			
Hypericum androsaemum	x	x					
H. elatum 'Elstead Variety'	x	x					
H. hircinum	x	x					

180

TREE OR SHRUB (E = evergreen, SE = semi-evergreen)	Flowers	Orna. fruit	Autumn leaf colour	Orna. adult leaves	Bark	Orna. young wood	Orna. young leaves
Ilex latifolia (E)	x	x		x			
I. pedunculosa (E)	x	x		x			
I. verticillata	x	x					x
Koelreuteria apiculata	x	x		x			x
K. paniculata	x	x	x	x			x
Ligustrum confusum	x	x					
L. delavayanum (E)	x	x				x	
L. quihoui	x	x					
L. sinense (SE)	x	x					
L. s. variegatum	x	x		x			
L. yunnanense (SE)	x	x					
Lithocarpus densiflorus (E)	x			x		x	x
Lonicera albertii	x	x		x			
L. × americana	x	x					
L. × brownii	x	x					
L. caprifolium	x	x					
L. ciliosa	x	x					
L. deflexicalyx	x	x					x
L. × heckrottii	x	x					
L. korolkowii	x	x					
L. ledebourii	x			x			
L. maackii podocarpa	x	x					
L. maximowiczii sachalinensis	x	x					
L. periclymenum	x	x					
L. quinquelocularis	x	x					x
L. tartarica	x	x					
L. × tellmanniana	x	x					
L. thibetica	x			x			
L. tragophylla	x	x					
Magnolia acuminata	x	x		x			
M. fraseri	x			x			
M. × highdownensis	x	x				x	
M. obovata	x	x		x			
M. officinalis	x	x		x			
M. sieboldii	x	x					
M. sinensis	x	x					

TREE OR SHRUB (E = evergreen SE = semi-evergreen)	Flowers	Orna. fruit	Autumn leaf colour	Orna. adult leaves	Bark	Orna. young wood	Orna. young leaves
M. tripetala		x		x			
M. virginiana (SE)	x	x		x			
M. wilsonii	x	x				x	
Malus × aldenhamensis	x	x		x			
M. angustifolia	x		x				
M. baccata	x	x	x				
M. coronaria 'Charlottae'	x		x				
M. × eleyi	x	x		x			
M. × floribunda	x	x					
M. glaucescens	x	x	x				x
M. × hartwigii	x	x					
M. 'Hopa Crab'	x	x					
M. ioensis	x					x	
M. kansuensis	x	x	x				
M. × lemoinei	x	x					
M. prattii	x	x	x	x			
M. prunifolia rinkii	x	x					
M. pumila 'Astrachanica'	x	x					
M. p. 'Elise Rathke'	x	x					
M. p. 'John Downie'	x	x					
M. p. 'Niedzwetzkyana'	x	x		x			
M. × purpurea	x	x		x		x	
M. sargentii	x	x					
M. × soulardii 'Red Tip Crab'	x	x	x				x
M. toringoides	x	x					
M. trilobata	x	x	x				
M. tschonoskii	x		x				
M. yunnanensis	x	x	x	x			
Meliosma beaniana	x	x					
M. cuneifolia	x	x					
M. oldhamii	x			x			
M. veitchiorum	x	x	x	x			
Osteomeles schwerinae (E)	x	x		x		x	x
O. subrotunda (E)	x	x		x		x	x
Oxydendrum arboreum	x		x				
Ozothamnus ledifolius (E)	x			x			
Paliurus spina-christi	x	x					

TREE OR SHRUB (E = evergreen SE = semi-evergreen)	Flowers	Orna. fruit	Autumn leaf colour	Orna. adult leaves	Bark	Orna. young wood	Orna. young leaves
Parrotia persica	x		x		x		
Pernettya leucocarpa (E)	x	x					
P. mucronata (E)	x	x					
P. pentlandii (E)	x	x					
P. pumila (E)	x	x					
P. tasmanica (E)	x	x					
Philadelphus coronarius 'Aureus'	x						x
Photinia amphidoxa	x	x	x				
P. beauverdiana notabilis	x	x	x				
P. davidsoniae (E)	x	x				x	x
P. prionophylla (E)	x	x					
P. serrulata (E)	x	x				x	x
P. villosa	x	x	x			x	
P. v. 'Flava'	x	x	x				
Physocarpus opulifolius 'Luteus'	x				x		x
Picrasma ailanthoides		x	x		x		
Pistacia chinensis		x	x				x
P. chinensis		x	x				x
Prinsepia sinensis	x	x					
P. uniflora	x	x					
P. utilis	x	x					
Prunus avium	x		x		x		
P. a. decumana	x		x		x		
P. a. plena	x		x		x		
P. × blireiana	x			x			
P. canescens	x				x		x
P. cerasifera atropurpurea	x	x		x			
P. cerasus	x	x					
P. × cistena	x			x			
P. dielsiana	x		x		x		
P. × hillieri	x		x				
P. × juddii	x		x				
P. maackii	x				x		
P. maximowiczii	x		x				
P. salicina	x	x	x				
P. sargentii	x	x	x				
P. serotina	x	x	x				
P. serrula	x				x		
P. spinosa 'Purpurea'	x			x			x

TREE OR SHRUB (E = evergreen SE = semi-evergreen)	Flowers	Orna. fruit	Autumn leaf colour	Orna. adult leaves	Bark	Orna. young wood	Orna. young leaves
P. subcordata	x		x			x	
P. ssiori	x				x		
Pseudolarix amabilis	x		x	x			x
Ptelea trifoliata	x	x	x				
P. t. 'Aurea'	x	x	x	x			
P. t. 'Glauca'	x	x		x			
Punica granatum	x						x
Pyracantha angustifolia (E)	x	x		x			
P. atalantioides (E)	x	x					
P. coccinea (E)	x	x					
P. c. lalandei (E)	x	x					
P. crenulata rogersiana (E)	x	x					
Pyrus pyrifolia	x		x				
P. regelii	x			x		x	
P. salicifolia pendula	x			x			x
P. ussuriensis	x		x				
Rhamnus imeretina		x	x	x			
R. purshiana	x	x					
Rhododendron albrechtii	x		x				x
R. araiophyllum (E)	x						x
R. argyrophyllum (E)	x			x		x	
R. arizelum (E)	x			x		x	x
R. auriculatum	x					x	
R. basilicum (E)	x			x			x
R. beanianum (E)	x			x		x	x
R. 'Bo-Peep' (E)	x						x
R. bureavii (E)	x			x		x	x
R. calendulaceum	x		x				
R. cinnabarinum (E)	x			x			
R. clementinae (E)	x			x		x	x
R. concatenans (E)	x			x			
R. coryphaeum (E)	x					x	x
R. cyanocarpum (E)	x						x
R. degronianum (E)	x			x		x	
R. erosum (E)	x				x		
R. exasperatum (E)	x			x	x	x	x
R. eximium (E)	x			x		x	x
R. falconeri (E)	x			x	x	x	x

TREE OR SHRUB (E = evergreen SE = semi-evergreen)	Flowers	Orna. fruit	Autumn leaf colour	Orna. adult leaves	Bark	Orna. young wood	Orna. young leaves
R. fictolacteum (E)	x			x		x	
R. fulgens (E)	x					x	x
R. fulvum (E)	x			x		x	x
R. habrotrichum (E)	x			x		x	
R. haemotodes (E)	x			x		x	x
R. hookeri (E)	x			x	x	x	x
R. h. 'Alix' (E)	x				x	x	x
R. lanatum (E)	x			x		x	x
R. lepidostylum (SE)	x			x			
R. lutescens (E)	x						x
R. luteum	x		x				
R. macabeanum (E)	x			x		x	x
R. makinoi (E)	x			x		x	x
R. mollyanum (E)	x			x		x	x
R. nipponicum	x		x		x		
R. niveum (E)	x			x		x	x
R. occidentale	x		x				
R. pachytrichum (E)	x					x	x
R. pentaphyllum	x		x				
R. praestans (E)	x					x	x
R. pseudochrysanthum (E)	x			x		x	x
R. quinquefolium	x		x				
R. reticulatum	x		x				
R. rex (E)	x			x			
R. schlippenbachii	x		x				
R. sinogrande (E)	x			x		x	
R. smirnowii (E)	x			x			x
R. strigillosum (E)	x			x		x	x
R. thomsonii (E)	x			x	x	x	x
R. tsariense (E)	x			x		x	x
R. tschonoskii	x		x				
R. ungernii (E)	x			x		x	x
R. vaseyi	x		x				
R. williamsianum (E)	x			x			x
R. xanthocodon (E)	x			x			
R. yakusimanum (E)	x			x		x	x
R. 'Yellow Hammer' (E)	x	flowers in spring and autumn					
Rhus glabra	x	x	x	x			
R. potaninii	x	x	x	x			

185

TREE OR SHRUB (E = evergreen SE = semi-evergreen)	Flowers	Orna. fruit	Autumn leaf colour	Orna. adult leaves	Bark	Orna. young wood	Orna. young leaves
R. typhina	x		x	x			
Robinia kelseyi	x		x	x			
R. pseudacacia	x			x			
R. p. 'Frisia'	x			x			
Rosa filipes	x	x					
R. foliolosa	x	x	x				
R. forrestiana	x	x					
R. 'Heather Muir'	x	x					
R. helenae	x	x					
R. macrophylla	x	x					
R. moyesii	x	x		x			
R. multiflora	x	x					
R. omeiensis	x	x		x			
R. o. pteracantha	x	x		x	handsome thorns		
R. roxburghii	x	x		x	x		
R. rubrifolia	x	x		x		x	x
R. rubus	x	x					
R. sericea	x	x					
R. s. chrysocarpa	x	x					
R. setipoda	x	x				x	x
R. soulieana	x	x		x		x	x
R. villosa	x	x					
R. v. 'Wolley-Dod's Rose'	x	x					
R. virginiana	x	x	x			x	
R. webbiana	x	x		x		x	
R. woodsii fendleri	x	x		x			
Rubus amabilis	x	x			x		
R. cockburnianus	x				x		
R. coreanus					x		
R. flagelliflorus (E)	x	x		x		x	
R. lasiostylus	x	x		x	x		
R. leucodermis	x	x		x	x		
R. thibetanus	x	x		x	x		
Salix alba aurea				x		x	
S. a. vitellina				x		x	
S. a. 'Britzensis'				x		x	
S. daphnoides	x					x	
S. fargesii	x					x	

TREE OR SHRUB (E = evergreen SE = semi-evergreen)	Flowers	Orna. fruit	Autumn leaf colour	Orna. adult leaves	Bark	Orna. young wood	Orna. young leaves
S. irrorata	x				x		
Sambucus caerulea	x	x					
S. callicarpa	x	x					
S. canadensis	x			x			
S. racemosa 'Plumosa Aurea'		x		x			
Schinus dependens	x	x					
Schizandra rubriflora	x	x					
Skimmia japonica (E)	x	x					
S. reevesiana (E)	x	x					
Sorbaria aitchisonii	x	x				x	
Sorbus alnifolia	x	x	x				x
S. a. submollis	x	x	x				
S. aria	x	x	x	x			x
S. a. 'Lutescens'	x	x		x	x		x
S. a. 'Decaisneana'	x	x		x	x		x
S. aucuparia	x	x					x
S. a. ssp. edulis	x	x					x
S. a. e. 'Beissneri'	x	x		x			x
S. a. xanthocarpa	x	x					
S. cashmeriana	x	x		x			
S. chamaemespilus	x	x				x	
S. commixta	x	x	x	x			
S. cuspidata	x	x	x	x		x	x
S. discolor	x	x	x				
S. esserteauiana	x	x		x			
S. e. flava	x	x					
S. folgneri	x	x	x	x		x	
S. gracilis	x	x	x				x
S. harrowiana	x	x		x			
S. × hostii	x	x		x			
S. hupehensis	x	x	x	x			
S. h. rosea	x	x	x	x			
S. × hybrida		x		x			
S. insignis	x	x					
S. intermedia	x	x		x			
S. japonica calocarpa	x	x	x	x		x	
S. 'Joseph Rock'	x	x		x			
S. koehneana	x	x		x			
S. lanata	x	x	x	x		x	x

TREE OR SHRUB (E = evergreen SE = semi-evergreen)	Flowers	Orna. fruit	Autumn leaf colour	Orna. adult leaves	Bark	Orna. young wood	Orna. young leaves
S. matsumarana	x	x	x				
S. megalocarpa	x		x	x			
S. meliosmifolia	x		x				x
S. pluripinnata	x	x		x			x
S. pohuashanensis	x	x					
S. poteriifolia	x	x		x			
S. prattii	x	x					
S. p. subarachnoidea	x	x		x			
S. rufo-ferruginea	x	x	x	x			
S. sargentiana	x	x	x				
S. scalaris	x	x		x			
S. scopulina	x	x					
S. tianshanica	x	x					
S. vilmorinii	x	x		x		x	
S. 'Wilfred Fox'	x	x	x	x		x	x
Stachyurus praecox	x		x			x	
Staphylea bumalda	x	x	x				
S. colchica	x	x					
S. holocarpa	x	x					x
Stephanandra incisa	x		x	x		x	
S. tanakae	x		x	x		x	
Stewartia koreana	x		x		x		
S. monadelpha	x		x		x		
S. pseudo-camellia	x		x		x		
S. sinensis	x		x		x		
Stranvaesia davidiana (E)	x	x	x				x
S. d. undulata (E)	x	x	x				x
Symplocos paniculata	x	x					
Tamarix parviflora	x					x	
Tilia oliveri	x			x			
T. petiolaris	x			x			
T. tomentosa	x			x			
T. tuan	x			x			
Vaccinium arctostaphylos	x	x	x				
V. corymbosum	x	x	x				
V. glauco-album (E)	x	x		x			
V. ovatum (E)						x	x

TREE OR SHRUB (E = evergreen, SE = semi-evergreen)	Flowers	Orna. fruit	Autumn leaf colour	Orna. adult leaves	Bark	Orna. young wood	Orna. young leaves
Viburnum alnifolium	x	x	x				
V. betulifolium	x	x					
V. davidii (E)		x		x			
V. dilatatum	x	x	x				
V. furcatum	x	x	x				
V. hupehense	x	x	x				
V. lantana	x	x	x	x			
V. opulus	x	x	x				
V. o. sterile	x		x				
V. setigerum	x	x	x				x
V. tomentosum	x	x	x				

189

❧ List of Common Names

Alder	Alnus spp.
All Saints' Cherry	*Prunus cerasus semperflorens*
Ash	Fraxinus spp.
Azarole	*Crataegus azarolus*
Barberry	Berberis spp.
Birch	Betula spp.
Bird Cherry	Prunus spp.
Blackthorn	*Prunus spinosa*
Bladder Nut	Staphylea spp.
Blueberry	*Vaccinium corymbosum*
Blue Pomette	*Crataegus brachyacantha*
Bramble	Rubus spp.
Buckeye	*Aesculus californica*
Buckthorn	Rhamnus spp.
Cascara	*Rhamnus purshiana*
Cherry (wild)	*Prunus avium*
Cherry-plum	*Prunus cerasifera*
Chinese Hawthorn	Photinia spp.
Clammy Locust	*Robinia viscosa*
Cockspur Thorn	*Crataegus crus-galli*
Cornelian Cherry	*Cornus mas*
Crab-apple	Malus spp.
Cranberry	*Pernettya mucronata*
Crown of Thorns	*Paliurus spina-christi*
Cucumber Tree	*Magnolia acuminata*
Dogwood	Cornus spp.
Elderberry	Sambucus spp.
False Acacia	*Robinia pseudacacia*
Firethorn	Pyracantha spp.
Goldenrain Tree	*Koelreuteria paniculata*

Guelder Rose	*Viburnum opulus*
Handkerchief Tree	*Davidia involucrata*
Hawthorn	Crataegus spp.
Hickory	Carya spp.
Holly	Ilex spp.
Honey Locust	Gleditschia spp.
Honeysuckle	Lonicera spp.
Hop Tree	*Ptelea trifoliata*
Indian Bean Tree, Golden	*Catalpa bignonioides* 'Aurea'
Japanese Cherry	*Prunus serrulata*
Japanese Maple	*Acer palmatum*
Japanese Snowball	*Viburnum tomentosum sterile*
Kentucky Coffee Tree	*Gymnocladus dioica*
Lead Plant	*Amorpha canascens*
Lime	Tilia spp.
Madrona	*Arbutus menziesii*
Maidenhair Tree	*Ginkgo biloba*
Manna Ash	*Fraxinus ornus*
Maple	Acer spp.
Mastick	Pistacia spp.
May	*Crataegus oxyacantha, C. monogyna*
Mezereon	*Daphne mezereum*
Mocker Nut	*Carya tomentosa*
Mock Orange	Philadelphus spp.
Mountain Ash	*Sorbus aucuparia*
Norway Maple	*Acer platanoides*
Pear	Pyrus spp.
Pecan Nut	*Carya pecan*
Pistachio	*Pistacia chinensis*
Plum	Prunus spp.
Pomegranate	*Punica granatum*
Privet	Ligustrum spp.
Rose	Rosa spp.
Rowan	*Sorbus aucuparia*
St. John's Wort	Hypericum spp.
Sea Buckthorn	*Hippophaë rhamnoides*
Scarlet Haw	*Crataegus coccinea*
Silver Berry	*Elaeagnus argentea*
Smoke Tree	*Cotinus coggygria*
Snake Bark	*Acer capillipes, A. davidii, A. pennsylvanicum, A. rufinerve*
Snowball Tree	*Viburnum opulus sterile*

Snowy Mespilus	*Amelanchier* spp.
Sorrel Tree	*Oxydendrum arboreum*
Stag's-horn Sumach	*Rhus typhina*
Strawberry Tree	*Arbutus unedo*
Sumach	Rhus spp.
Syringa	Philadelphus spp.
Tamarisk	Tamarix spp.
Tutsan	*Hypericum androsaemum*
Tanbark Oak	*Lithocarpus densiflorus*
Umbrella Tree	*Magnolia tripetala*
Washington Thorn	*Crataegus phaenopyrum*
Wayfaring Tree	*Viburnum lantana*
Whitebeam	*Sorbus aria*
Willow	Salix spp.
Wig Tree	*Cotinus coggygria*
Witch-hazel	Hamamelis spp.
Woodbine	*Lonicera periclymenum*
Yellow Wood	*Cladrastis lutea*